EDUCATION AND TRAINING

SKILLS-BASED SOCIOLOGY

Series Editors: Tim Heaton and Tony Lawson

The *Skills-Based Sociology* series is designed to cover the core skills for Sociology A level (and equivalent courses) and to bring students up to date with recent sociological thought in key topic areas. Students are given the opportunity to develop their skills through exercises which they can carry out by themselves or in groups, as well as given practice in answering exam questions. The series emphasises contemporary developments in sociological knowledge, with a critical focus on recent social theories such as post-modernism and the New Right.

Published

EDUCATION AND TRAINING
Tim Heaton and Tony Lawson

Forthcoming

THEORY AND METHODS
Mel Churton

CRIME AND DEVIANCE
Tim Heaton and Tony Lawson

MASS MEDIA
Marsha Jones and Emma Jones

STRATIFICATION AND DIFFERENTIATION
Mark Kirby

HEALTH AND ILLNESS
Michael Senior with Bruce Viveash

Further titles in preparation

EDUCATION AND TRAINING

Tim Heaton
and
Tony Lawson

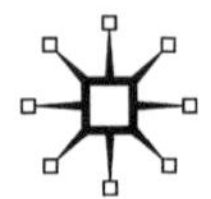

Published by
PALGRAVE MACMILLAN
Houndmills, Basingstoke, Hampshire RG21 6XS and
175 Fifth Avenue, New York, N.Y. 10010
Companies and representatives throughout the world

PALGRAVE MACMILLAN is the global academic imprint of the Palgrave Macmillan division of St. Martin's Press, LLC and of Palgrave Macmillan Ltd. Macmillan® is a registered trademark in the United States, United Kingdom and other countries. Palgrave is a registered trademark in the European Union and other countries.

ISBN 0–333–64612–6

This book is printed on paper suitable for recycling and made from fully managed and sustained forest sources.

A catalogue record for this book is available from the British Library.

10 9 8 7 6 5 4 3
11 10 09 08 07 06 05 04

Printed and bound in Great Britain by
J. W. Arrowsmith Ltd, Bristol

To **Sarah Andrew** and the sociology students of King Edward VII Upper School,
Melton Mowbray

To **Liz Clarke**: much loved and much missed in Leicester

Contents

Acknowledgements

The authors wish to thank the following for granting us permission to reproduce extracts, figures and tables: Philip Allan Publishers Ltd, Guardian Newspapers Ltd, Her Majesty's Stationery Office, The Independent Newspaper Publishing plc, the Institute of Employment Studies, Macmillan Press Ltd, the National Extension College, National Foundation for Educational Research, Thomas Nelson & Sons Ltd, Olympus Books UK, Penguin Books Ltd, Polity Press/NCC Blackwell, Taylor & Francis Group Ltd, Stanley Thornes Publishers Ltd and Times Newspapers Ltd.

We are also grateful to the Associated Examining Board (AEB) for allowing us to use questions from past A Level examination papers. All answers and hints on answers are the sole responsibility of the authors and have not been provided or approved by the AEB.

Every effort has been made to trace all the copyright-holders, but if any have been inadvertently overlooked the publishers will be pleased to make the necessary arrangement at the first opportunity.

The authors are most grateful to Frances Arnold, Catherine Gray and Keith Povey for their editorial help.

Acknowledgements

1 Introduction

The philosophy behind the book

The aim of this book is threefold. Firstly, we wish you to take an active part in your own education. The subject core for sociology A level developed by the Schools Curriculum and Assessment Authority identifies the skills of *interpretation, application* and *evaluation* as the central skills that candidates must demonstrate in any A level sociology examination, whether advanced or advanced supplementary. Interpretation means that you should be able to look at different types of text, such as tables or newspaper articles, and be able to communicate your understanding of them. Application is the ability to take sociological and non-sociological material and use it in relevant ways to answer the questions set. Evaluation means being able to assess sociological debates and arguments through a consideration of evidence.

The best way of developing these skills is to practise them yourself. We have therefore designed a series of exercises that are tied to these three skills, and if you carry them out you should be able to improve your performance in these areas. You will be able to identify the skills each exercise is designed to develop by looking out for the following symbols: **i** for interpretation, **a** for application and **e** for evaluation. However we also want you to understand the interconnections between all the information in this book, so you will also find that there are *link exercises* for you to do. These will not only help you perform skilfully, but increase the sophistication of your understanding of the sociology of education and training.

Our second aim is to present you with sociological knowledge that is appropriate to and useful for your examination performance, as the ability to convey *knowledge* and *understanding* is another skill that all A and AS level examinations include. We decided that what we did not want to do was to present the knowledge you easily could glean from other textbooks. We felt it was pointless to try to cover ground that is more than adequately covered elsewhere. But we do want you to be as up-to-date as possible with the material you are familiar with, so that you can apply it in the examination. We have therefore focused on developments in sociology during the 1980s and 1990s.

We have not attempted to tell you all there is to know about sociology in this period, because to develop your sociological skills you should be finding out for yourself what has been happening in society and sociology during this time. We have, however, tried to give you an overview of the debates that have been going on and the sociologists who have been writing about education and training in this period. You will find that much of the material concerns the theories and ideas of the New Right and of the postmodernists, and how other sociologists have responded to these developments during this period.

Our third aim is to help you to pass the examination, so we have included a series of exam questions, sometimes with answers and sometimes not, but always there is some task for you to do yourself. We believe that if you carry out the activities connected to these questions you will help yourself to pass the examination. It may be that you will prefer to conduct these activities with a teacher, and she or he will be able to build upon the ideas and activities to improve further your performance. However you can also use the examination activities as supplements to your classroom work, as you go through the course, or as a revision aid as you near the examination.

The important thing to remember is that we cannot do it all for you. You will gain most from this book if you approach it in an active way and are prepared to take the information and skills and apply them in the examination itself. If you just read the text and miss out the exercises, you will only be doing half of what is necessary to pass the exam.

Subject content

The content of this book is broken down into seven areas. In Chapter 2 we consider the background and context to the development of educational policies and systems in Britain in the 1980s and 1990s. Chapter 3 looks at the changes in policy and education systems that occurred in the 1980s and 1990s and the sociological research on them. The book then moves on to various explanations of differential educational attainment. Chapter 4 looks at class differences in educational performance. Chapter 5 addresses the debates on gender inequalities in educational achievement. Explanations of ethnic differences in educational attainment are covered in Chapter 6. We then go on to consider the role or function of schooling and training. Chapter 7 looks at the purpose of education and training from a functionalist perspective; whilst Chapter 8 offers a conflict analysis.

2 Educational policy and systems in Britain: the background to changes in the 1980s and 1990s

By the end of this chapter you should:

- be aware of how educational policy has been shaped by certain key objectives;
- have a critical understanding of early educational policies in Britain;
- be familiar with comprehensive schools and the conflicting views which exist of them;
- appreciate the arguments for and against private schools;
- understand that educational policy since 1976 has been introduced for social, political and economic reasons.

Introduction

Chapters 2 and 3 examine the significance of educational policies in Britain. Educational policies are important for three reasons. Firstly, they shape the education systems in which teachers, lecturers and students work. Secondly, they determine in part the degree to which societies can become meritocratic – that is, the talented rise in the social structure. Thirdly, they shape what is taught in schools and colleges. In this chapter we provide an overview of the debates surrounding educational policies up to the 1970s, while Chapter 3 focuses on the issues that emerged from policy developments in the 1980s and 1990s. Attention is also given in this chapter to private sector schooling. This exists outside state provision, and is not constrained by the same government educational policies that we will be focusing on.

When reading Chapters 2 and 3 it is essential that you do not treat them in isolation from the rest of the book. Subsequent chapters will examine differential educational achievement by social class, gender and ethnicity; and the role of education and training in society. All of these can be understood and explained with reference to the educational policies discussed in these chapters, and it is essential that you are able to make the links. You will be helped to make the connections through a series of link exercises in the other chapters.

Important principles and concepts of the education system

Reforms in the British education system since the Second World War have often had two objectives in mind:

1. To create a meritocracy, through equality of educational opportunity.
2. To create a highly trained and efficient workforce by transferring vocational skills.

1. Creating a meritocracy through equality of educational opportunity

A meritocracy is a situation where individuals are rewarded on the basis of merit or ability and effort and not according to social background. The concept of meritocracy is important in the study of education because it provides the justification for the social system as it currently operates. If everyone is rewarded for their skills and abilities rather than who their parents were, then people will see their position in society, whether well-rewarded or not, as a legitimate position – that is, one that is deserved and therefore fair. Educational reform since 1944 has often been associated with attempts to make the education system, and therefore society, more meritocratic.

Equality of educational opportunity refers to the idea that education systems should provide the same opportunities for all students to achieve to their fullest ability regardless of their social background. It is important to note the difference between reforms that are concerned with 'equality of educational access', such as opening up higher education to more social groups, and 'equality of educational outcome', which might for example be concerned with encouraging female students to succeed in science subjects. The creation of the Open University is an example of the former and the GIST (Girls Into Science and Technology) project is an example of the latter.

It is also important to recognise that this principle was part of the postwar 'social democratic consensus', in which the main political strands in Britain were in broad agreement on the shape of social and educational policies. This agreement focused on the creation of a welfare state as a way of eliminating disadvantage and promoting equal opportunity. However this consensus was not unchallenged: critics on the right were suspicious of what they saw as egalitarian policies in the 1950s and 1960s, and critics on the left argued that the reforms did not actually produce equality of opportunity.

Exercise 2.1

Discuss with another sociology student whether equality of educational opportunity exists in your school or college. Try to justify your decisions to each other. You could begin this exercise by reflecting on whether males and females are offered an equal educational experience in your school or college.

2. Creating a highly trained and efficient workforce by transferring vocational skills

The importance of schooling for the economy has long been recognised by sociologists and politicians alike. They have argued that a society's economic performance is linked to the skills and enterprise of its citizens. Though the purpose of education may also include other aims, the transfer of marketable skills from one generation to the next is a central part of economic success. The role of the education system in this process is seen as vital, though it should be remembered that there have traditionally been avenues other than schools for the acquisition of vocational skills, such as apprenticeship schemes.

Exercise 2.2

In what ways do you think schooling can or does equip pupils with the necessary skills for employment? The following examples should help you to get started.

- Schooling teaches numeracy.
- Schooling develops interpersonal skills.

Early educational policies

The 1870 Forster Act

This Act established state provision for elementary education. The introduction of a state system of education was a product of several factors. Firstly, there was a need to create a literate workforce in Britain, who would have the skills to produce goods as efficiently as their industrial competitors. Secondly, Val Rust (1991) argues that education systems were developed to fit the needs not just of modern industry, but of modern society as a whole. That is, education systems were designed to promote a sense of national identity, unifying different groups within the modern nation-state and fostering a sense of citizenship. The main problem with the Act was that there was no provision for secondary education. Those secondary schools that did exist were fee paying. Therefore the schooling system that prevailed served to divide children along class lines – the working class were in effect denied a secondary education.

The 1944 Education Act

This Act established compulsory and free secondary education for all (up to the age of 15), based on the principal of equality of educational opportunity. The 1944 Act created a tripartite (three-part) system of secondary education. It was claimed that the three types of school would have 'parity of esteem' (equal status). It was through the selective '11-plus' exam that children were channelled into the schools most suited to their talents and abilities. The more academic went to grammar schools, those showing an aptitude for applied science and art went to technical schools, and the rest went to secondary modern schools for a practical education. The Act also established that education should be a partnership between central government, local government through the LEAs (local education authorities) and the schools. Though initially intended to create three types of secondary school, the system never really established technical schools, with the result that secondary education was bipartite rather than tripartite. The lack of technical schools can be seen as an important argument for the development of vocational education in secondary schooling during the 1980s.

Exercise 2.3

a — 1. Find out which schools in your area were or still are part of the tripartite system of secondary education.

i e — 2. With the help of a sociology textbook, identify two arguments that have been made for the tripartite system of education and two arguments that have been made against it.

a e — 3. Interview two people who were educated under the tripartite system of schooling. Find out the type of school they went to. Ask them whether they felt there was 'parity of esteem' with other schools in the area and get them to explain their answer. What arguments would they make for and against the tripartite system? (Do their answers match those you found for question 2?)

The comprehensive system – the mid 1960s to the present day

Comprehensive schools are non-selective institutions that offer free schooling for all types of student under one roof (in 1987, 86 per cent of secondary schools were comprehensive). This system of schooling was introduced following intense criticism of the tripartite system; in particular, the way the selective basis of the system created 'wasted talent' among those who happened to 'fail' the 11-plus. Attacks on the selection process, based upon what were seen as flawed IQ tests, were influential in convincing LEAs, whether Conservative or Labour, of the necessity for comprehensive schooling. However traditionalists were unhappy with the abolition of the grammar schools, which were seen as centres of excellence, and argued that comprehensivisation could only lead to a lowering of educational standards. However social reformers argued that comprehensive schools would not only offer greater social equality, but would also better serve the economic interests of society by 'dredging the pool of talent' (Willis, 1983). This meant that comprehensives would allow previously unrecognised talented individuals from the working class to be identified and given the opportunity to contribute to the economic success of society. Comprehensives were therefore seen by both left and right as an attempt to engineer social equality in society. They have subsequently been the focus of much research and comment, as they have provided a battleground for those of different political outlook.

Exercise 2.4

One of the major arguments for comprehensive schools is that they 'mix' together children from diverse social backgrounds and therefore break down divisive social barriers.

With the help of a sociology textbook, identify two other arguments for comprehensive schools.

ITEM A

Exercise 2.5

1. With reference to the table in Item A, what percentage of candidates passed five GCSE exams (grades A–C) at 11–18 comprehensive schools?

2. Identify one implication for comprehensive school students of the differential educational achievement shown in Item A. (Hint: the information in Item A will help you to answer this question.)

3. As Item A indicates, the mass media often claim that comprehensives have largely failed to improve educational standards. With the help of a sociology textbook, identify and explain two reasons why comprehensives may have failed to raise educational standards. (Hint: look out for debates about the effects of streaming and the Assisted Places Scheme.)

ITEM A

Comprehensives 'fail' at A-level

By Donald MacLeod
Education Correspondent

ONLY ONE in twelve 16-year-olds in state comprehensive schools go on to get three A-levels, the passport to higher education and better jobs, according to a study released yesterday.

In independent schools more than 40 per cent reach this threshold and in grammar schools the figure is 47 per cent, say Professor Alan Smithers and Pamela Robinson, of Manchester University's School of Education. Professor Smithers says he was so shocked by the figures that he had them checked three times.

Their study for the Council for Industry and Higher Education questions some of the optimism about the increasing numbers staying on at school or college. It calls A-levels, 'a minority sport', and says vocational education in England is 'messy' and seen as second best. 'There is effectively no mainstream post-16 education for most of the school population,' it concludes.

The Smithers/Robinson figures highlight how poorly the majority of pupils at comprehensive schools are doing both at GCSE and A-level compared with 16-year-olds at independent and grammar schools. One consequence has been that the middle classes have strengthened their grip on university places; not only are they more likely to apply but they more likely to get in.

The considerable increase in the numbers of A-level students in state schools and further education colleges looks like a triumph for comprehensives in encouraging more young people to stay on at school. But, the report adds, the picture is different if one looks at the proportion of students gaining five good GCSE passes and three A-levels. Only a quarter of comprehensive pupils gained five A–C grades at GCSE, compared to more than 80 per cent in grammar and private schools.

Professor Smithers and Ms Robinson point out that the strength of the highly selective and highly specialised English system is that the few who remain in school or college reach very high standards. It allows universities and polytechnics to produce graduates in a short time with relatively few drop-outs.

But the 'backwash' effect on the 85 per cent who do not manage the academic hurdles is serious. The report concludes: 'Perhaps the worst feature of the English system is the way it treats the ordinarily intelligent child.'

While 18-year-olds in England come out very well in international terms, 10-year-olds and 14-year-olds perform badly.

EXAM PERFORMANCE BY TYPE OF SCHOOL 1988

Exam Passes	Independent	Grammar	Comprehensive (11–18)	Sixth Form/ Tertiary College	Comprehensive (11–16)	Other
Three A Levels						
Numbers	21,690	7,770	31,820	11,760	–	840
Percentage of candidates passing all three exams	70.7	61.9	48.0	53.6	–	40.2
Percentage of fifth-formers going on to pass all three exams	44.6	47.7	9.4	6.3*	–	2.9
5 GCSE, Grades A-C						
Numbers	39,785	16,686	94,077	–	47,275	5,239
Percentage of candidates passing all all 5 exams	80.7	84.7	28.7	–	25.2	14.8

**Drawn mainly from comprehensives (11–16)*
Source: Statistics of Education, School Leavers (1988): Statistical Bulletin 1/91, London: DES

(*Source: D. MacLeod, The Independent, 5 December 1991.*)

Private schools

Private schools – or, as they are often known, independent or public schools – exist outside the state sector and are not always required to follow government educational policies. For example private schools do not have to teach to the national curriculum, nor make their pupils take the SATs. Most private schools tend to offer a traditional academic education (including subjects such as Latin) and charge fees for entry. In 1981 the government tried to make private education more accessible to low-income families by offering to pay all or part of a bright pupil's fees through the Assisted Places Scheme. Some New Right theorists support the Assisted Places Scheme because in their view the traditional academic curriculum of the private sector is superior to the 'progressive' curriculum of the comprehensive sector. They therefore see the Assisted Places Scheme as part of a desired privatisation process in the education system. However the scheme has been criticised (Whitty, 1989) for providing a taxpayer's subsidy to the private schools, while sending mainly middle-class, rather than poor working-class children to them. It has also been argued that state financial support for the private schools lends important ideological support to these schools (Walford, 1993).

ITEM B

The private sector is now expanding, between 1979 and 1994 the percentage of pupils at private schools rose from 5.8 per cent to just over 7 per cent of the total school population. A small part of this increase was due to the introduction of the Assisted Places Scheme in 1981, which provided grants to a limited number of less well-off children who, it was thought, would benefit from a private education. In fact very few of the families that have taken advantage of this scheme are from the working class.

(Source: Adapted from M. O'Donnell and J. Garrod, Sociology in Practice, Walton on Thames, Nelson, 1990.)

ITEM B

Exercise 2.6

i

1. According to Item B, what was the increase in the percentage of pupils attending private schools between 1979 and 1994?

i

2. Referring to Item B, why might it be argued that the assisted places scheme is failing in its intent?

Exercise 2.7

i a e

Refer back to Item A (page 8) and use the information in the item to make a case for independent (private) schools.

Other arguments in favour of private schools

1. They give parents greater freedom of choice.
2. Many famous schools such as Eton are a precious part of the national heritage and culture.
3. They are not constrained by the national curriculum and have the freedom to experiment with new 'progressive' methods of teaching. A good example of a private school that takes advantage of these 'freedoms' is Summerhill School.
4. They contribute to diversity in the education system, because they are themselves so diverse.
5. They provide opportunities for a specialised curriculum, so that particular talents can be developed.

ITEM C

Ex-private-school students dominate the top jobs in British institutions, including the government, the civil service, the church, the legal system, the armed forces and the financial system in the city. Furthermore, those who control these institutions come overwhelmingly from a few exclusive schools. For example Eton, Harrow, Winchester and Westminster.

1992 saw the publication of the *Whitehall Companion*, a 1000-page directory that contains biographies of the 980 senior civil servants. The *Whitehall Companion* reveals how far the mandarins of Whitehall share a similar social and educational background. Eight of the twelve biggest departments are run by permanent secretaries, all of whom are men, none of whom are from ethnic minorities, all but one of whom attended either Oxford or Cambridge University (the so-called 'Oxbridge' connection) and all of whom went to private fee-paying schools.

Those who occupy the top jobs give their sons and daughters the unfair advantage of sponsored mobility. This is achieved by sending them to these same schools and by choosing new recruits for the top jobs from among those who have been to these schools. This restrictive, elite self-recruitment is known as the old school tie (boy) network.

(Source: Adapted from M. Denscombe, Sociology Update, Leicester, Olympus Books, 1993.)

ITEM C

Exercise 2.8

1. Using Item C, in no more than fifty words make a case against private schools.

Other arguments against public schools

1. Those from private schools who govern may not fully concern themselves with conditions in the schools attended by 93 per

cent of the population as their children continue to be educated in private schools.
2. Comprehensive schools will not be truly comprehensive and non-selective until 100 per cent of pupils attend them.
3. Fee-paying schools split British society into two: those who can afford to pay and do go, and those who can not afford to pay and do not go. Thus the existence of private schools is divisive.
4. They are unfair in that they provide an education with small class sizes on the basis of ability to pay rather than talent.
5. In a society that claims to be a meritocracy, the existence of public schools gives an advantage to a small group in society.

Developments in educational thinking and policy since 1976

Background

The 'great debate' on education began in 1976, when the Labour prime minister of the time, James Callaghan, raised two issues of concern.

1. Work

Education was not geared up to the world of work. It was claimed that schools were failing to produce young workers with marketable skills and that this was a major factor in the decline in Britain's industrial competitiveness. While Jim Callaghan saw this decline in relative terms, comparing the economic performance of Britain against that of its industrial competitors, sociologists in the 1980s and 1990s were more interested in the long-term changes that were happening in the world economy in the 1970s as an explanation for Britain's decline. The economic background to the 'great debate' has therefore been the focus of much sociological work, particularly from those sociologists who argue that there has been a fundamental change in the processes of production, under the impact of new technologies and new systems of working. Central to the development of a 'postmodern' economic system is the creation of a global market, through a high-tech information revolution that has made access to all parts of the world relatively easy.

It is therefore argued by postmodernists that traditional 'Fordist' methods of working, such as product standardisation and a semi-skilled labour force, are inefficient in a global economy. Fordism emerged as the dominant way of organising production in the early part of the twentieth century. Its most significant features were the breaking down of tasks into smaller and smaller actions, so that the activities of workers could be closely controlled. Management consisted of coordinating the activities of large numbers of workers, often positioned along assembly lines, to achieve the most efficient production of large numbers of identical goods. 'Post-Fordists' such as Murray (1988) suggest that computer technologies have allowed industries to respond to a growing demand by consumers for diversity in goods, through organising work in different ways. For example 'just-in-time' systems of production are made possible through the use of computerised stock-control systems, so that large numbers of production components are not kept in warehouses, thus losing money for the entrepreneur through tying up capital. Instead computers are used to order and deliver necessary parts only at the point of production when they are needed.

One result of post-Fordist production is a change in the way labour is used and therefore in the type of labour needed by post-Fordist industries. Organisational hierarchies have been flattened and workers are called upon to be much more flexible in the way they work, employing greater skills than the traditional 'Taylorist' worker, who performed low-skill repetitive tasks. As Britain's competitiveness in this global economy declined, there was perceived to be a need for a more highly skilled workforce. It was the lack of appropriate response from the education system to this need that underpinned the 'great debate'.

However, how far post-Fordist techniques have penetrated industry is a matter of much dispute. While it is clear that a global economy has taken shape, in which the market is world-wide, this does not mean that every firm, or even the majority of firms are post-Fordist. Indeed Ainley (1993) argues that post-Fordist production techniques do not result in a universal demand for highly skilled workers. Rather, post-Fordism polarises the workforce into a core of highly skilled and a periphery of deskilled workers – a dual labour market. The level of demand for a skilled workforce in Britain is therefore open to dispute.

2. Standards

Educational standards were falling under the influence of 'progressive' teaching. Progressive education was an influential postwar development among British educators, according to New Right sociologists such as Marsland (1988). Progressive education placed the child at the centre of the educational experience and advocated a process of individualised learning, preferably through discovery methods. Critics argued that the employment of 'discovery learning' techniques in schools was holding back children through lack of teacher direction. Progressive education, it was claimed, undermined traditional morality through the promotion of values associated, for example, with feminism and antiracism, and reduced access to the 'high culture' of Britain, represented by Shakespeare in the English curriculum. In the 1960s the authors of the *Black Papers* (Cox and Boyson, 1975) were calling for a return to traditional values and standards through restoration of the grammar schools and reversal of the postwar moves towards greater equality. The *Black Papers* represented the emergence of New Right ideologies with respect to education.

Educational policy following the 'great debate'

The concern about relevance and quality in British education remained long after Callaghan's brief term of office. The Conservative governments of the 1980s and 1990s systematically set out to halt the alleged decline in British education through a series of sweeping educational changes. The policies introduced attempted to vocationalise schooling and raise the performances and efficiency of individual schools by creating a climate of competition. It should be remembered that these policies were influenced by the work of the New Right 'think tanks', who had developed an ideological challenge to the social democratic ideas that had dominated both major parties since the Second World War. However the New Right was itself divided: between a 'libertarian' wing, who were in favour of the free market in every sphere of activity, and an 'authoritarian' wing, who on social issues were concerned to establish social order and obedience, above the rights of individuals.

Simon (1988) claims that the whole package of reforms was partly introduced as an attempt to depoliticise the curriculum, widen parental choice and control, instil market forces into education, and enhance the powers of central government and individual schools in the control of education. This was to be achieved primarily through undermining the local education authorities' power to control schools and introducing a national curriculum, which would be taught in all state schools. It is significant that the egalitarian goal of creating a meritocracy through equality of educational opportunity had largely disappeared from the political agenda.

The vision of a state system of education organised along the lines of a market, with parental choice and devolved management, has been advocated by New Right supporters such as Caldwell and Spinks (1992). While they recognise that there are alternative ways of organising the school system, they argue that pressure from parents and local communities will see the emergence of their preferred system, where state intervention is kept to a minimum and a true free market in education grows up, in which a 'culture of service' predominates. However this has been criticised by Hartley (1994), among others, for not telling the whole story of a 'free market' in education. Hartley argues that local control of schools is accompanied by the apparently contradictory process of central strategic control, through the introduction of the national curriculum and quality control mechanisms through government inspection. According to Hartley, the reason for these parallel developments is that, in a postmodern economy, the administration (central government) can no longer administer on its own, but needs the cooperation of those administered – the clients – to accomplish control. Thus social order in general, and in schools, compliance and the transfer of skills from one generation to the next, is carried out by 'coproduction' – where the state and the subjects together administer a late capitalist society, which involves the processes of centralisation and decentralisation being conducted simultaneously. It is to these developments in the 1980s and 1990s that we will turn in Chapter 3.

ITEMS D AND E

Exercise 2.9

e

1. Working with another sociology student, identify two arguments for and two arguments against education directly serving the needs of industry. (If you get stuck on this task, return to it after you have read Chapters 7 and 8.)

i e

2. Study Items D and E. Identify two arguments for and two arguments against the claim that educational standards are falling. You may be able to collect examination statistics from the past few years from your own school or college to provide some evidence.

i

3. You should try to keep yourself up-to-date with the debate on educational standards. It would be a good idea for you to collect recent exam statistics to supplement those we have provided. You could do this nationally by referring to newspapers and periodicals such as *Social Trends* and *Sociology Update*, and locally by looking in your school's annual prospectus.

a

4. Find out from teachers/lecturers at your school/college what Simon (1988) means when he says that the reforms:

(a) depoliticise the curriculum;
(b) widen parental choice and control;
(c) instil market forces into education;
(d) enhance 'the powers of central government and individual schools in the control of education'.

a

5. Can you suggest any contradictions in the New Right educational aims that Simon identifies?

ITEM D

Concern over Standards

The urgent need to raise standards – the original reason for introducing a strongly prescriptive national curriculum – was emphasised by a series of worrying reports and damning statistics. A study by the National Institute for Economic and Social Research found that the proportion of 16-year-olds achieving the equivalent of GCSE grades A to C in maths, science and the national language was 66 per cent in France, 62 per cent in Germany, 50 per cent in Japan and just 27 per cent in England.

Another study by Dr John Marks, one of the government's advisers, showed that less than 10 per cent of State school pupils achieved GCSE grades A to C in English, maths, science, French and either history or geography – the foundations, as he put it, of a broad education. The government-funded Adult Literacy and Basic Skills Unit found that 40 per cent of school leavers had the reading ability expected of an average 11-year-old; the same proportion had not the maths skills expected of a 14-year-old. An opinion poll discovered that less than half the school leavers questioned knew when World War II ended.

At the same time, curiously, the GCSE pass-rate rose for the sixth year in succession – from 32 per cent in 1987, the last year of O-levels, to a record 52 per cent – while the A-level pass-rate soared to a record 82 per cent. Both sets of statistics reawakened concerns about grade inflation. Her Majesty's Inspectors having earlier reported that they had evidence that 'could point to a gradual erosion of standards'.

Later, after studying how GCSE was marked, the Inspectors said the problem was not so much grade inflation as the systematic under-examination of the harder aspects of each subject. In English, for example, candidates achieving high grades often displayed originality, but their vocabulary, spelling, grammar and punctuation were not of the standard required for good-quality communication. In history, the better candidates could evaluate sources of evidence, but their understanding of causation and their ability to produce coherent essays were less well developed. In science, those gaining good grades could handle data and analyse information, but were much less confident in their understanding of key ideas.

The findings appeared to bear out the warnings of GCSE's critics that its emphasis on 'skills' would lead to a reduction in knowledge and intellectual rigour.

Although the Labour party notably failed to exploit the government's weak performance, nothing could disguise the fact that, nearly 15 years after the Tories came to power, state education was continuing to fail an estimated one pupil in three. In his annual report on the nation's schools, Professor Stewart Sutherland, Her Majesty's Chief Inspector, drew attention to the 'stubbornly persistent minority' of poor work that led to two million children receiving an unsatisfactory or 'downright poor' education.

He announced immediate inquiries into why unsatisfactory teaching persisted; standards of behaviour in schools, particularly the prevalence of bullying; and why a declining proportion of pupils are taking A-level mathematics and science. But he said the most urgent need was for a review of the length of the teaching week, which varied between schools by as much as five hours and resulted in some children ultimately receiving a year's less teaching than others.

(Source: J. Clare, 'Education', in P. Allan et al. (eds), Focus on Britain 1994: Review of 1993, Oxfordshire, Philip Allan, 1994.)

ITEM E

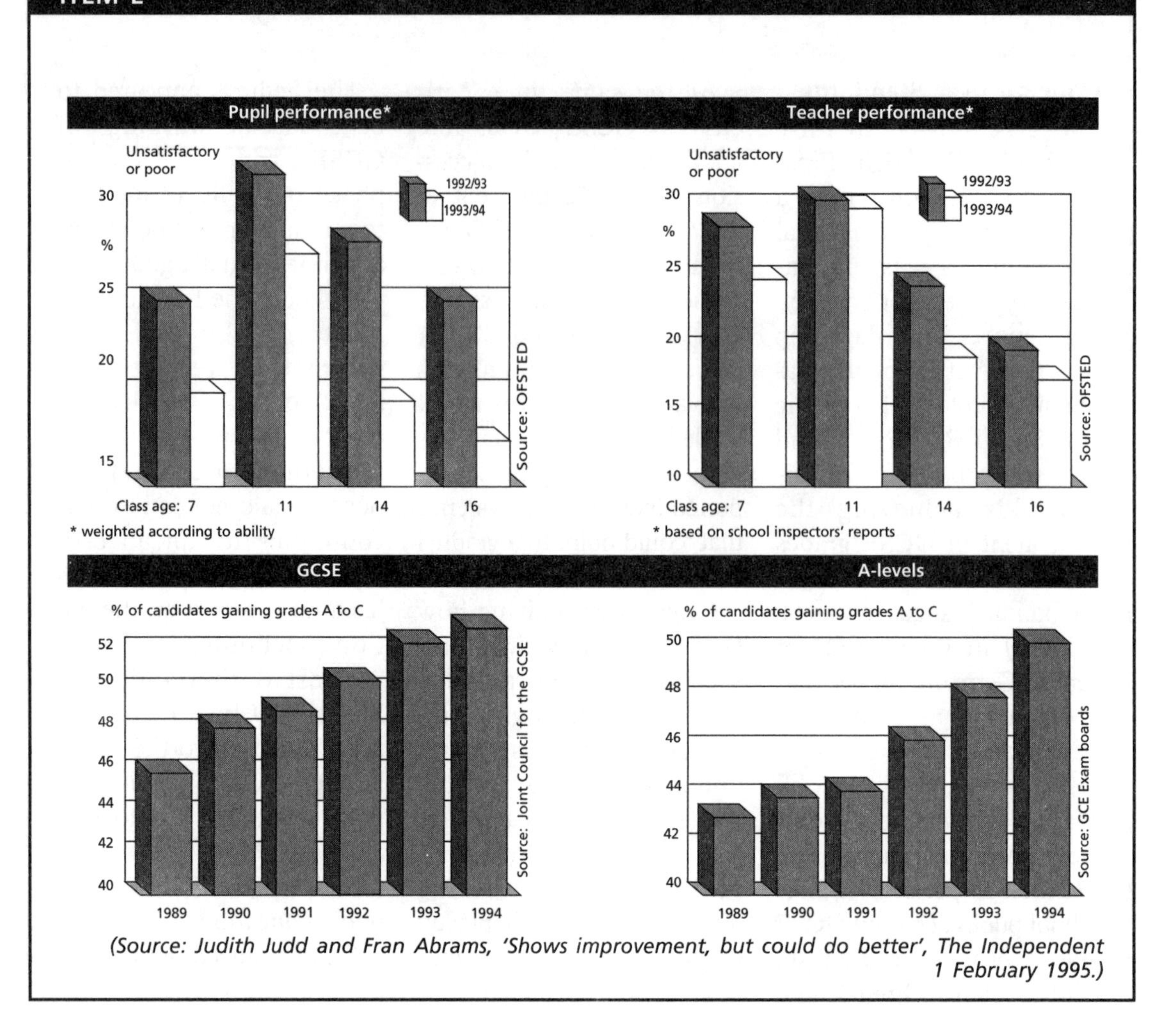

(Source: Judith Judd and Fran Abrams, 'Shows improvement, but could do better', The Independent 1 February 1995.)

3 Changes in educational policy and systems in Britain in the 1980s and 1990s

By the end of this chapter you should:

- understand the reasons for changes to examinations and assessment in the 1980s and 1990s and the competing views expressed about the changes;
- have a critical understanding of the new vocationalism;
- have reflected on student answers to an exam question;
- appreciate conflicting debates surrounding the 1988 Education Act;
- recognise the implications of the Dearing Report;
- be sensitive to changes in education and training for 16–19-year-olds and higher education. You should understand the reasons for the changes and the conflicting views expressed about the changes;
- be familiar with the privatisation process taking place in schools;
- have practised structured exam questions yourself.

Introduction

Under the influence of New Right ideas, Conservative governments in the 1980s and 1990s have been attempting to change the educational climate in Britain. By emphasising vocationalism, standards, parental choice and teacher accountability, they aim to achieve a more 'entrepreneurial' education system. To this end, three broad categories of change can be identified in education and training policy since the 1980s:

1. Changes in examinations and assessment
2. The new vocationalism
3. The 1988 Education Reform Act

Changes in examinations and assessment

Four major changes have occurred with regard to examinations and assessment since the mid 1980s.

1. GCSE

The General Certificate of Education (GCE O-level) and the Certificate of Secondary Education (CSE) have been replaced by the General Certificate of Secondary Education (GCSE). The aim of the GCSE is to unify the examination system at 16, so as to avoid the old O-level/CSE hierarchy. The GCSE is therefore aimed at the top 60 per cent of the ability range, although in practice it is sat by about 80 per cent. The GCSE is also designed to test what candidates 'know, understand and can do', rather than just examine the facts they have learned for the examination. Since the introduction of the GCSE, the proportion of candidates who are gaining the equivalent of a pass in the old O-level has been steadily rising. As indicated earlier, this has provoked a controversy over the standards of the GCSE. Some New Right commentators have expressed a concern that the GCSE is less demanding than the O-level and that therefore 'standards are falling'. The examination boards argue that they have maintained the standards of the old O-level, while introducing new forms of assessment, that allow more students to demonstrate to markers what they can do.

(Useful source of information: S. Walker, 'GCSE Social Science: the story so far', *Social Science Teacher*, vol. 15 no. 1, 1985.)

2. AS courses

Advanced Supplementary (AS) courses, roughly 'half an A-level', have been introduced to run alongside Advanced (A) levels. Their introduction was a response to concern about the narrowness of the post-16 curriculum. Unlike many of Britain's industrial competitors, students specialise in particular subjects at the relatively early age of 16. This specialisation, it is argued, is bad for Britain's economic performance as it discourages students from pursuing scientific subjects beyond the age of 16. However, as Conservative governments during the 1980s and 1990s have consistently defended A levels as the 'gold standard' of the education system, the opportunities to change the post-16 curriculum have been limited by the insistence on maintaining A levels. Therefore AS courses were introduced as an attempt to broaden the experiences of post-16 students without affecting A level provision. The original intention was to allow those specialising in arts or sciences to study subjects beyond those of their immediate interest by following a complementary AS course. However the takeup of AS nationally has been relatively small, with only the social science subjects having any significant entry.

(Useful source of information: J. Coyle, 'What will follow Key Stage 4? Developments in Advanced Supplementary and Advanced level Sociology', *Social Science Teacher*, vol. 20, no. 2, 1991.)

3. Vocational qualifications

Two new qualifications aimed at bridging the academic and vocational divide have been created. Firstly, there is the job-specific National Vocational Qualification (NVQ). NVQs are industry-specific qualifications that are designed to test the competence of those taking them. That is, NVQs test not just knowledge, but skills and understanding also. These competences are tested in application, rather than just in examinations, so that NVQ candidates have to demonstrate their competence in work or simulated work situations. It is thus the performance of candidates, rather than their knowledge, that is the basis of NVQ assessment.

Moreover NVQs allow prior learning to be accredited and they adopt a modular approach, so that students can build up their qualification through a planned process rather than leaving everything to the final examination. Another important dimension of NVQs is that students are empowered through being encouraged to take more responsibility for their own learning. This is achieved, according to Stanton (1990), largely through the action planning process, where students, in consultation with their tutors, chart their own way through the course.

Secondly, the broad vocational General National Vocational Qualification (GNVQ) has been developed by various examination boards, under the umbrella of the National Council for Vocational Qualifications (NCVQ). These courses are not job-specific, but are designed to meet the vocational needs of related groups of occupations, such as health and social care. They have been developed using the model of NVQs and incorporate much of the practice associated with the more specific qualifications. For example there is an emphasis on core skill modules, such as numeracy and information technology. The GNVQ is related explicitly to A levels, in that the courses are described in A-level-equivalent terms. Thus an Advanced GNVQ is the equivalent of two A levels. GNVQs operate across the 14–19 curriculum to offer an alternative route to jobs and higher education for older students.

These developments have been generally welcomed, not least by many students for whom they offer a non-academic alternative. This can be seen in the increasing post-16 stay-on rates. Moreover they have been welcomed by many educationalists as an alternative to the A level route to higher education for those students who have found the traditional advanced levels inappropriate. One of the criticisms of traditional A levels has been the low completion and high failure rate associated with them. For example a significant minority of students follow an A level course for two years, but emerge from it with no qualifications. Many others drop out from A levels as they experience difficulty with the highly academic and abstract nature of many of the courses.

Concern has been expressed about the standard of GNVQs, most notably by Smithers (1993), who argues that they are not the equivalent of A levels and represent a downgrading of the important theoretical aspects of vocational training adhered to by our industrial competitors. Others, such as Jones (1993), argue that GNVQs are just as rigorous as A-levels but in a different way, and identify more clearly than A-levels what an individual is capable of. Another criticism is that GNVQs are no more likely than A levels to ensure that those who begin the course will emerge with the full qualification at the end. For example a survey of 12 GNVQ colleges (FEU, 1994) showed that the completion rate for the intermediate GNVQ science course was 60 per cent across the 12 colleges, compared with 90 per cent, who completed the first year of their A level course.

A more fundamental criticism of the development of these courses, with their credit accumulation and continuous assessment, has come from the postmodernists. Usher and Edwards (1994) do not accept the argument that continuous assessment is somehow 'better' than end-of-course examination. They argue that continuous assessment is a more stressful form of assessment and ties the student into a huge web of bureaucratic documentation; that independent thought is squeezed out by every action and piece of work being open to assessment and codification as a 'competence'. They see the development of this type of education as an example of the increased surveillance associated with postmodern societies, as outlined by Foucault (see for example Foucault, 1982). The concept of surveillance is used by postmodernists to describe the processes of social control in postmodern societies. Premodern societies depended on physical force to control the population. Social control in societies characterised by modernity is more likely to be achieved through the rule of law. In postmodern societies, individuals tend to 'police' themselves through ways of thinking and behaving (discourses) that define what is seen as 'normal' or 'abnormal' in society. Surveillance in this sense does not include the direct gaze of the teacher. Rather it consists of the competences that have to be demonstrated in order to gain the qualification. In effect, Usher and Edwards argue that students become the NVQ, as their public identity is defined by their progress towards achieving the competences. They exercise surveillance of themselves as they chart their own progress through the NVQ course, carrying out appropriate behaviours for the stage they are at.

(Useful sources of information: S. Maguire, 'Training for a Living? The 1990's Youth Labour Market', *Sociology Review*, vol. 3, no. 1, 1993; F. Koubel, 'General National Vocational Qualifications: Some Considerations for Social Science Teachers', *Social Science Teacher*, vol. 22, no. 3, 1993.)

4. Coursework

Coursework has been introduced as part of the assessment for examination courses followed by 14–18 year olds. Coursework is where the student offers material developed by him or herself for assessment outside the main examination. This may take the form of projects or classroom activities of various types. It was pioneered within the GCSE programme, but has been adopted in many A-level courses also. The emphasis on coursework has been boosted by the emergence of GNVQs, where students have to build up a 'portfolio of evidence' based on a variety of activities. However there has been government opposition to coursework in academic examinations, and as a consequence the percentage of coursework in most academic examinations has been restricted to 20 per cent. Concern about coursework has centred on the opportunities for candidates to cheat and obtain help from others, notably parents. While Scott (1990) found that there was some input from parents in terms of providing opportunities and resources for their children, it was not widespread. Coursework seems to be a popular option with students as it provides them with opportunities to gain marks outside the examination room.

The introduction of coursework is part of a wider movement in education towards experiential learning. Experiential methods of teaching do not rely on the 'teacher–expert' teaching students an accepted body of knowledge. Rather it is a way of teaching that relies on students exploring for themselves issues of interest, and thus gaining knowledge of something through their own experience of it. While experiential learning has been welcomed by many types of educationalist, postmodernists such as Usher and Edwards (1994) argue that experiential learning fits in well with the postmodern culture we live in. Postmodernists argue that all knowledge is relative, that there is no such thing as the absolute truth. Instead there are only multiple and partial realities based on the perspectives of individuals and groups in society. Postmodern societies are characterised by a shift away from book learning to an emphasis on images and experience as sources of knowledge. There can be, in postmodern societies, no right or wrong pieces of knowledge, because what we know depends on where we stand in social formations, such as what groups we belong to or identify with, and the sense and understanding we bring to bear on our experience. Postmodernists describe this as the 'situatedness' of the individual in the social formation. As Baudrillard (1983) argues, when what is 'real' is no longer for certain or accepted by everybody, there is more emphasis on lived experience as a source of knowledge. Experiential learning therefore expresses at the level of education what we are experiencing in the wider society.

Usher and Edwards argue that the perceived effects of experiential learning are contradictory. It is seen by the New Right as an important counterbalance to the influence of progressive teachers, who are believed to dominate the world of education. The assumption here is that experience of the 'real' world will lay bare the falseness of left-wing ideology. More left-wing views see experiential learning as an emancipatory technique, freeing the individual learner from the tyranny of received knowledge delivered by an authoritarian teacher. Usher and Edwards stress how this contradication is itself a 'real' one, existing at the same time in the same situation, and never to be resolved with victory for one viewpoint or another.

(Useful source of information: T. Heaton and S. Andrew, 'Coursework: the students' perspective', *Sociology Review*, vol. 2, no. 4, 1993.)

Link exercise 3.1

From your own experiences, explain how any two changes to examinations and assessment fit in with new vocational thinking. (Hint: consider the ways in which the courses and assessment methods give school leavers transferable skills, that is, skills they can utilise in the workplace.) This exercise may best be attempted when you have read the section on new vocationalism later on in this chapter.

Exercise 3.1

Working with two other sociology students, hold a debate on the merits and drawbacks of the changes in examinations and assessment. One of you should act as a chair to the debate, one should argue the merits of the changes and the other should argue their drawbacks. The chair should ensure that the two speakers have an equal amount of time to make their case and that the debate is conducted in an orderly fashion. The two debaters should carefully prepare their arguments by doing some thorough background research into the changes. The articles referred to above could act as a useful starting point for this research. Each debater should know exactly what the new courses and forms of assessment are, how they differ from their predecessors and the merits or drawbacks of the changes. If you are feeling brave, try to hold the debate in front of an audience, perhaps your sociology class. The audience could have a vote on who made the most convincing argument.

Exercise 3.2

Keep yourself up-to-date on the issues surrounding examinations and assessment by reading the educational media. You should jot down any arguments that add to those you came across during Exercise 3.1.

New vocationalism

New vocationalism refers to the educational initiatives that have emerged in the 1980s and 1990s in an attempt to make educational provision more responsive to industry's needs, for example the Technical and Vocational Education Initiative. Of course there has always been a concern to match the educational system to the demands of industry, but new vocationalism differs from previous attempts in three important ways. Watson (1993) argues that (1) new vocationalism attempts to bridge the gap between general and vocational education, rather than seeing them as separate; (2) new vocational qualifications are awarded after proof of acquisition of particular competences and not by serving a particular length of time in an apprenticeship; and (3) flexible 'transferable' skills replace the narrow job-specific skills of previous attempts at vocational education.

The six most prominent developments in new vocationalism have been:

1. The Youth Training Scheme (YTS).
2. Employment Training (ET).
3. The Technical and Vocational Education Initiative (TVEI).
4. The Certificate of Pre-vocational Education (CPVE).
5. City Technology Colleges (CTCs).
6. General National Vocational Qualifications (GNVQs).

The government claims that, through such developments, employers will receive workers who have the necessary skills to make effective use of modern technology, and thereby improve the productivity and economic performance of individual firms and the country as a whole.

1. YTS

This has its origins in the Youth Opportunities Programme (YOP), which ran from 1978–83. From 1986 YTS offered a two-year training programme for 16-year-old school leavers who were unemployed after leaving school. The scheme consisted of structured, work-based training, with a minimum of 20 weeks on-the-job training over the two-year period. By 1988 all 16–17 year olds were guaranteed a place on a YTS programme if they wanted one. However they lost their entitlement to income support at the same time.

In 1990 YTS was replaced by Youth Training (YT). In 1991 responsibility for Youth Training provision passed from the nationally organised Manpower Services Commission (MSC) to local Training and Enterprise Councils (TECs) in England and Wales and Local Enterprise Companies (LECs) in Scotland. The key difference between YTS and YT is that trainees are now offered a programme that varies in length according to the needs and development of the person being trained. Youth trainees are also now able to work towards National Vocational Qualifications (NVQs).

Moore and Hickox (1994) see the introduction of YTS and its successors as part of the New Right agenda, which, while leaving existing educational arrangements alone, has provided an alternative agency (eventually the Training Agency) offering courses that might prove attractive to those young people (and adults under the ET scheme) who are not keen to follow a traditional educational route to qualifications. Morever the providers of YTS courses were able to intervene directly in the further education sector, which undermined the principle of educational autonomy from the state.

2. ET

Employment Training (ET) was introduced in 1988 in order to meet the individual training needs of unemployed adults. This programme merged with Employment Action (EA) in 1993 and now bears the title 'Training for Work'. As with YT, Training for Work operates under the auspices of the TECs/LECs. The aim is to provide the unemployed, especially the long-term unemployed, with skills and attitudes that will be attractive to employers. However the merged Training for Work programme has been criticised because it represents a reduction in the training entitlement of the unemployed from 26 to 20 weeks. Moreover there is no mandatory training element to the work experience offered under Training for Work, and the take-up of places has therefore been slow and the drop-out rate high (see Kirby, 1993).

3. TVEI

Now known as the Technical and Vocational Extension (TVE), the TVEI was not a course. It was a way of organising and managing the education of 14–18 year olds across the whole ability range. Its central purpose was to widen and enrich the curriculum so that young adults were prepared in a practical and relevant way for the world of work. Notable developments within the original TVEI framework included work experience placements with local employers, records of achievement, and providing or widening the provision of information technology in schools and colleges. The TVEI was seen as a way in which schools could provide access to the 'enterprise culture', whereby young people would be exposed to 'entrepreneurial spirit'. The TVEI was financed through the Manpower Services Commission and was designed to challenge existing practices in schools. This was achieved, according to Weiner (1990), through a 'carrot-dangling' process, in which extra funds were made available to schools pursuing certain types of vocational activity. But she also argues, along with Finn (1985), that such initiatives, rather than being committed to equal opportunity, signalled the end of any commitment to the principle that had been central to educational policy since the Second World War.

4. CPVE

The CPVE was a one-year, full-time course for post-16-year-old students in schools and colleges. The course consisted of three components:

1. The core, which included areas such as applied numeracy, science, technology and information technology.
2. Vocational studies, which included modules such as business and administrative services, and distribution.
3. Additional studies: these were not compulsory, and included GCSEs and leisure studies.

In addition to these three components, students undertook a work experience programme for a minimum of 15 days.

The main successes of the CPVE and other foundation vocational courses were increased motivation and attendance (Spours and Young, 1988), thereby showing that vocational courses did have a constituency amongst young people. However, although the CPVE was seen as meeting the needs of some underachieving students, it was also criticised for introducing new social divisions, as those graduating from the CPVE found it difficult to access more academic courses, such as the GCSE.

The CPVE was replaced in 1992 by the Diploma in Vocational Education (DVE). This course is open to a wider age range (14–19) and has three levels: foundation, intermediate and national. It signalled the emergence of a national system of vocational qualifications, which were equated directly with traditional academic qualifications through the GNVQ system.

5. CTCs

A limited number of CTCs were set up for 11–19 year olds in large towns and inner city areas. They are independent of local authority control and, in part, were established with the aid of industrial sponsorship. While conforming to the requirements of the National Curriculum, emphasis is given to science, mathematics and technology. For example 60 per cent of the timetable for 14–16 year olds is devoted to these subjects. CTCs have fostered close links with industry and offer work experience at an early age. They are modelled on the 'magnet schools' in the United States, where schools are allowed to offer specialisms to attract particular types of student.

Criticism of the CTCs has concentrated on the lack of industrial support for their establishment, with the result that the government has had to inject large amounts of cash (Ball, 1990a). The consequence of this has been, according to critics, to skew local markets in schools in such a way as to make the job of local education authorities more difficult. Moreover CTCs have been established as much in middle-class suburbs as in inner city areas, thus reducing their 'revitalisation role'. OFSTED inspectors of some CTCs have at times been critical of the education provided in these colleges.

6. GNVQs

We have already looked at the development of General National Vocational Qualifications in the section on 'Changes in Examinations and Assessment'. GNVQs are an important element of new vocationalism as they are an attempt to produce examination qualifications that equal those obtained by the academic route of GCSE, A levels and traditional university degrees.

Exercise 3.3

1. The chart below gives two arguments for and two arguments against YT. Copy out and then complete the chart by identifying four other arguments for and against YT. When considering the arguments for YT you will find it useful to consult the literature on YT in your local careers library. The following articles will be useful when addressing the arguments against YT: D. Finn, 'Education for Jobs: the route to YTS', *Social Studies Review*, vol. 4, no. 1 (1988); S. Maguire, 'Training for a Living? The 1990's Youth Labour Market', *Sociology Review*, vol. 3, no. 1 (1993).

Arguments for YT	**Arguments against YT**
1. You get paid a wage or allowance while you learn.	1. YT is a way of disguising the 'true' rate of youth unemployment.
2. You can gain vocational qualifications whilst working.	2. YT lacks status and many school leavers feel stigmatised by joining a YT programme.

2. Try to contact two people who have undertaken or are currently undertaking a YT programme. Show them your list of arguments for and against YT. Do they agree with the arguments you have identified? Try to get them to back up their views with their actual experiences. Overall, are they in favour of YT or not? Can they add to the list of arguments for and against YT? Share and discuss your findings with another sociology student.

3. In no more than 100 words, write your conclusions about the desirability of YT. (Hint: it is important that you state which of the two views of YT you find most plausible, and why.)

ie 4. Take any new vocational initiative other than YT and investigate the arguments for and against its introduction. Which viewpoint do you find most convincing, and why? You may find it useful to look at past copies of *The Times Educational Supplement* or the education features in 'quality' newspapers. Making use of relevant CD ROMs will prove helpful. Teachers in your school or college could also be a valuable source of information. Your school or college may have a CPVE/DVE and/or a TVEI/TVE coordinator who may be able to help.

ITEM A

Exam question and student answers

You should now be familiar with new vocationalism and the various viewpoints expressed about it. The question and answer exercise that follows is based on a question in the AEB's A-level June 1992 examination. It should help you to clarify your understanding of the debates surrounding new vocationalism and give you an insight into what constitutes good and bad practice when writing answers to examination questions.

Before you begin this exercise you must carefully read the following:

- Item A and the question
- The student responses
- Comments on the responses

Once you have completed the reading, mark the remaining two student responses. You should gauge the standard from the previously marked responses and comments. You should award each response a whole mark between 0 and 8. Make sure you justify your marking with comments, as in the other three student responses.

ITEM A

The view that education is failing to train young people in the skills needed for jobs has influenced educationalists. The government created an agency called the Manpower Services Commission (MSC) which began to pay for courses which were directly connected with training people in specific skills, rather than in the sort of general education which was typical of schools. Gradually the philosophy of skill-training, called 'vocationalism', and the large amount of money spent by the MSC changed the nature of education after the age of 16. Supporters of vocational schemes argue that as Britain has fallen behind other nations because of an unskilled workforce, the new courses will help remedy this problem, by creating new attitudes to work and new skills amongst young people.

(Source: Adapted from S. Moore, Sociology Alive, Stanley Thornes, 1987.)

Question

Item A suggests that the aim of the new vocationalism is to 'create new attitudes to work and new skills amongst young people'. Some sociologists have suggested alternative aims. Using information from Item A and elsewhere, evaluate sociological accounts of the new vocationalism. *(8 marks)*

Student answers

CANDIDATE A

Durkheim has highlighted his views and argues that the various education systems, including vocational courses, exist to provide the workforce with the various skills required. Before industrialisation these skills were provided by parents in certain trades (for example blacksmiths), but then the division of labour became too specialised and a scheme was needed. Many sociologists (especially Marxists) believe that education is not needed and that on-the-job training is sufficient as education overeducates the workforce and allows the capitalist economy to control its workforce. Durkheim also believes that the vocational system transmits the norms and values of society so that people do not deviate from mainstream culture.

Bowles and Gintis, however, argue that the system creates a set of myths, which in turn create a submissive, passive worker ready to do a lot of work for very little recognition. They believe that a meritocracy has developed, and this has led people to believe that their success is dependent on their educational achievement and that those who work the hardest will reach the top. But this is not always true. Marxists believe that privilege breeds privilege, and that no matter what education people receive the middle class will always reach the top as they have the means to get there. Marxists believe that the system is for the working class, yet it teaches them how to cope with their low place in society, not how to improve themselves.

Mark and comments

2 marks. This answer is an attempt to apply the ideas of Durkheim and Bowles and Gintis to the issue of vocationalism. However the answer does not focus precisely enough on the issue of vocationalism and much irrelevant material is included. In passing, the answer suggests that vocational schemes were needed to provide the workforce with skills that parents could no longer give their children (a positive view), and that the system is intended to produce a particular attitude in workers (a negative view). Though other bits of the material could have been made relevant, they were not applied to the question set. Nor did the answer interpret Item A effectively, or attempt to assess the two positions that were suggested.

CANDIDATE B

Marxists would disagree that the aim of the new vocationalism is to create new attitudes and skills amongst young people, they believe that the creation of the YTS by the MSC and other training schemes have been introduced by the capitalists, who use their power and control of the state as a way of gaining a pool of cheap labour to further their profits. The young are easily exploited, have little public voice and are unlikely to be unionised. Westergaard and Resler claim that these attitudes were actually capitalist ones that reinforced capitalist ideology and domination. They encouraged workers to accept the status quo and the belief that the situation was their own fault because of their educational 'failure'. This could be used to distract attention from the inequalities of the capitalist system.

Other sociologists see these schemes as a way in which the government disguises unemployment figures and so directs attention away from the failings of policies. Functionalists see the policies of the government on new vocationalism as an extension of the meritocratic educational system, whereby everybody has the same chance to achieve success.

These work schemes would further collective goals and benefit the interests of society as a whole, and ensure and maintain stability, not conflict, amongst those who because of unemployment may become marginal in society.

I think that, on balance, sociological accounts have tended to be more critical of vocational schemes than supportive.

Mark and comments

5 marks. This answer is a more successful attempt to apply Marxist and functionalist positions to the issue of new vocationalism. There is also a suggestion of a third position concerning unemployment figures. The use of Marxist and functionalist ideas here is more focused on the schemes and the answer also includes appropriate evidence. In addition it employs information from Item A as a starting point for a discussion of the Marxist position. The answer displays appropriate knowledge, accurately reproduced. An attempt at evaluation, although limited, does emerge from the main body of the answer, where the bulk of the evidence supports a criticism of the schemes. To score more, this would have to be extended somewhat, for example by looking at the ideological positions of the supporters and critics of the schemes.

CANDIDATE C

Some sociologists, for example, Paul Thompson, a Marxist, believe that schemes such as 'YT' produce a pool of workers who are prepared to do low-skilled, low-paid jobs. This is echoed by many who believe that vocational schemes are slave labour. The Marxists especially criticise them, saying that they support capitalism. This is because they provide cheap labour, which is done by youths who are relatively fit and healthy. Other sociologists believe that vocationalism does not succeed because there are no jobs for trainees to go to once they have finished the course. They criticise the government because YT trainees cannot claim benefit and thus have to rely on the often meagre earnings that employers pay them. They also claim that the government can keep down unemployment figures since those on a vocational scheme are not registered as unemployed.

Item A says that the 'new courses will help . . . by creating new attitudes to work and new skills amongst young people'. However sociologists disagree, saying that young people become bored and feel dejected if they have to do basic jobs such as sweeping floors. They also believe that employers would rather have workers with academic skills and therefore few employ Youth Training students. On the other hand YT can be useful in such industries as engineering, where practical skills are acquired by experience.

In conclusion, on the basis of the evidence presented one is inclined to favour the sociologists' view that YT is not the answer. The government seems resistant to putting money into a scheme to help create jobs. Until it does, vocational training will continue to be unsuccessful.

Mark and comments

4 marks. Again, this answer reveals some knowledge of the schemes offered under new vocationalism. However it offers a very one-sided, negative view of the schemes. While evidence is supplied to support this negative position, such as the work of Paul Thompson, the only positive view of the schemes is an interpretation of Item A. It is therefore unsurprising that, by depending mainly on sociological accounts, the writer has chosen to support the critics of vocational schemes. This answer is therefore an unbalanced, albeit straightforward, account of the issue under consideration and can only attract a limited number of marks.

CANDIDATE D

New vocationalism has its foundations in the 1988 Act. It has advantages, such as training young people in the skills needed for jobs and the workforce. The government has introduced MSC, YT and ET, which are all beneficial to society. Functionalists would say youth training skills are important for industry. Conservative sociologists would agree with Item A and say that the new vocationalism provides specific skills rather than the general education that is typical of schools. Criticisms of the new vocationalism is that sociologists which are liberal and social democratic would completely disagree. They say that vocationalism exploits young people. Industry is using the young and the government is just disguising the unemployment statistics.

Mark and comments

To be completed by you.

CANDIDATE E

Item A suggests that 'new vocationalism' is aimed at training people, teaching them skills and better attitudes to work, and providing a skilled workforce. Dan Finn claims that a document was leaked to *Time Out* showing the government's real aims were to reduce unemployment statistics, provide cheap labour, lower wages and ensure social control over the young to prevent crime. He says that the government's claim that training school leavers will reduce youth unemployment is false and a cover-up, since training cannot create more new jobs. He also believes that such training schemes indoctrinate the young into being an obedient, docile and highly conformist workforce that will not threaten the status quo. Stan Cohen argues they actually de-skill the workforce and Paul Willis *et al.* argue that they keep youth in 'suspended animation' before getting a job.

Others have argued that new vocationalism has created a two-tiered system, in which schools such as CTCs and those which have opted out have better resources, better teachers, 'enrichment programmes' and can be selective, thus attracting only the best pupils. Therefore new vocationalism has reduced equality of opportunity in schools and parity of esteem, turning the clocks back to the tripartite system and its inequalities. It is also argued that the long-term plan of the 'New Right' is to privatise education, which would be setting the clock back further and creating a great deal of inequality. Many criticise the new schemes for not addressing the issues of gender and race, nor the issue of cultural definitions of knowledge that reduce equality of opportunity by enforcing the white, male, middle-class view of what constitute valuable skills and knowledge.

The views of Marxists such as Finn and Willis are perhaps questioned because they are influenced by Marxist ideology and have a vested interest in showing how new vocationalism is exploitative. They also claim that new vocationalism supports their theory that the function of education is to fulfil the needs of capitalists and the economy, since it has put the needs of industry before the development of the individual's capabilities; and through vocationalism the government has been able to gain greater control over what is taught and how it is taught, outlawing subjects such as peace studies and methods such as progressive teaching that oppose their political beliefs.

Mark and comments

To be completed by you.

Vocationalists (those who promote the vocational element in education) are not a new phenomenon and can be found in every post-Second World War period. Moore and Hickox (1994) suggest that the importance of vocationalist strands in education is associated with the perceived need to increase the skill levels of British society in order to improve economic performance in an increasingly competitive world. The expansion of vocational education and training in the 1980s and 1990s is therefore associated with the need to increase the number staying on beyond the age of 16, by providing new types of courses, new ways of delivering content to students and new ways of assessing students. Vocationalists therefore claim that vocational courses are more 'relevant' than traditional courses because they closely correspond to the 'real' needs of students and the 'real' needs of the economy.

However Moore and Hickox also argue that vocationalism in the 1980s and 1990s has become detached from its usual 'liberal' proponents and become attached to the New Right agenda of changing the culture of British institutions, such as the education system. The aim of New Right theorists is to promote an 'enterprise' culture in education, rather than the 'liberal' and 'radical' culture of the 1960s, with its emphasis on individual fulfilment and the empowerment and upward social mobility of disadvantaged groups, such as the working class and ethnic minorities (see for example DES, 1974). Some New Right vocationalists are therefore critical of the traditional academic curriculum, because they see it as elitist and irrelevant to the real world of work. Finn (1987) identifies this New Right critique as also being hostile to the vocational programmes of the 1970s, with their emphasis on trade union membership and workers' rights.

The concern of New Right vocationalists is therefore to use central control of the curriculum to promote an education system that encourages an entrepreneurial spirit in schoolchildren, and in which the content of the curriculum is much more directly related to the skills requirements of industry, through an emphasis on the acquisition of competencies rather than abstract knowledge. The New Right vocationalists therefore look to the German model of education, as described by Barnett (1986), as a way of ensuring that Britain produces a workforce with the high levels of skill required for a post-Fordist economy.

This approach, with its emphasis on central control, has been criticised for going against the central belief of the New Right: that the market should decide the content and outcomes of the education system. The New Right vocationalists argue that education is too important a resource to be left to market forces, where existing views on what constitutes useful education could crowd out the newer vocational approaches. The New Right vocationalists are also in conflict with other New Right strands, such as that of Scruton (1984), where the emphasis is on a traditional, subject-based curriculum, combined with respect for traditional authority.

The whole vocational approach has also come under criticism from some sociologists, such as Moore and Hickox (1994). They argue that it is impossible to forecast with any degree of certainty what the future needs of industry might be, and it is therefore impossible to create a vocational education system that is responsive to those needs. Moreover Jones and Moore (1993) argue that the notion of competence employed by the New Right is a very narrow one and does not include the deeper intellectual competencies that are necessary to develop the flexible workforce needed in a post-Fordist economy.

Student answers D and E obtained 3 and 6 marks respectively.

The 1988 Education Reform Act

The 1988 Education Reform Act is arguably the most wide-ranging piece of educational legislation since the 1944 Education Act. The five most significant aspects of the Act are outlined below.

1. The national curriculum

This was implemented in an attempt to create a broad and balanced, standardised, formal curriculum. By formal curriculum we mean the subjects that are offered to students for study in school. The introduction of the national curriculum was significant because it shifted the balance of power over the school curriculum. No longer were a diverse set of interest groups (local education authorities, teachers, exam boards, university academics) controlling the curriculum, but the national government. Ball (1990a) argues that the introduction of the national curriculum was made possible by the 'discourse of derision' established by New Right thinkers, which laid the blame for perceived educational failure at the doors of those who had traditionally controlled the curriculum. Educational 'experts' were attacked by the New Right as being responsible for the mismatch between the needs of the economy and the skills that children learned in schools.

The national curriculum is essentially academic and traditional. In some ways this conflicts with the vocational emphasis of initiatives such as TVEI, CPVE and YT. What has been created is a stratified system of 'core', 'foundation' and 'optional' subjects for children educated under the state sector to follow. The important changes made to the national curriculum (and national assessment) following the 1994 Dearing Report will be introduced to you in Exercise 3.6 (pages 41–2). The introduction of the national curriculum was an important landmark in the history of state education in Britain as it represents, for the first time, an attempt to control the content of education nationally. Despite the involvement of many educationalists and teachers in the formation of the national curriculum, it has been heavily criticised by teachers for being overprescriptive (trying to control too much of what is actually taught), bureaucratic (involving a huge increase in paper work) and responsible for squeezing other worthwhile educational experiences out of the curriculum, for example GCSE sociology.

Moreover there have been many disagreements over the content of national curriculum subjects. For example there has been a long-running dispute over what aspects of history should be included. Successive government ministers have intervened to put forward a particular view of history, stressing traditional approaches. Sylvester (1994) points out that this ignores elements of history (for example women's history) that are important in a multicultural society such as Britain. Postmodernists would also argue that, given the fragmented and diverse nature of postmodern societies, in which individuals have many conflicting educational needs, the attempt to impose a common curriculum on everyone is unlikely to meet those needs (Donald, 1992). For example sociology is not part of the national curriculum and this has had the effect of decimating the number of students taking GCSE sociology. Therefore the national curriculum does not meet the needs of students with an interest in the social.

However there is a much more fundamental criticism of the national curriculum, and this needs to be addressed here. Postmodernists have argued against the existence of any fundamental truths in society that can be translated into a national curriculum. For example, one of the main elements of the national curriculum is science, which the postmodernists would describe as a 'metanarrative' – a 'story' or myth, not a collection of truths, that attempts to explain the whole of existence.

On the contrary, the postmodernist Baudrillard (1983) argues that it is not possible to penetrate the appearance or surface of things to see what is 'really there'. To Baudrillard the only reality is the surface reality of the images of the media age – the 'signs' we absorb from the media, which form a new type of reality: the 'hyperreality'. Therefore, according to Baudrillard, our 'knowledge' of the world is not gained from experience itself, but from our experience of media images. What we 'know' about the United States, Israel or South Africa is drawn from our experience of television pictures about them. Similarly, what we 'know' about science is drawn from the hyperreal and not from learning the 'truth' about the world in schools.

There is, in the postmodern view, a collapse of the 'economy of truth' (Hebdige, 1989) in the contemporary world, that is, the notion that there is any verifiable truth is both irrelevant and misleading. Therefore to present a national curriculum that is supposed to encompass everything a child in Britain should know is an enterprise doomed to failure. All information, according to the postmodernists, is shifting and precarious. What is today's 'knowledge' will be tomorrow's 'falsehood'. But postmodernists go further than this, arguing that any attempt to find out what is 'really going on' is pointless, and therefore the idea of identifying what is 'science' or 'history' – as the national curriculum attempts to do – is useless. What the national curriculum therefore represents is not knowledge but a type of ideology; a 'discourse' (see Foucault, 1979) or perspective that is not true, but is powerful. The national curriculum is powerful because it is a way of organising information, so that the world is seen as being organised in one particular way as opposed to another.

Critics of this view argue that science is more than just a 'metanarrative' – it is a distinct way of producing 'truth' that transcends, or goes beyond, individual or cultural experiences. What this means is that scientists in different societies and from different ideologies can agree that some things have been proved as 'true' about the underlying reality of the universe. Scientists do not just examine surface realities, but can verify knowledge through their methodologies. There is thus a body of knowledge called science that can be presented to children as the 'truth' of things.

2. National assessment

This involves standardised assessment tests (SATs) in certain subjects at the ages of 7, 11, 14 and 16. These tests were introduced as a way of monitoring standards in schools and keeping parents informed of their children's progress. National testing has proved to be one of most controversial aspects of the national curriculum arrangements, with teachers boycotting them in 1993 and 1994. There are two features of the testing arrangements that many teachers object to. First, they argue that the testing arrangements force them to 'teach to the test'. They spend so much time preparing their students for the SATs that there is little time for any other form of education. Second, the results of the tests are compiled into 'league tables' of schools, giving parents information about how a school is performing. Critics of league tables argue that they are a very crude measure of a school's effectiveness. A school may appear to be doing very badly in the league table, but it actually provides an effective learning environment for lower ability pupils. Some pupils might have done better than if they had gone to another school that concentrates less on low ability students, yet this second school's test scores may be better because it attracts more able students in the first place.

3. Open enrolment

This places an obligation on schools to enrol all comers to their full capacity and provides parents with a wider choice in the type of state school they can send their children to. Moreover it exposes schools to internal market forces as they seek to compete for pupils. The creation of a market in education has been one of the main policies of successive Conservative governments since 1979. The aim of the New Right theorists who have influenced the government is to introduce into the state sector as many features of the private sector as possible. The New Right wishes to introduce the idea of consumers (parents and children) exercising choice in a system characterised by diversification (that is, the introduction of many different types of school), which would offer consumers real choices. Through open enrolment and the league tabling of examination results, parents will be able to identify 'star' schools, and these will become popular. Conversely 'sink' schools will be forced to change their practices for the better or they will suffer a decline in their fortunes, which logically could lead to closure.

The New Right argues that this will encourage the spread of good practices throughout the school system. Critics of open enrolment have argued that, in practice, oversubscribed schools can choose who they accept or reject, so that there is only limited parental choice in the system. Given that popular schools can choose their pupils, these critics argue that selection is being introduced through the back door. This has the effect of recreating the inequalities and hierarchies in schools that existed before the reforms of the 1960s (Elliott and MacLennan, 1994).

4. Local management of schools (LMS)

This increases the financial responsibilities of head teachers and governors as they are given direct control of 90 per cent of their school budget. The budget is largely determined by the size of the school roll and therefore one of the effects of LMS is to encourage competition between schools for pupils. LMS has had a number of consequences, but head teachers and governors have been enthusiastically in favour of the devolution of decision-making into their hands (Simkins, 1994) as it can increase staff commitment. Conversely, as Ball (1990b) notes, staff may be faced with unfamiliar demands on their time for marketing and finance-raising activities, which they may resent or be ill-prepared for. New Right theorists argue that giving autonomy to schools in this way will increase diversity and choice in the education system, as schools will seek to specialise in different areas. However Moore (1990) notes that schools in Chicago, when given autonomy, have tended to emphasise traditional academic criteria rather than new specialisms. Thus autonomy may lead to a new uniformity rather than increased diversity.

5. Grant maintained schools (GMS)

This part of the Act allows head teachers and governors to 'opt out' of local authority control, providing the majority of parents whose sons and/or daughters attend the school vote for it. Unlike LEA schools, GM schools receive their budgets from central government through the Funding Agency for Schools. This quango (a non-elected, government-appointed organisation) offers GM schools increased autonomy as they have full control over their budgets and a complete say in how their schools are run and organised. GM schools that have 'opted out' of LEA control so far have been influenced by one of two factors. They have either been under threat of closure by the LEA, or have wished to offer a fairly traditional curriculum.

Rather than promoting choice and diversity, as postmodernists would suggest, GM schools are mainly a type of reconstructed grammar school, with a heavily academic emphasis. Moreover the autonomy of GM schools is circumscribed by central government control. Like LEA schools, under LMS they have been given operational control (that is, day-to-day control) over their budgets. However the government retains allocative control (that is, the government decides the total funds to be allocated) in terms of the overall education budget, which necessarily curtails what GMs would like to achieve.

Exercise 3.4

In the 1970s Young (1971) wrote about the social construction of educational knowledge. He claimed that powerful groups in society ensured that the formal curriculum taught in schools was stratified into high- and low-status subjects. Some might argue that Young's ideas can be applied to the national curriculum, as established in 1988. This is because there is a clear distinction between core and foundation subjects.

Your task is to find out what were the core (possibly high-status) and foundation (possibly low-status) subjects. When you have done this, copy out and complete the table below. You should also write a short evaluative paragraph that reflects the extent to which the core subjects can be deemed high status and the foundation subjects low status.

The National Curriculum – status of subjects

Core or high-status subjects	Foundation or low-status subjects
	History Music

Exercise 3.5

1. You will see on the next two pages a series of jumbled up statements relating to the 1988 Education Reform Act. Your task is to identify which are the arguments for the Act and which are against it. When you have made your choices, record your answers in a table that clearly separates the arguments for the 1988 Education Act from the arguments against it. Aim to put the statements into your own words rather than simply copying them out. The following example should help you to get started. An argument for LMS is: LMS allows head teachers to spend their budget as they see fit.

2. When you have completed the task, do some further research into the 1988 Education Reform Act (this could be an ongoing research programme). You could begin by seeking the opinion of teachers in your school or college, and by keeping a close eye on the educational press. Add to the list of arguments you have written down so far. You should aim to end up with at least three arguments for and against each aspect of the 1988 Education Reform Act.

ARGUMENTS FOR AND AGAINST THE 1988 EDUCATION REFORM ACT

Open enrolment

Schools will be forced into a competitive market place because of open enrolment. Schools will raise standards and offer an improved service in the hope of attracting students from nearby educational institutions. The quality of the whole education system will improve as a consequence.

GMS

It will prove more difficult for Local Education Authorities to co-ordinate resources and services for all schools in an area as opted out, schools move out of its control.

LMS

LMS may lead to a fall in educational standards if experienced (costly) teachers are replaced by inexperienced (cheaper) teachers.

National Assessment

. . . standardised national testing provides a reliable means by which society can evaluate the success of individual schools and the education system as a whole.

Open Enrolment

Competition between schools is likely to create a climate of hostility and suspicion between educational institutions, rather than mutual support and cooperation.

National Curriculum

It will help to ensure that there is some consistency in what is taught in schools across Britain. Repetition and lack of continuity between primary and secondary schools will be avoided. Students who have to move from one part of the country to another will find the transition less disruptive.

GMS

Grant maintained schools have a greater control over their budget. This allows school governors and head teachers to spend money as they see fit. Money which used to be held back by the LEA for adminis-tration can now be spent on books and equipment, and employing more teachers.

National Curriculum

It is a prescriptive and burdensome monster. We are left with a very cluttered curriculum.

National Assessment

. . . testing is not useful unless a lot of money is provided to support the children who are 'failing'. This is unlikely to happen.

GMS

There is the great danger that a two tier education system will emerge as some schools opt out of LEA control. This is because the well funded grant maintained schools will attract more students (and money) than the under-funded LEA schools.

National Assessment

. . . testing can put undue stress on pupils. Moreover, it is likely that schools will 'set' students to help them cope with the tiered tests at the ages of 11 and 14. Evidence suggests that setting can have a detrimental effect on the educational achievements of 'lower band' students.

LMS

LMS offers head teachers greater control over their school budget. This gives head teachers and their governors the opportunity to pursue their own spending priorities.

Open Enrolment

It is possible that over-subscribed schools will have to turn away some pupils. This creates the danger that popular schools, like CTCs, will select their pupils on the basis of ability. It is possible that the national curriculum tests will be used for this purpose.

National Assessment

Testing will provide parents with vital information on their children's educational progress and will help them to support their future educational needs.

National Curriculum

. . . if all students have to follow a core curriculum, it may prevent the division between 'girls' subjects and 'boys' subjects, thus reduce stereotyping.

National Curriculum

The government seems to have conveniently omitted from the national curriculum those subjects to which they are politically opposed. For example, environmental science, sociology, and politics.

National Curriculum

The National Curriculum is too eurocentric. It allows few opportunities for ethnic minority students to explore and draw on their cultural routes.

Changes to the national curriculum and assessment – the Dearing Report

In response to the many criticisms of the national curriculum and the standardised assessment tests (including those highlighted in Exercise 3.5) the government performed a political somersault in 1994 by accepting Sir Ron Dearing's recommendations to slim down the highly prescriptive national curriculum and simplify the burdensome testing procedures. The following exercise will familiarise you with the changes and the various views expressed about them.

ITEM B

Exercise 3.6

Read Item B and complete the following tasks.

i 1. Explain what changes have been made to the national curriculum and national assessment.

i e 2. Draw up a two-column table and make a list of the positive and negative aspects of the changes.

It would be a good idea to do some further research to help you complete these tasks in greater detail. You could begin by searching for other newspaper articles on Dearing's recommendations – try to access them via your local public library or by using a relevant CD ROM.

ITEM B

National curriculum is torn up

JUDITH JUDD
Education Editor

MINISTERS YESTERDAY abandoned Government's 10-subject national curriculum and tests introduced only five years ago for pupils aged five to 16.

The decision to accept proposals from Sir Ron Dearing to cut back testing and the compulsory content of lessons and to give teachers more say is a victory for teachers.

Their boycott of national testing last summer, which compelled John Patten, Secretary of State for Education, to set up the inquiry proved one of the most successful pieces of industrial action in recent years, although last night they were divided about whether to end the action.

Sir Ron's recommendations to restrict testing at the ages of 7, 11 and 14 to three rather than nine or ten subjects also accord with the views of Baroness Thatcher who, as Prime Minister, wanted only English mathematics and science as compulsory subjects. She was defeated by Kenneth Baker, the former Secretary of State and architect of the original proposals.

The biggest change proposed by Sir Ron, the former Post Office chairman, is for pupils aged 14–16. As revealed in the *Independent on Sunday*, he wants to reduce the compulsory content of the curriculum to allow some 14-year-olds to pursue vocational courses in subjects such as bricklaying instead of the traditional academic diet.

Some teachers believe this will create a twin-track system with pupils divided into sheep and goats as they were in grammar and secondary modern schools.

Working parties will begin an immediate review of all national curriculum subjects and the arrangements will be introduced in September 1995 with no further changes for five years. A core of material which must be taught will be separated from optional material.

In primary schools there will be cuts in the content of the curriculum prescribed by law of about 50 per cent in subjects other than English, mathematics and science.

Fourteen-year-olds will have to study only those three subjects and short courses in technology and a modern language. Once time is allowed for physical and religious education, about 40 per cent of the timetable will be free for other subjects. Schools will be able to spend less time on science than at present.

Traditionalists have lost the battle for simple factual tests. The 10-level scale on which pupils are placed after national tests at 7, 11 and 14 will be retained though simplified and will end at 14. The GCSE will be the national test for 16-year-olds and present grades will be kept.

The number of subjects to be tested at 14 still has to be decided and will not be increased until after 1996. Lady Blatch, Minister of State for Education, would like most subjects included.

Sir Ron said: 'I hope teachers will see this as an honest and constructive response to their concerns. I think they will welcome very much the trust these proposals place in schools and teachers.'

Mr Patten said: 'The decisions consolidate the key benefits of the national curriculum but they also liberate teachers from bureaucracy and overprescription.'

Ann Taylor, Labour's education spokeswoman, said the report was the Government's 'latest and greatest U-turn'. She likened Mr Patten to 'the arsonist who called in the fire brigade'.

The Association of Teachers and Lecturers said that it had already advised members to mark this summer's tests but the National Union of Teachers said its boycott would continue.

David Hart, general secretary of the National Association of Head Teachers, said: 'I hope the teaching profession can see the victory that it has in its hands.'

(Source: J. Judd, The Independent, 6 January 1994.)

ITEM C **_Exercise 3.7_**

This exercise will help you to develop the skills of interpretation, application and evaluation, as well as furthering your knowledge and understanding of the issues raised so far.

Read Item C and complete the questions and sentences below. Make sure that you write out the questions and statements as headings for your answers.

i a 1. The Norwood Report (1943) defined three types of child to fit three types of school. Identify each type of child and the type of school each should attend.

i 2. (a) What does Chitty mean in Item C when he states that the 1944 Education Act 'provided no clear definition of the content . . . of primary and secondary education'?

i (b) Which aspect of the 1988 Education Reform Act overcomes this 'deficiency'?

i 3. Why do some sociologists claim that the 1944 Education Act led to a bipartite (two-part) rather than a tripartite (three-part) education system?

i e 4. What two criticisms were made of the education system of the 1950s and 1960s?

i a 5. Table 1 in Item C shows that between 1976 and 1990 an increasing number of pupils attended independent schools. Suggest one reason for this increase.

i 6. What was the aim of the 1976–79 education 'consensus'?

i 7. The 1979 Conservative Party manifesto talked about . . . in order to. . . .

i 8. What is the Assisted Places Scheme?

a 9. Identify two implications, positive and/or negative, of a 'voucher scheme' of schooling.

i 10. Two 'educational objectives of the victorious politicians of 1987' were. . . .

i 11. The introduction of national testing under a national curriculum was/is seen as desirable because. . . .

i a e 12. With reference to the information in Table 2 of Item C and elsewhere, assess the extent to which educational reforms in Britain over the last 55 years have created a meritocratic society. (This question is perhaps best attempted when you have read Chapters 7 and 8.)

i 13. The national curriculum consists of. . . .

i 14. Assessment of students' progress in the national curriculum will occur at the ages of. . . .

i 15. Local management of schools is where. . . .

i 16. What are city technology colleges?

i 17. What are grant maintained schools?

i 18. The 1988 Education Reform Act has shifted the control of education away from. . . . towards. . . .

i 19. Identify two pieces of evidence to support the claim that the 1988 Education Reform Act has not been an 'unqualified success'.

i 20. Two ways in which the government hopes to speed up the 'opting out' process are by. . . . . .

i 21. Study Figure 1 in Item C and calculate to the nearest whole percentage point the amount by which spending on education in Germany outstripped that in the UK between 1980 and 1988.

i a e 22. Chitty claims in the opening paragraph of Item C that 'the modern education system both reflects and serves to perpetuate the existing class structure . . . it seems clear that the present Conservative government is more determined than ever to create a divided system, particularly at the secondary level, which discriminates against the vast majority of working-class children'. Using information in Item C and other sources, evaluate this statement. (This question is perhaps best attempted when you have read Chapters 7 and 8.)

ITEM C

The Education System Transformed

Education has been a major focus for change and reconstruction under recent Conservative governments. Talk has been of extending choice and of greater parental responsibility. But are we seeing the return of a divided system like that in the 1940s and 1950s?

CLYDE CHITTY

IT WAS the Taunton Commission of 1867, describing its own proposals for the three-tired division of education, which pointed out: 'It is obvious that these divisions correspond roughly, but by no means exactly, to the gradations of society'. Today, the division of education is less clear-cut and the correspondence is often blurred, but it remains true that the modern education system both reflects and serves to perpetuate the existing class structure. Indeed, following a period of rapid and significant advance in the 1960s and early 1970s when a genuine attempt was made to ameliorate the harsh correlation between educational opportunity and the class-and-occupational structure of the nation, it seems clear that the present Conservative government is more determined than ever to create a divided system, particularly at the secondary level, which discriminates against the vast majority of working-class children.

Background to the present debate

According to an unequivocal statement in a White Paper with the title Educational Reconstruction issued by the Board of Education in July 1943:

> There is nothing to be said in favour of a system which subjects children at the age of 11 to the strain of a competitive examination on which not only their future schooling, but their future careers, may depend.

However, the rest of the document failed to take note of this stricture and proceeded to recommend that children should undergo a selection procedure at the age of 11. Secondary education should be provided in three main types of school, to be known as grammar, modern and technical schools. It was accepted that there should be free interchange between the different types and perhaps, in special circumstances, a combination of all three types on one site or in one building (Board of Education 1943, pp. 6, 9–10).

In the same year, a special committee of the Secondary School Examinations Council produced a full-scale report on *Curriculum and Examinations in Secondary Schools*, known as the Norwood Report. This argued that the evolution of education had 'thrown up' three 'rough groupings' of children with different 'types of mind'. There were pupils who were 'interested in learning for its own sake'; those 'whose interests and abilities lie markedly in the field of applied science or applied art'; and those who deal 'more easily with concrete things than with ideas'. According to the authors of the report, each of these three groupings, from at least the age of 11, required a particular type of curriculum suited to it peculiar needs and future prospects:

> In a wise economy of secondary education, pupils of a particular type of mind would receive the training best-suited for them and that training would lead them to an occupation where their capacities would be suitably used: that a future occupation is already present to their minds while they are still at school has been suggested, though, admittedly, the degree to which it is present varies. Thus, to the three main types of mind . . . there would correspond three main types of curriculum (SSEC 1943, pp. 2–4).

Both these documents appeared at a time when Britain and its allies were inflicting severe defeats on the Axis powers, encouraging a number of politicians to think seriously in terms of postwar reconstruction. Preparations for a new and far-reaching Education Act had, in fact, been under way at the Board of Education since July 1941, when R. A. Butler became president. In marked contrast to the situation that was to prevail in 1987–88, the wartime coalition government sought advice and recommendations from a wide range of organisations, and, in the course of three years, over 100 reports and memoranda were sent to the board, making proposals about every aspect of educational policy. It seemed particularly iniquitous to many that the vast majority of children were still denied a proper secondary education, with their entire school career having to be spent in public elementary schools and with little or no prospect of decent employment at the age of 14.

1944 AND ALL THAT

The outcome of all these discussions was the 1944 Education Act, which established secondary education for all pupils as an integral part of an education system which was to be seen as a continuous process – ranging from the primary sector to further education. The act came to be regarded by many as a cornerstone of the postwar Welfare State, but it had a number of grave weaknesses and shortcomings which undermined its good intentions. Above all, it provided no clear definition of the content or structure of primary and secondary education. The word 'curriculum' did not appear in the act, and there was no statutory requirement for the inclusion of any subject in the school timetable, with the exception of religious education. With regard to structure, it seemed to be assumed that pupils would move on from their primary school to one or other of three types of secondary school (grammar, technical and secondary modern); but multilateral and comprehensive schools were not officially proscribed.

As things turned out, the secondary structure that emerged in this country in the late 1940s and 1950s was a bipartite rather than a tripartite system, comprising grammar schools on the one hand and secondary modern schools on the other – the former taking, from 1950 onwards, one in five of all children at age 11. Unlike the situation elsewhere in Europe – and particularly in West Germany, where the *realschule* or technical school has always been a powerful rival to the *gymnasium* or grammar school – the technical school never developed as a viable option in this country. Priority was given in the postwar years to the speedy establishment of a new system of secondary modern schools; and the majority of local authorities were singularly reluctant to divert scant resources to the development of secondary technical education. This caution may have resulted from a certain amount of confusion as to the exact function of technical schools; or it may have been due to the cost of the equipment required. Whatever the precise reason, as late as 1958, secondary technical schools still accounted for the education of less than 4 per cent of the secondary age-group. And a number of Conservative politicians, notably Dr Rhodes Boyson, continue to argue that the divided system could have been saved if local authorities had built a sufficient number of technical schools.

A COMPREHENSIVE CHANGE?

In a recent letter to the former general secretary of the National Union of Teachers (published in *The Guardian* on 28 February 1992). Prime Minister John Major accused the Labour Party of being solely responsible for 'ushering in' the comprehensive system of secondary schools in the 1960s. By any standards, this is a gross misrepresentation of the facts. For the movement which gathered momentum after the election of a Labour government in 1964 was based on the pioneering work of a number of local authorities (both Labour and Conservative) in the 1950s and attracted support, initially at least, from right across the political spectrum.

In order to understand the current debate, it is important to appreciate why the divided system of education came in for such heavy criticism in the 1950s and 1960s. In the first place, the educational sociology of the period was very much the sociology of access: its chief concerns were the ways in which educational opportunity was weighted against children from working-class families. To many sociologists, it seemed grossly unfair that grammar schools remained largely middle-class institutions. At the same time, educationists began to question the belief that every child was born with a given quota of 'intelligence' which remained constant throughout his or her life and which could be accurately measured by mental tests applied at the age of 10 or 11. And all this new research was taking place at a time when technological change and economic advance were making new demands on the education system and emphasising the need to raise the educational level of the population as a whole.

The policy-makers of the 1960s saw a direct and indisputable correlation between educational reform and economic well-being: a skilled and educated workforce would facilitate economic growth which would, in turn, constitute a firm basis for sustained educational expansion. But this beguilingly simple philosophy was shattered by the economic recession of the early 1970s which served to undermine all the liberal and expansionist tenets of the previous decade. The Callaghan government of 1976–79 was anxious to distance itself from 'progressive' educational opinion and tried to build a new educational 'consensus' around more central control of the school curriculum, greater teacher accountability and the more direct subordination of secondary education to the perceived needs of the economy (see Chitty 1992, p. 31). But this was by no means 'radical' enough for the Far Right of the Conservative Party, which now began to question the nature and purpose of a 'national system of education, locally administered'. For the policy advisers who gathered around Margaret Thatcher in the 1980s, it was not enough simply to return to the divided system of the postwar period. Admittedly, they wanted to see a greater variety of schools at the secondary level, with a corresponding enhancement of parental choice. But their ultimate objective was the break-up of the state education system, with all schools owned by individual trusts and their survival dependent on their ability to satisfy their customers. The 1988 Education Act would be a step on the road to the complete privatisation of the service.

THE 1988 EDUCATION ACT

It was not until the end of her second administration that Margaret Thatcher felt strong enough to reorganise the education system. Up to that point (1986–87), her policies had proved something of a disappointment to her Far Right supporters. Admittedly, the 1979 Conservative Party manifesto had talked in terms of 'extending parents' rights and responsibilities, including their right of choice in order to 'help raise standards by giving them greater influence over education' (Conservative Party 1979, p. 25); and the government had introduced an Assisted Places Scheme in 1981 whereby 'less well-off parents' would be able to claim part or all the fees at certain private schools from a special government fund.

But Keith Joseph (Education Secretary 1981–86) had failed to overcome his civil servants' opposition to the introduction of a voucher scheme (whereby all parents would be issued with a voucher to spend at the school of their choice); and local authority administration of the education service remained virtually intact. By 1986–87, the Prime Minister was coming under increasing pressure from the Right to dismantle the state education system in its existing form. In an interview with the editor of the *Daily Mail*, published on 13 May 1987, she proclaimed triumphantly:

> We are going much further with education than we ever thought of doing before. Although we've spent all that money per pupil, and with more teachers, there is still so much wrong, so we are going to do something determined about it. . . . There is going to be a revolution in the running of the schools.

This 'revolution' would apparently include: a reduction in the powers of the local education authorities, a reversal of 'this universal comprehensive thing' and 'the breaking-up of the giant comprehensives' (ibid). And a month later, the same determination was in evidence. Asked by a caller to a pre-election radio and television programme in the BBC series *Election Call*, broadcast on 10 June 1987, what she regretted she had not actually achieved during eight years of Conservative government, the Prime Minister replied:

> In some ways, I wish we had begun to tackle education earlier. We have been content to continue with the policies of our predecessors. But now we have much worse left-wing Labour authorities than we have ever had before – so something simply has to be done (reported in *The Guardian* 11 June 1987).

After eight years of comparatively unexceptional policy-making, a real break with past traditions and accepted procedures came in 1987/88. The culture of the education system – its hegemonic ideas and organising principles – was challenged and transformed. The third Thatcher administration possessed the confidence and determination to adopt radical strategies for dismantling both the comprehensive secondary system so painstakingly built up since the 1950s and 1960s, and the constitutional settlement devised in 1944. As Brian Simon has argued (Simon 1988, p. 15), the educational objectives of the victorious politicians of 1987 were strictly two-fold: 'first, to break the power of the local authorities which traditionally had been directly

Table 1: Private education: on the increase and spreading into the 'State' sector?

Pupils in independent schools as a proportion of all pupils:[1] by sex and age[2]

Great Britain					**Percentages**
	1976	**1981**	**1986[3]**	**1989**	**1990**
Boys aged:					
Under 11	4	4	5	5	5
11–15	7	6	7	8	8
16 and over	16	17	19	19	20
All ages	6	6	6	7	7
Girls aged:					
Under 11	4	4	5	5	5
11–15	6	6	6	7	8
16 and over	13	12	14	15	16
All ages	5	5	6	7	7
All pupils	5	5	6	7	7

[1] At January.
[2] Ages are as at December of the previous year for 1976 and 1981. Thereafter ages are as at previous August for England and Wales and December for Scotland.
[3] Includes estimates for Scotland.

(*Source*: Department of Education and Science, 1992.)

responsible for running their own "systems" of education . . . and second, to erect (or reinforce) an hierarchical system of schooling both subject to market forces and more directly under central state control.'

The 1988 Education Act – and the 1987 Education Bill from which it emerged – can be seen as the direct outcome of discussions that had been taking place in Downing Street under the Prime Minister's guidance since the departure of Keith Joseph from the DES in May 1986. For those present, the chief concern was to secure the abolition of a 'national system, locally administered'. But it was accepted that it would be very difficult to move directly towards a privatised system of schooling, and it was therefore important to find ways of gradually reaching this goal over the lifetime of another parliament. Short-term measures would include the creation of new types of school at the secondary level and the introduction of a system of per capita (that is: per pupil) funding as stage one of a phased introduction of the education credit.

The one issue on which the Prime Minister's advisers failed to reach agreement concerned the desirability or otherwise of a centrally-imposed national curriculum. The neo-liberal wing of the Far Right objected to the idea of imposing a standard curriculum on all state schools; but supporters argued that in at least one major respect, a national curriculum could be compatible with the furtherance of free-market principles. It would, after all, act as justification for a massive programme of national testing at important stages in a child's school career, thereby providing crucial evidence to parents of the worth of individual schools.

THREE MAJOR CHANGES

Turning now to the act itself, it seems sensible to concentrate on three major changes affecting schools brought about by the legislation. The first of these was the introduction of a national curriculum for all state schools alongside a national system of assessment for pupils from 5–16 years. The 1988 Act defined mathematics, English and science as the three core subjects, with a second group as foundation subjects: a

Table 2: Conservative Cabinet members seem to favour private education for their children.

The Cabinet's choice of schools

Minister	Children	Schools attended
John Major	2	State primary, private secondary
Kenneth Clarke	2	State primary, private secondary
Norman Lamont	2	Private
Douglas Hurd	3*	Private
Tom King	2	Private
Kenneth Baker	2	Private
John Gummer	4	Two state primary, one private secondary, one fee-paying choir school
Tony Newton	2	State
Michael Howard	2	Private
John MacGregor	3	Private
Michael Heseltine	3	Private
Lord Mackay	1	Private
Peter Brooke	3	Private
David Hunt	4	Private
Ian Lang	2	Private
Peter Lilley	0	
David Mellor	2	Private
Chris Patten	3	State primary/one private
Malcolm Rifkind	2	Private
John Wakeham	3	Two at private
William Waldegrave	4	Private
David Waddington	5	Private

* From first marriage; two young children from second marriage not included

(*Source*: *The Guardian*, 19 February 1992.)

modern foreign language (though not for primary-school children), technology, history, geography, art, music and physical education. For most subjects there were to be attainment targets at 7, 14, and 16; and these would provide standards against which pupils' progress and performance could be assessed. It was originally envisaged that much of the assessment would be carried out by teachers as an integral part of normal classroom work: but, in the words of the 1987 National Curriculum Consultation Document published by the DES: 'at the heart of the assessment process, there will be nationally-prescribed tests done by all pupils to supplement the individual teachers' assessments' (DES 1987, p. 11).

The second major change concerned the introduction of a system of school management known as the Local Management of Schools or LMS. This was the innovation which had many of the features of an educational voucher scheme. School budgets for staffing, premises and services were now to be delegated to individual schools; and the delegated budget would be funded by a formula which would be largely determined by the number of pupils on the school roll. Accompanying this was a change in admissions regulations which meant that schools in future would be obliged to admit pupils to their capacity.

The third major change involved the creation of a new tier of schooling comprising City Technology Colleges (CTCs) and Grant-Maintained Schools. The CTC Plan, already announced by Education Secretary Kenneth Baker in a speech to the 1986 Conservative Party Conference, envisaged the setting up of around 20 11–18 schools, each of them to be financed partly by private capital, to be independent of local authority control, and to be sited with the main purpose of providing a new choice of secondary school for inner-city pupils. Grant-Maintained Schools were to be those schools which chose to 'opt out' of the locally-maintained system and receive their finance direct from the DES.

These, then, were three of the most far-reaching of the changes introduced by the 1988 Education Act. With its 238 clauses and 13 schedules, it received the royal assent on 29 July 1988 and was described by Peter Wilby and Ngaio Crequer in the *Independent* of the previous day as 'a Gothic monstrosity of legislation'. It increased the powers of the Education Secretary to a quite extraordinary extent and restored to the central government a control over the school curriculum it had not possessed since the interwar period. While gathering more power to the centre, it introduced important limitations on the functions of the local education authorities which were now forced to give greater autonomy to schools and heads and governing bodies. Above all, it ef-

Figure 1: The UK's declining rate of growth on educational spending

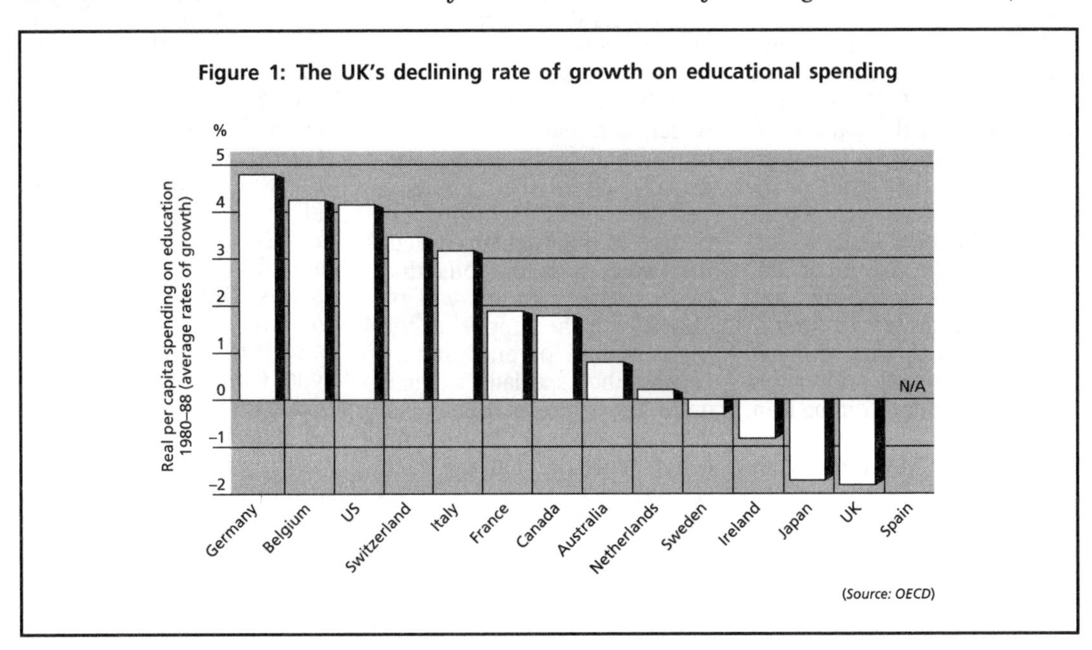

(Source: OECD)

fectively ended that ill-defined partnership between central government, local government and individual schools that had been such an important feature of the postwar consensus established in the 1940s.

1992 WHITE PAPER AND FUTURE PROSPECTS

The Thatcherite programme of 1979 could claim a good deal of popular support following th economic troubles of the previous three years. It did not at that time include proposals to reorganise the education system and the health service, and there is little evidence of widespread popular or professional support for this later stage of the Thatcherite agenda. Indeed, it seems clear that a succession of clear parliamentary majorities for the Conservative Party has enabled a small, unrepresentative collection of Far Right pressure groups to dominate the education debate without any claim to be speaking on behalf of a significant section of the electorate.

The project has not, however, met with unqualified success. The Right is angry that much of the curriculum planning of the past four years has been in the hands of the despised professionals; by the time of the 1992 general election, only 219 of the 25,000 state schools in England and Wales had chosen to opt out of local authority control (somewhat significantly, more than 100 of these coming from the 25 lowest-spending authorities); and by 1993, when the CTC programme comes to a premature close, only 15 colleges will be in existence.

The government has recently published a new White Paper, *Choice and Diversity: A New Framework for Schools* (DFE 1992) in order to accelerate the demise of the local education authorities. The opting-out process will be 'streamlined' and speeded up, with responsibility for channelling funds to grant-maintained schools handed over to a new statutory body, the Funding Agency for Schools. It is clearly intended that LEAs will have a much-diminished role, with limited responsibilities in such areas as special needs, transport and the monitoring of attendance, together with permission to compete with other bodies to provide services to grant-maintained schools.

At the same time, secondary schools will be encouraged to specialise in one or more subjects of the National Curriculum. And this seemingly innocent proposal represents a considerable threat to the comprehensive principle. For in an area such as Wandsworth in South London, which is already experimenting with the idea of its secondary schools being able to 'sell themselves' by having 'expertise' in a particular curriculum area, it is obvious that two or three schools will be able to win the support of the 'right sort of parents' simply because their specialist strength gives them the status of revamped grammar schools. In other words, what we face after half a century of 'secondary education for all' is a return to the divided system of the 1940s and 1950s.

REFERENCES AND FURTHER READING

Board of Education (1943) *Educational Reconstruction* (White Paper), HMSO.

Chitty, C. (1992) 'From great debate to great reform act: the postwar consensus overturned, 1976–88', in A. Rattansi and D. Reeder (eds) *Rethinking Radical Education: Essays in Honour of Brian Simon*, Lawrence and Wishart.

Conservative Party (1979) *The Conservative Manifesto*, Conservative Central Office, April.

DES (Department of Education and Science) (1987) *The National Curriculum 5–16: A Consultation Document*, DES, July.

DFE (Department for Education) (1992) *Choice and Diversity: A New Framework for Schools* (White Paper) (Cm 2021) HMSO, July.

SSEC (Secondary School Examinations Council) (1943) *Curriculum and Examinations in Secondary Schools* (The Norwood Report) HMSO.

Simon, B. (1988) *Bending the Rules: The Baker 'Reform' of Education*, Lawrence and Wishart.

Clyde Chitty is Lecturer in Education at the University of Birmingham.

The 1992 Education White Paper

- Opting out made easier for schools and spending by local authorities on literature against opting out curbed
- New Funding Agency for Schools to take over responsibility for channelling funds to independent schools
- All schools free to specialise in one or more subjects in addition to teaching all national curriculum subjects
- A new School Curriculum and Assessment Authority (SCAA) to be established
- A new Education Association to take over responsibility for running schools which inspectors judge to be failing its students
- Rights of parents of special needs students to be strengthened and special schools may be able to opt out
- Firm action promised to get rid of the 1.5 million surplus school places. Annual reports to the government on this issue from the local areas

(Source: C. Chitty, Sociology Review, vol. 2, no. 3, Philip Allan Publishers, 1993.)

The expansion of education and training for 16–19 year olds

Educationalists have pointed out that one of the main problems with the education system, in relation to the industrial performance of the British economy, has been the low staying-on rate in post-compulsory schooling. Raffe (1993) suggests that there are four main reasons why this has traditionally been the case. He argues that national culture, and especially working-class culture, has held schooling in low esteem and that many 16-year-old students have perceived themselves as being designated 'failures' by the system. Also, while A levels have borne a high risk of failure, vocational qualifications have not yet achieved parity of esteem and therefore the lure of the labour market has persuaded many 16 year olds to go into employment. However, as jobs became scarcer during the 1980s these factors began to be less important in disuading young people from staying on at school.

Moreover the further education sector, as a major provider of vocational education, was criticised during the 1980s for failing to respond quickly enough to the needs of a changing economy and for ignoring individual needs in the courses they offered (see Theodossin, 1986). The colleges were also seen as providing expensive courses, which potential customers were not particularly keen on.

Hence a major objective of government educational policy since the mid 1980s has been to increase the provision and quality of education and training for 16–19 year olds. A range of new courses have been offered by schools, sixth form colleges, further education colleges, tertiary colleges and the TECs/LECs. The substantial increase in staying-on rates is illustrated in Item D.

ITEM D

Exercise 3.8

1. In what year did the sharp increase begin in the number of males continuing with education and training (Item D)?

2. Study the information in Item D. Identify the percentage of males and the percentage of females staying on in 1991.

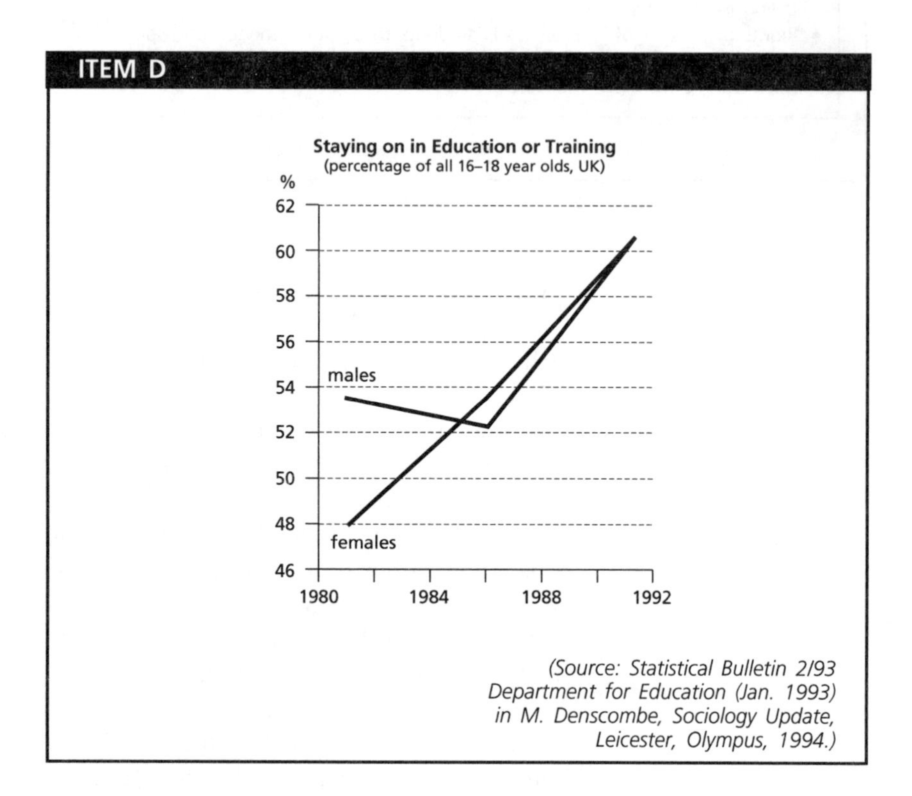

Maguire (1993) offers five reasons to account for the huge increase in participation in post-compulsory education.

1. The increased number of well-qualified students following improvements in GCSE results.
2. The fall in the number of employment opportunities available to young people as a result of the recession of the late 1980s and early 1990s.
3. The decline in the number of training places available because of cutbacks in YT funding.
4. Changes to the social security arrangements whereby 16–17 year olds lost their entitlement to income support.
5. The wider provision of courses and places in further and higher education.

The increases in the number of students following courses in the 16–19 sector would seem at first sight to be desirable. It is argued that this increase will open up opportunities to study at the higher education level and provide industry with better-educated and skilled workers. However there are also problems with such a rapid expansion. The Audit Commission and the Office for Standards in Education (OFSTED, 1993) has pointed out that 30 per cent of those following post-16 studies do not complete or are unsuccessful in their courses. Maguire (1993) shows particular concern for those students who extend their education for one year only. She maintains that one-year students are unlikely significantly to improve their employment prospects by undertaking an extra year. Indeed she suggests that they may be disadvantaged because they have to compete with younger and cheaper 16 year olds in an increasingly competitive employment market.

As well as expanding, in the 1980s the further education sector became subject to the 'marketisation' that has been a key policy of successive Conservative governments. Post-16 colleges' connections with local government authorities have been severed and they are now centrally funded through the government-appointed Further Education Funding Council, which retains allocative control over the sector. This extends the relative control over budgets that local authority schools were given through the Local Management of Schools initiative, so that colleges directly control the bulk of the money they receive. The aim of freeing the 16–19 sector from local authority control was to introduce greater competition into the sector, so that quality education could be offered and a greater number of students could be persuaded to continue their education after reaching the age of 16.

The day-to-day or operational control of the further education sector was handed over to revamped governing bodies, in which local authority representatives were displaced by local business personnel, who would ensure that the colleges were more responsive to the local labour market. As Sieminski (1993) argues, these local markets were increasingly shaped by a change from Fordist methods of production towards neo-or post-Fordist methods, in which there is a need for a highly skilled and flexible labour force to produce the quality goods required in a highly differentiated market. The role of the further education sector was to provide a flexible labour force.

In order to ensure that competition between further education colleges increased the quality of provision, the finance a college received was tied (1) to the number and type of students it attracted and (2) to the expansion of student numbers over a number of years. Therefore different types of student were worth different amounts to a college. The aim of this was to ensure that recruitment concentrated on those types of students the government defined as desirable.

There was also a commitment to increasing the quality of the education the students received (DES *et al.*, 1991) by linking the outcomes of the colleges (in terms of the qualifications students gained) with the cost of delivering the curriculum. For example Müller and Funnell (1991) argue that post-16 colleges can adapt the workings of industry and operate a total quality management (TQM) system, which would place the learner at the heart of the procedures of the college and 'give ownership' of learning to learners themselves. This would provide a 'value added' dimension to the education the students received, so that the service performed by the colleges would not just be measured in terms of the qualifications gained, but also by the quality of the educational experiences students had received.

However critics of this approach have argued that the development of a new curriculum in the further education sector, through the introduction of NVQs and GNVQs, may not be as empowering to the students as New Right advocates suggest. Supporters of vocational education argue that there are benefits for students in the 'competence' approach to education. Here students are encouraged to acquire 'transferable skills' through gaining specific competences during the course of their studies (see Guy, 1991), and are rewarded for their practical achievements and not just academic knowledge. Critics argue that the potential for personal development in such teaching style innovations as action planning and project-based work have been restricted by the narrow focus of vocational courses on 'competence' (see Raggatt, 1991). Thus the creativity supposedly developed by the new vocational courses is argued by Cathcart and Esland (1990) to be an illusion, as prepackaged material is substituted for individually generated projects. It may be – according to Edwards (1991), amongst others – that a core of workers will be trained to be flexible for steady, full-time work, while the periphery of workers are trained to be flexible in a different way, that is, to move in and out of employment as the local labour market expands and contracts.

The expansion of higher education

The growth of higher education in Britain has occurred in two waves. The first wave followed the Robbins Report (1963) and led to the expansion of the 'old' universities and the creation of new 'red-brick' universities and polytechnics. The second wave was more recent and reflected the Government's concern to increase the participation rate of young adults and adult returners in higher education. The rate of increase in the number of students taking degree and equivalent courses, though rising to over 1.5 million, has therefore not been constant, but has been shaped by economic factors (such as a fall in student numbers after the financial cuts of 1981) and government policy towards the higher education sector.

Moreover this growth in student numbers has increased the diversity of students taking up degree work. The introduction of the Open University and the redesignation of polytechnics as universities following the 1993 Education Act has allowed a shift away from the traditional university course, which was originally designed as a three-year residential experience, mainly for young middle-class males (see Halsey, 1993).

While the expansion of the higher education sector has created greater equality of opportunity for women, this is not so for the working class: the *number* of students of working-class origin may have grown as the system has expanded, but the *proportion* of the working class receiving higher education has remained fairly static. The expansion of the higher education sector has therefore led to increased opportunities for middle-and upper-class children, relative to their numbers in the population.

The higher education sector has, like all other sectors of education, been subject to increasing marketisation of its services. The pressure to change the curriculum and teaching methods is related to the development of what are called post-Fordist production techniques in the economy as a whole and the consequent need for 'flexible' and 'multi-skilled' workers by industry. The term Fordism is used to describe the method of manufacturing that was dominant from the beginning of the twentieth century until the 1950s and 1960s. Fordism was characterised by the mass production of standardised goods for a mass market, in which consumer demand was undifferentiated. Workers under Fordism were required to perform under the control of Taylorist principles, whereby they required little skill and their every move was directed towards greater production of a standard product. Taylorism was developed by F. W. Taylor as an organisational structure, in which tasks were broken down into the simplest of operations, so that less skilled workers could be employed on fragments of production rather than highly skilled workers producing an entire product individually. Fordist organisations were therefore characterised by hierarchial bureaucracies, in which management's main task was the integration and coordination of the actions of many highly specialised, but unskilled, workers.

Post-Fordism is a move towards a different kind of economy, in which services such as leisure facilities, retailing and finance are just as important as the manufacturing of goods. Moreover, in a post-Fordist economy markets are no longer 'mass' and undifferentiated. Rather there are multiple markets with specialised needs and demands. These demands are being met by both manufacturing and service industries through the development of new computer technologies, which, for example, allow the high-speed transfer of information or the development of 'just-in-time' production, so that industry can respond quickly to constant changes in demand by the consumer. Therefore, because post-Fordist organisations have to be responsive and flexible, innovating constantly to maximise profits, they need, for their core activities, flexible and multiskilled workers who are not resistant to changes in working practices. It should be noted that the ideas of post-Fordism have been challenged by sociologists such as O'Reilly (1992), who argues that the extent of post-Fordist practices and multiskilling in society is actually limited, and that those that do exist are not creating a new type of postmodern society, but are only extensions of long-standing worker exploitation.

The supposed role of education in this shift from Fordist to post-Fordist methods of production is to produce the flexible and multiskilled workers the new arrangements need. As the core workers in post-Fordist organisations have to be highly skilled, the role of the higher education sector is crucial for developing a workforce with the requisite skills and attitudes to make post-Fordist organisation successful and profitable. Indeed Edwards (1993) argues that the institutions of post-compulsory education are themselves subject to post-Fordist changes in working practices as the government requires them to be more 'productive' and 'efficient', taking more students through their courses at a lower cost. Traditional roles in higher education are therefore breaking down as lecturers are required to take on new roles, such as marketing, counselling, budgeting and so on. This is combined with the loss of security of employment and the increased use of part-time and temporary staff (the casualisation of the workforce) that is associated with post-Fordist organisations.

The search for greater flexibility in higher education has led to a number of developments, such as the modularisation (or unitisation) of degrees, the creation of distance learning and the ending of the 'binary' division of universities and polytechnics, which means increased competition between higher education institutions. Moreover the unified university sector is expected by the government to attract a greater proportion of its income from private sources, making state support for the system less important. Postmodernists argue that one characteristic of the higher education sector that is symptomatic of the development of a postmodern society is the dissolving of the boundaries of time and space that are traditionally associated with a university education.

In general terms, postmodernists suggest that 'modern' societies are typified by rigid 'temporal and spatial' boundaries. For example a 'modern' curriculum in the universities would have very distinct boundaries between subjects, which would be studied in separate locations (university departments) and at separate and distinct times (for example a person would 'go' to a physics lecture and then 'go' to a chemistry lecture). Education in a modern society would therefore be a closed and bounded system, forming a distinct segment of an individual's life. In a postmodernist society these boundaries dissolve and melt into each other, so that distinctions of time and space become less important. For example the differences between traditional academic subjects begin to disappear, as these subjects contribute to developments with each other. Spatial and temporal rigidities also dissolve. The traditional university course lasted for three years at an identifiable university site. The development of distance learning and the success of the Open University suggest that this is no longer necessarily the case, as university degrees can be obtained over differing numbers of years and without the necessity of residing in a university situation. Rustin (1994) argues that it is the ideology of 'flexibility', held and promoted by the administrators in the university sector, which is the cutting edge of this dissolving of traditional boundaries.

In the marketisation process, students themselves have been subject to privatising forces, as the government has allowed the value of the student grant to decline as a proportion of income and introduced a system of student loans, which are to be paid back when the student gains employment. Healey (1989) argues that the case for student loans is usually couched in terms of the benefits for both higher education and student motivation and rarely in terms of savings to public expenditure, which, he suggests, constitutes the underlying reason for their introduction. But as Jarvis (1990) has suggested, the real impact of student loans may be that 'future indebtedness' acts as a disincentive to working-class students when considering higher education.

Another consequence of the changes to higher education in the 1980s has been the onset of 'credential inflation' in Britain (Collins, 1981). This concept emerges from the idea developed by Dore (1976) of a 'diploma disease' – the overproduction of educated personnel in developing countries, which were unable to absorb the numbers of highly skilled graduates emerging from the higher education sector. This led to high levels of graduate unemployment and under-employment and social discontent among the most educated section of society. The process in the United States and Britain has led to many students going on to follow post-graduate degrees in order to increase their employment chances in a labour market characterised by an oversupply of highly educated workers.

ITEM E

Students jobs market gets tougher by degree

Charles Hymas
Education Correspondent

GRADUATES FACE continued intense competition for jobs despite a rise in vacancies among employers, researchers will report this week. Too many degree-holders are chasing too few good jobs with an average of 90 applications for each graduate post.

It means that up to 12 per cent of graduates can expect to be unemployed. Many more will have to take short-term or temporary jobs because the traditional 'blue chip' posts are more difficult to get, according to the study by the Brighton-based Institute of Employment Studies.

At the same time, companies are concerned that too many graduates still lack the communication skills and business awareness that they want. However, employers' attitudes are changing:

'Companies are increasingly recruiting graduates for specific tasks and relatively few can expect to follow long-term careers into higher management with a single employer,' say the researchers.

Not only are employers targeting particular universities or courses, but a substantial minority are raising academic entry standards, demanding better degrees or A-level results. It amounts to a fundamental change in the graduate job market that is a result not only of the recession but also the big expansion in the number of students in higher education (see graph). Almost 700,000 left with degrees between 1988 and 1992; the figure is projected to rise by about 27 per cent between 1993 and 1997.

This year's degree-holders will also be competing against a large pool of graduates who failed to get jobs in previous years or stayed on to do postgraduate courses. The changes mirror what has happened in the United States, with its mass higher education system.

Developments likely to be imported to Britain include higher drop-out rates, rising under-utilisation of graduates (estimated to be true of one in five American graduates) and more selective recruitment practices, with employers looking for both academic pedigree and work experience.

The government has put the brakes on the expansion of higher education, which 30 per cent of young people now enter compared with 14 per cent in the 1980s. However, the researchers warn there is a latent and unprecedented demand for places in higher education which conflicts with that policy.

They say this stems from the rapid rise in the proportion of 16-year-olds staying on in education (from less than half in 1983–84 to three-quarters in 1993–94), the rise in pupils getting good GCSE and A-level grades, limited job opportunities, and the growth in access to university for people without the traditional academic qualifications.

Without an increase in government funds, alternative funding has to be considered, which could require students or parents to contribute more:

'Rising student poverty and the financial pressures on higher education mean that the issue will need to be resolved if university is to remain an attractive option for young people, and current standards of degree quality are to be maintained.'

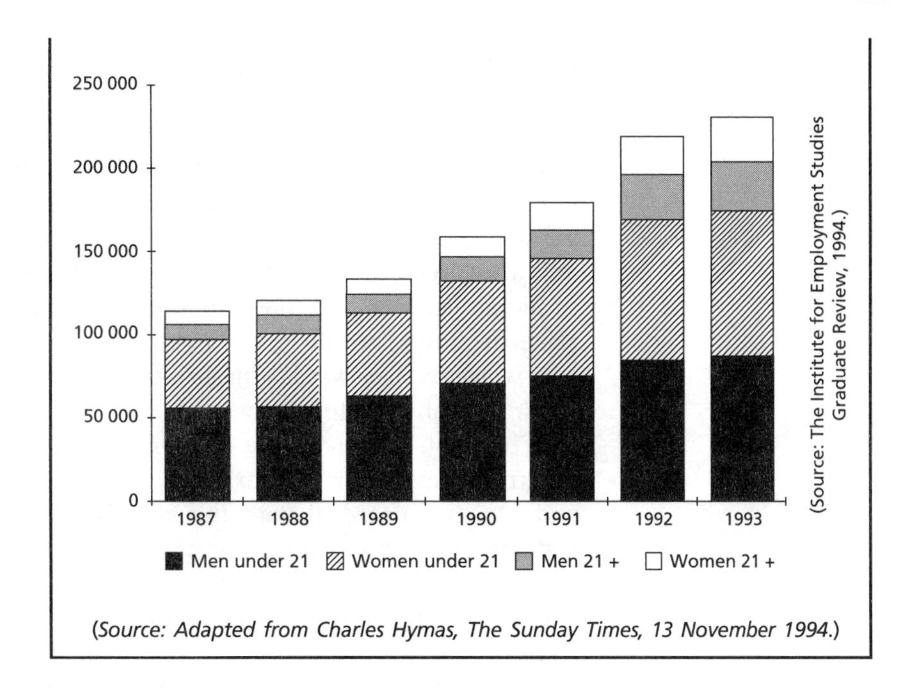

(Source: Adapted from Charles Hymas, The Sunday Times, 13 November 1994.)

ITEM E

Exercise 3.9

i 1. Look at the graph in Item E. Which group has shown the largest expansion in admissions to full-time and sandwich first degree courses?

i a 2. Look at the quotation that begins 'Companies are increasingly recruiting'. How might this quotation support a postmodern view of work?

i 3. What reasons does the article suggest for the continuing high demand for higher education?

i a 4. What evidence can be drawn from the article to support the idea of a 'diploma disease'?

i 5. Identify from Item E, two negative consequences, other than 'credential inflation', of the expansion in the number of students attending higher education institutions.

The privatisation of state schools

Government policy in the 1980s and 1990s was geared towards raising standards, increasing parental choice and making education responsive to industry's needs (Burgess, 1994). However a number of sociologists claim that they are, in effect, policies of privatisation. For example Green (1994) argues that the American postmodernist Rorty (1982) supports the views of the New Right, with their emphasis on the free workings of the market and their assumption that the private sector is always superior to state provision. American New Right sociologists Chubb and Moe (1990) claim that bureaucratic state control inhibits effective performance by schools and that the solution to disatisfaction by 'consumers' is to open up the school system to the market. They argue that, by introducing the financial disciplines of the market place to schools and freeing them from unresponsive bureaucratic control, standards will be raised as schools will be forced to respond to the demands of the consumer. Chubb and Moe argue that the private sector in schools has a strong motive to please parents, and therefore opening up the state sector to these same incentives would make schools more responsive to what parents want, or they would simply close. The work of Chubb and Moe has been criticised for its methodology, where the statistical connection between effective state schools and low levels of bureaucratic control is very weak. For example Green (1994) argues that Chubb and Moe do not deal with the fact that the most effective school systems, such as Japan's, have high levels of centralised control.

In Britain the New Right has supported the development of the grant maintained sector ('opting out') and the city technology colleges, which, though still under the financial control of central government, have created a semi-independent sector. The driving force behind this privatisation is open enrolment, or what is called the 'marketisation of education'. Edwards and Whitty (1992) argue that the introduction of market mechanisms, through parental choice, will lead to children from less advantaged backgrounds being concentrated in certain schools, while 'better' schools will be filled with the children of the middle class. As popular schools become crowded they will begin to select their entrants, usually on the basis of ability, so that different schools will increasingly be differentiated according to ability – a new selective system.

ITEM F **_Exercise 3.10_**

Use Item F and other sources (possibly newspaper articles and the paragraph above) to support the claim that state schooling is being privatised.

ITEM F

Since election in 1979, the Conservative governments have gradually encouraged what may be seen as a 'privatisation' process for schooling, by supporting existing private schools, both ideologically and financially, and by reducing the psychological barrier between the state and private sectors. The 1980 Education Act, for example, introduced the Assisted Places Scheme to enable some children to attend academically-selective private schools, their parents paying no fees or only a part of the fees on a means-tested scale. Some £65 million was spent on this scheme in 1991/92. The scheme has acted as a firm financial and ideological support for the private sector. A further £5 million was spent on private music and ballet schools.

The 1988 Education Reform Act further softened the dividing line between the maintained and private sectors by legislating for the introduction of City Technology Colleges and Grant Maintained Schools. The CTCs are designated as independent schools, but are funded jointly by the state and industry and commerce, while the Grant Maintained Schools are still officially within the state system, but are funded directly by the Department for Education rather than through the Local Education Authority system. At the same time, there has been an increasing need for parents of children in the state-maintained sector to make donations to the schools to ensure that adequate facilities are available. All of this blurs the boundary between the state and private sectors . . . such that, increasingly, the state-maintained sector cannot be understood without reference to the nature and diversity of the private sector. The private sector is not an isolated oddity of voyeuristic interest, but directly interacts with the nature and quality of education available in the maintained sector.

(Source: G. Walford, 'Education and Private Schools', Sociology Review, vol. 3, no. 2, Philip Allan Publishers, 1993.)

Structured exam questions

It is important that you now assess your understanding of the debates covered in Chapters 2 and 3. To do this you need to spend time answering questions: a, b, c and d from the AEB's A level November 1992 examination (reproduced below). Do not attempt question e at this point as it will be set for you later on in the book.

Before attempting to answer the questions, observe our advice on tackling them. When you have completed your answers, hand them in to your sociology teacher/lecturer for marking.

Questions

(a) What does the author of Item G mean when he writes that some subjects such as economics, politics and sociology have been omitted from the National Curriculum 'for deliberate ideological reasons' *(2 marks)*

The question is one of interpretation and application. As two marks are available, you should work out where the two marks lie. You should conclude that you have to discuss the ideological dimension and suggest why this was deliberate.

(b) Identify two 'academic costs associated with comprehensive education' and two 'social costs associated with academic selection' (Item H). *(4 marks)*

Again, interpretation and application is the skill dimension of the question. Be careful to offer the appropriate number of reasons in each section. Refer back to Item H and the context of the phrases to help you work out what they mean.

(c) With reference to information in Item H and elsewhere, assess sociological explanations of the role of private education in Britain. *(6 marks)*

The wording of the question requires you to refer to Item H (interpretation and application) and other sources (knowledge and understanding) and then assess (evaluation). Note also that the question requires you to evaluate 'explanations', so you need to address more than one. Make sure that you look at the strengths and weaknesses of those you choose. Only by so doing will you come to a balanced conclusion.

(d) Apart from the National Curriculum (Item G) and the Assisted Places Scheme (Item H), discuss the importance of any one other educational change since 1980. *(5 marks)*

ITEM G

The subservience that lies at the core of the National Curriculum

It has been argued by some Marxist writers on education that teachers are simply tools of an ideological state apparatus and serve only to reproduce the ideas of the dominant group in society.

I have always had certain reservations about this view, but they are hard to sustain in the light of your report that only 4 per cent of teachers believe that the Education Reform Act to be wrong in principle. This presumably means widespread support among teachers for the National Curriculum.

The National Curriculum is an exercise in knowledge and control; it is tightly prescriptive and not only sets out what subjects are now to count as knowledge, but will also define what those subjects are and test them regularly to make sure that the content is taught.

Most important of all, however, is what is missing. None of the subjects of the National Curriculum enables direct and explicit learning about contemporary society. For deliberate ideological reasons, subjects such as economics, politics and sociology are excluded. The education of informed, democratic citizens cannot be a central concern either of the Government or, it seems, of teachers if areas such as the political system, racism, economic policy, the welfare system, etc., are left either to haphazard indirect comment via subjects such as history, geography or to vague 'cross-curricular themes'.

(Source: Adapted from Dr C. Harber © The Guardian (letter page) February 1990.)

ITEM H

The Assisted Place Scheme was established under Section 17 of the 1980 Education Act, and the first pupils to participate in it entered their schools in the following September. The central justification for the Scheme was that it would make it possible for 'bright children from less affluent homes' to attend independent schools of proven academic worth from which they would otherwise have been excluded by their parents' inability to pay. Their presence in the Public Schools is justified as an extension of parental choice, a restoration of academic opportunities to many children who would not be fully stretched in schools which have to cope with a full range of ability. Opponents of the Scheme see it as an unnecessary and offensive declaration by the government that the state sector is incapable of providing for very able children, and as a government-sponsored withdrawal of middle-class support from schools so evidently identified as second-best.

The Assisted Places Scheme has therefore revived long-standing arguments about the academic costs associated with comprehensive education and the social costs associated with academic selection.

(Source: (eds), A. Hargreaves and D. Reynolds, Education Policies: Controversies and Critiques, London, Falmer Press, 1989.)

Note that there are two educational changes you cannot use (interpretation and application), but apart from these you have a free choice. Make sure that you keep within the time constraint. Choose the educational change you are most familiar with, and when discussing its importance, refer to its advantages and its problems (evaluation). If possible, make reference to any sociological studies that support the points being made (application).

(e) Using ideas from Item G and elsewhere, outline and evaluate the Marxist approach to the sociology of education. *(8 marks)*

You should be able to work out for yourself the skills required here. Although the question assumes that there is only one Marxist approach, you will be rewarded if you challenge this in your discussion. It is important to make your evaluation through a balanced consideration of the insights the Marxists have provided and the limitations they have.

4 Explaining class differences in educational achievement

By the end of this chapter you should:

- be able to describe class differences in educational achievement;
- be able to assess different explanations of class differences in educational achievement;
- appreciate the way government educational policies can affect the educational achievements of different social classes;
- have given critical thought to the concept of social class in post-modern societies;
- have reflected on student answers to exam questions;
- have practised structured exam questions yourself.

Introduction

Despite, or perhaps because of, the educational changes of the last fifty years, class inequalities in educational achievement remain as firmly entrenched as ever. In this chapter we will consider the disparities in attainment by class in the 1990s and then offer a set of explanations to account for such differential educational performance. Four types of explanation will be advanced: (1) genetic explanations, which focus on innate differences in intelligence; (2) outside school explanations (non-genetic), which find the answers in terms of the home backgrounds of different social classes; (3) inside school explanations, which look at systems of organisation and social processes inside schools; and (4) a structuration approach, which combines elements of the outside school and inside school explanations.

Evidence of class differences in educational achievement

Sociological evidence suggests that working-class pupils underachieve in the education system compared with middle-class pupils. Items A and B below provide some evidence of the disparities that exist.

ITEM A

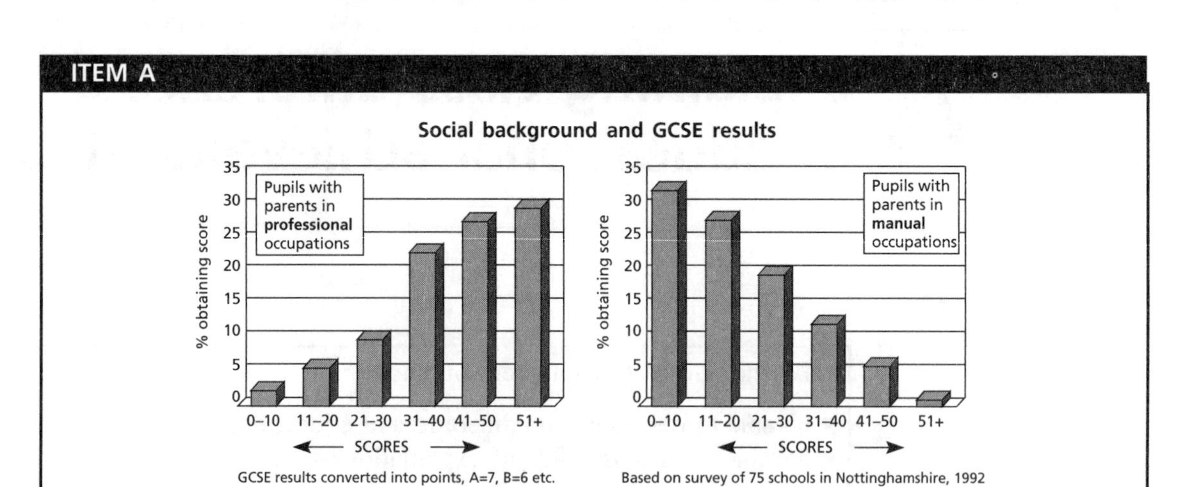

(*Source: D. Jesson and J. Gray, in M. Denscombe, Sociology Update, Leicester, Olympus Books, 1993.*)

ITEM B

Highest qualification held:[1] by socio-economic group of father, 1990–1991 (Great Britain, percentages)

	Professional	Employers and managers	Intermediate and junior non-manual	Skilled manual and own account non-professional	Semi-skilled manual and personal service	Unskilled manual	All Persons
Degree	32	17	17	6	4	3	10
Higher education	19	15	18	10	7	5	11
GCE A level[2]	15	13	12	8	6	4	9
GCSE, grades A–C[2]	19	24	25	21	19	15	21
GCSE, grades D–G[2,3]	4	9	7	12	12	10	10
Foreign	4	4	4	3	2	2	3
No qualifications	7	19	18	40	50	60	35

1. Persons aged 25–59 not in full-time education. See appendix, Part 3: Education.
2. Or equivalent.
3. Includes commercial qualifications and apprenticeships.

(*Source: General Household Survey 1994, reproduced in Social Trends, vol. 24, London: HMSO.*)

ITEMS A AND B

Exercise 4.1

i

1. According to Item B, what is the difference between the percentage of those from the professional category holding a degree and those from unskilled manual backgrounds?

i a

2. Use the information in Items A and B to support the claim that differential educational achievement exists by social class.

i a

3. Explain why sociologists would not want to generalise about the relationship between social class and educational performance on the basis of the Nottinghamshire study referred to in Item A.

i a

4. Sociologists could level the criticism that terms such as 'professional' and 'manual', as in Item A, are too broad. Suggest a way in which the 'manual' category could be usefully subdivided.

Exercise 4.2

i

Official statistics can go out of date quickly. Try to update the statistics we have presented on class inequalities in educational attainment. You could start this search by referring to the most recent editions of *Sociology Update* and *Social Trends*. If your search is successful, repeat questions 1 and 2 in Exercise 4.1.

Explanations of class differences in educational achievement

Now that you have some appreciation of the extent of class inequalities in educational performance, we will move on to address what have become established explanations for such inequalities. Four explanations will be considered.

1. Genetic explanations
2. Outside school explanations
3. Inside school explanations
4. A structuration explanation

1. Genetic explanations

Genetic accounts of class differences in educational attainment are suggested by some psychologists. Four main points are put forward in this explanation.

1. Intelligence is fixed and can be measured in a scientific way.
2. Objective intelligence quotient (IQ) tests have shown that working-class students are less intelligent than middle-class students.

3. 'Measured' differences in 'natural' intelligence account for class inequalities in educational achievement.
4. Class inequalities in educational performance continue over time because intelligence is largely genetically inherited – the inequalities are in effect passed down from one generation to the next.

Exercise 4.3

1. Below are five questions taken from an IQ test. Try to answer the questions yourself for fun!

(a) Underline the odd-man-out.
Byron Shelly Keats Chamberlain Chaucer

(b) Underline the phrase which completes the sequence. Alfred had his cakes; Bruce had his spider; Canute had his waves. Which comes next: Charles with his Nell; John with his barons; Keats with his poetry; Henry with his wives; or Richard with his hunchback?

(c) Underline which two of these six drawings do not make a pair.

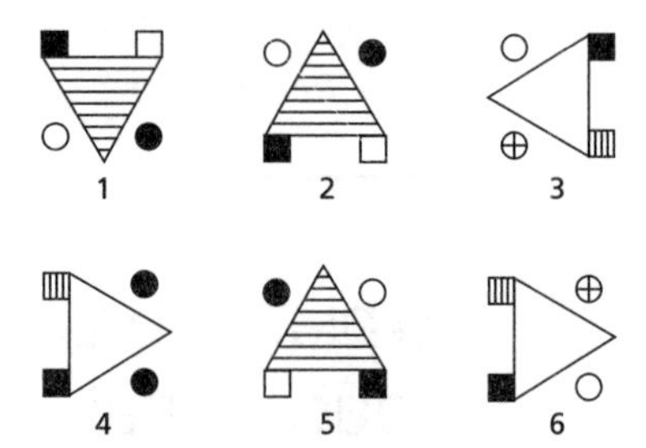

(d) Underline which of these is not a film star.
BALEG
RAYLOT
OROPEC
PALSREM
DABTOR

(e) Underline which of these is not a girl's name.
SAYDI
BLISY
SHOLT
TEEMILCNEN

(Source: H. J. Eysenck, Know your own IQ, Harmondsworth, Penguin, 1962.)

2. A number of sociologists have questioned the methodological basis of genetic explanations. It is argued that the IQ tests are culturally loaded in favour of middle-class children and are therefore not objective. Justify this claim in the light of the IQ questions you have just attempted.

3. With the help of a sociology textbook, give two other criticisms sociologists have made against genetic explanations of class differences in educational achievement.

It is important to note that it is not just psychologists who put forward genetic explanations, but sociologists also. Peter Saunders (1994) argues that there is a strong body of evidence to support a link between intelligence and social class. However Saunders does not rely on intelligence testing on its own, but argues that, in a truly meritocratic society, we should expect to find some connection between social class and occupational success. He argues that, as the middle class has expanded through occupational changes, the proportion of working-class children who make it into the middle class are much the same as you might predict if intelligence was the key factor influencing class membership. His conclusion is that Britain is a society largely based on talent. However his work has been criticised for denying the importance of IQ testing while at the same time using the concept of IQ in his calculations of the intelligence of different classes. It is also important to note that Saunders is critical of the conclusions Herrnstein and Murray (1994) came to concerning race and intelligence. He suggests that class is socially selected and therefore subject to a 'sorting out' process, where, over generations, the less intelligent filter to the bottom of the class system, whereas race is fixed at birth and therefore is not subject to this same sifting process (see Chapter 6).

2. Outside school explanations

Within a more sociological framework, the effects of home background have been stressed. Three distinct social (as opposed to genetic) explanations have emerged from the outside school approach. These all adopt a macro approach, looking at the structures of society to examine educational underachievement.

- Material deprivation theory
- Cultural deprivation theory
- Cultural difference theory

Material deprivation theory

This explanation focuses on income inequality and the material social problems that go with it. It is argued that working-class households have lower incomes than their middle-class counterparts, and as a consequence they experience material deprivations such as an unhealthy diet and unsatisfactory housing conditions. These deprivations are said in turn to hinder their chances of success at school (as judged by test and examination results). Douglas's (1964) study *The Home and the School* offers partial support for the materialistic approach. For example he demonstrates that unsatisfactory housing conditions did in fact depress school test performances at the time of the study.

One implication of the material deprivation theory is that, as the material conditions of the working class improve, then differential educational achievement can be eliminated. However improvements in social conditions since the 1960s have not brought about a decrease in the gap between working-class and middle-class educational achievement. Yet the statistical link between material deprivation and educational underachievement still remains, with schools drawing their pupils from the most deprived areas of cities performing less well than those in more affluent suburbs.

Exercise 4.4

A spider diagram has been started for you to show the way in which material deprivation depresses the school performance of working-class students. Copy out and complete the diagram yourself by indicating three other ways in which a lack of income may contribute to working-class underachievement in schools.

Material deprivation and depressed school performance

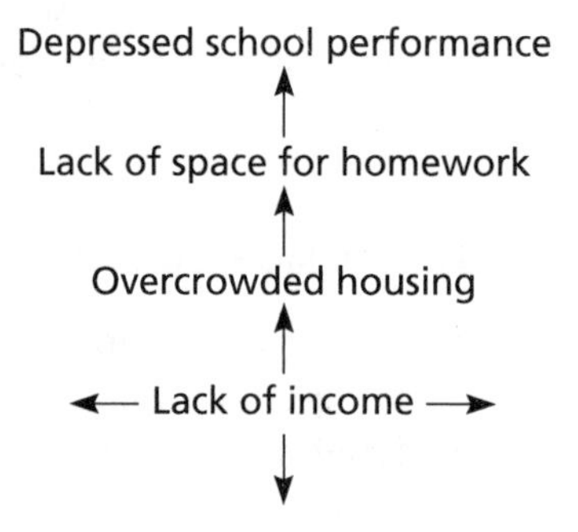

Cultural deprivation theory

Cultural deprivation theory primarily locates class differences in educational attainment in terms of the varying attitudes towards education that emerge from different class cultures. It is claimed that working-class attitudes and values are in some way 'inferior' or less beneficial for education than the middle classes' value systems, and as a consequence the working-class home acts as a 'deficit system'. This idea is based on the assumption that most working-class parents share a value system that encourages their children to drop out of school early and devalues what they learn there. However this is to assign to the working class as a whole, features that may only pertain to part of it. It ignores, for example, the long tradition of educational self-help of other sections of the working class.

A number of studies, including Douglas (1964) and the Plowden Report (1967), have pointed out that working-class parents offer less encouragement and support towards their children's education than middle-class parents do, and that this helps to explain in some part the differences in educational performance between the social classes. However others, such as Tizard *et al.* (1981), argue that the apparent lack of interest by working-class parents in their children's education may mask their lack of confidence or knowledge in dealing with schools, rather than an indifference to their children's fate.

Exercise 4.5

Working with another sociology student, identify four possible examples of 'deficient' parental attitudes or values that may contribute to working-class underachievement in schools. The following example should help you to get started.

1. Working-class parents are less likely to attend parent evenings.

Compensatory educational policies

During the 1960s one solution to cultural deprivation was attempted with compensatory education programmes. These were an attempt to provide additional educational provision for the 'culturally deprived' to try to offset those attitudes and behaviours that were said to restrict educational achievement. In the USA, the government's compensatory package was 'Operation Head Start' and in Britain the government established 'educational priority areas'. It should be noted that these programmes were genuine attempts to promote equality of opportunity and had the effect of channelling funds into areas of deprivation. Central to the operation of these schemes was the belief that, if you were able to encourage positive attitudes towards schooling early enough, then the negative effects of working-class culture could be countered.

The history of these schemes suggests that the effects of such interventions are varied and depend on a number of factors, including how 'success' is actually measured. They are also subject to changes in political attitudes. While the postwar social democratic consensus held sway, then the schemes were seen as an appropriate way of encouraging meritocracy. However left-wing critics argued that the schemes were based on middle-class professionals' misconceptions of working-class culture, rather than on any real research. Right-wing opponents disliked the increased state intervention that the schemes involved, seeing them as overly bureaucratic and a drain on tax-payers' money.

Exercise 4.6

This exercise is designed to broaden your understanding of compensatory education.

Read a sociology textbook that covers 'Operation Headstart' and 'educational priority areas' and make brief notes on them by jotting down the different aspects of the policies and the criticisms that have been made of them. We would recommend either *Sociology Themes and Perspectives*, 4th edition, by M. Haralambos and M. Holborn (1995) or *A New Introduction to Sociology*, 3rd edition, by M. O'Donnell (1992) for this task.

Material and cultural deprivation theories – an evaluation

The strengths of the theories are as follows:

1. They are an improvement on earlier genetic-based theories because they recognise the importance of social (as opposed to biological) causes of class inequalities in educational attainment.
2. The explanations have served to generate a great deal of further sociological research into class inequalities in educational performance.
3. Most of the empirical support for the two theories is of a quantitative nature and is therefore high in reliability.

Exercise 4.7

Below are a number of partly completed statements relating to the weaknesses of the material and cultural deprivation approaches. Your task is to complete these statements by selecting the appropriate finish to the sentences from the three alternatives provided.

1. The explanations have only looked at factors outside the school. . . . . .

2. The explanations are to some extent deterministic because. . . . . .

3. Cultural deprivation theory implies that the working-class child is in some way deficient. . . . . .

Matching sentence endings:

(a) they see the child's performance as being determined by external social forces.

(b) it could be that they are simply different. Many argue that it is the education system that is deficient because it is not prepared for the working-class child.

(c) they have ignored the influence of social processes operating inside schools, for example the effects of streaming.

Exercise 4.8

One further criticism that can be made of the material and cultural deprivation approaches is that there is no attempt to link the cultural with the material. This is a major weakness, for it is necessary to understand the way in which material factors shape cultural behaviours. The 'flow' diagram below illustrates one of the possible links. Your task for this exercise is draw two other 'flow' diagrams that further illustrate the material and cultural connection.

The necessity to work night shifts (material constraint)

Non-attendance at parent evenings (cultural behaviour)

Cultural difference theory

This theory focuses on the mismatch between working-class culture and the middle-class culture of schools. It is most often associated with Bernstein's (1975) language codes theory and Bourdieu's (1973) and Bourdieu's and Passeron's (1977) cultural capital theory. As an explanation for class differences in educational attainment, it can be considered to be more sophisticated than the cultural deprivation theory. This is because the theory draws on the notion of cultural difference rather than cultural deprivation (deprivation almost implies inferiority), and the fact that its theorists recognise that the education system is in some way responsible for the underachievement of working-class pupils.

Bernstein's examination of the relationship between social class, mode of cognitive expression and educational attainment can at times be complex (see for example Bernstein, 1975). What follows is a simplified version of some of his earlier thoughts on this subject, developed in the 1960s and 1970s.

First, people's position in the class structure determines the mode of cognitive expression (language code) they are socialised into.

Second, working-class children are generally socialised into a restricted language code, characterised by the following:

1. A limited vocabulary.
2. Context-bound speech – that is, particular to the context in which it is spoken.
3. Grammatically simple.
4. Short and descriptive sentences.

A typical sentence is: 'Me ma learnt me to read'.

Third, middle-class children are generally socialised into an elaborated language code (although they have access to the restricted code). This form of language is largely confined to the middle classes and includes the following characteristics:

1. An extensive vocabulary.
2. Context-free speech – that is, independent of the context in which it is spoken.
3. Grammatically complex.
4. Long and analytical sentences.

A typical sentence is: 'My mother taught me how to read'.

Fourth, the different language patterns people adopt affects their educability (their potential to be educated). This is because the formal teaching of schools and externally set examinations are carried out in the elaborated language code.

Fifth, middle-class children are more likely to succeed at school because they are able to draw on the elaborated language code, which is essential for educational success. For example they will be able to write essays that demonstrate abstract analysis.

Finally, working-class children are more likely to underperform at school because the language code they adopt clashes with the speech patterns used in schools – it is in effect inappropriate for educational success. For example they may write essays that are overly descriptive and lacking in analysis.

Exercise 4.9

Using the account of Bernstein's thoughts above, write a short paragraph (no more than 60 words) that summarises his language code theory of differential educational performance. You could start your paragraph in the following way:

'Working-class students underperform educationally in comparison with middle-class students because . . . '

Bourdieu's work, like that of Bernstein, is complex and we offer only a simplified version of his ideas, which were developed in the 1970s (see Bourdieu, 1973; Bourdieu and Passeron, 1977).

First, social groups with control over economic capital (wealth) can ensure that their sons/daughters also pick up cultural capital (knowledge, demeanour, language, tastes, lifestyle).

Second, the possession of cultural capital is essential if educational capital (qualifications) is to be obtained. This is because schools are essentially middle-class institutions that assess pupils in terms of their grasp of 'high' (middle-class) culture.

Third, working-class students underachieve in the education system because they do not have the same access to cultural capital, for example trips to the cinema, the theatre and museums. Working-class culture is in effect too distant from the 'academic' culture embedded in schooling to allow for educational success.

Thus a major function of schools is to pass on privilege from one generation to another. Given the ideological importance of the concept of meritocracy in justifying social arrangements, schools ensure that the children of the working class will remain working class because they are handicapped in the acquisition of cultural capital by their home background.

However critics of this approach to working-class underachievement argue that the cultural differences between working-class children and middle-class schools are not as important as the material disadvantages suffered by working-class children. While being aware that real cultural differences do exist, Lynch and O'Neill (1994) argue that it is poverty that often lies behind this tension. They give the example of school rules concerning shoes, which were resented by working-class parents, not because of shape or colour, but because they could not afford separate shoes for home and school. Hence the major problem facing working-class children is that their parents have insufficient material resources to take advantage of the opportunities that schools provide.

Moreover we should be careful not to stereotype social class groupings into automatic 'successes' or 'failures'. Aggleton (1987) shows how some middle-class children with cultural capital resist schooling in ways similar to working-class children and come out of school with poor qualifications. Aggleton argues that there is a conflict between the culture of the home backgrounds of these middle-class resisters, which stresses personal fulfilment and creativity, and the stifling regimentation of most school life. The major difference between these middle-class resisters and their working-class counterparts is that, in the labour market, the middle class do not seem to be impaired in the same way as the working class, so that their cultural capital pays off, despite their lack of formal qualifications.

An evaluation of cultural difference theories (Bernstein and Bourdieu)

Strengths:

1. They recognise that the working-class child is culturally different rather than deficient.
2. They appreciate that the education system is in some way at fault because it is not responsive to a range of cultural backgrounds – it is too middle class.

Weaknesses:

1. They both lack empirical support.
2. They are both deterministic. They assume that working-class culture is inevitably passed on. They do not acknowledge that some working-class students do break away from their culture, have a high level of cultural capital and adopt elaborated language codes.

3. Inside school explanations

These explanations adopt a micro sociological framework, turning inwards to look at the internal workings of schools. Two areas of the schooling process have received particular attention by interactionist sociologists interested in explaining class differences in educational attainment:

1. Streaming (banding or setting)
2. Teachers' expectations

Both these areas constitute part of what is called the hidden curriculum. The hidden curriculum is all the unofficial or informal learning that takes place inside schools and the classroom. Sociologists argue that, through the hidden curriculum of streaming and teacher expectations, educational success and failure are socially constructed. What is meant by this is that failure or success in schools is not a natural phenomenon, linked to genetic ability alone. Rather the experiences that children have in schools shape and influence the qualifications they emerge with at the end of their schooling.

While it is obvious that the formal curriculum (time-tabled subjects such as history, biology and so on) has an important effect on what is learned in schools, sociologists have argued that factors such as the structure of the school or the way teachers deal with different types of pupil also have an important effect on educational outcomes. Marxist sociologists in particular have suggested that this hidden curriculum is the most important part of schooling, because it legitimates inequality through the application of the label 'failure' to those from a working-class background. Those so labelled end up in working-class occupations, believing that their low position in the social hierarchy is a result of their own inadequacy.

Exercise 4.10

This exercise has been designed to get you to think about the way in which streaming and teacher expectations affect educational outcomes. The fictitious characters are deliberately stereotyped so that the effects of the hidden curriculum become immediately visible to you.

You should now read the case studies and then answer the questions that follow. You should initially do this on your own, but compare and discuss your responses with at least two other sociology students when you have finished.

Fictitious background

Each student is enrolled at Leicester City Comprehensive School (11–18), and all are 14 years of age. They are streamed into three sets for maths, English and foreign languages and are taught in mixed ability groupings for all their other subjects. School uniform is worn between the ages of 11 and 16.

Student A

- Mother lives off state benefits as a single parent.
- Smells.
- Comes to school in 'tatty' clothes and has been sent home twice this year for 'inappropriate dress'.

- Very quiet in class.
- Rarely works in class and is frequently seen 'doodling' and day dreaming.
- Sits on her own and is not liked by the other students.
- Her English and design teachers have described her as 'lazy' and 'thick'.
- In the lowest sets for maths, English and foreign languages.

Student B

- Mum is a school nurse and a school governor. Dad is an accountant.
- Well dressed.
- Works reasonably quietly.
- Homework is often late but always handed in.
- Very popular with the 'bright' pupils.
- Described at her last school as an 'underperforming' student.
- Had three detentions this year for smoking in the toilets.
- Predicted GCSE results: five Ds, one C, two Es, one B.
- In the middle band for maths, English and foreign languages.

Student C

- Mum works in a pub. Dad is a paint sprayer.
- Often fails to wear the school uniform. Three letters have been sent home already this year.
- A noisy and disruptive pupil.
- Has handed in three pieces of homework since starting school.
- Plays truant and feels that school is a laugh.
- Very popular with the 'lower ability' students.
- Described by his geography teacher as a 'good for nothing'.
- In the lowest sets for maths, English and foreign languages.
- Hates teachers.

Student D

- Dad is a primary school head. Mum is the owner of a local book shop.
- Has a new school uniform each year.
- A very quiet worker.
- Homework is always handed in on time.
- Very popular with the 'bright' students.
- Quick to ask questions in class.
- In the top sets for maths, English and foreign languages. Obtained a B grade in GCSE maths at the age of 13.
- Sits on the school council.

Student E

- Mum is a single parent and works as a childminder.
- Often fails to wear a school uniform. Mum was called in by the head last week to make her conform.
- Very 'noisy' in class.
- Homework is handed in late.
- Popular with all the students in her year.
- Described in her last report as an arrogant student.
- In the top set for English and bottom sets for maths and foreign languages.
- Hates all her teachers other than her tutor.

1. Which social class is each student from?

2. How are the teachers in the school likely to respond to each student?

3. What will be each student's reaction to schooling?

4. What are the likely educational qualifications and jobs each student will obtain?

Streaming

The issue of streaming in schools is an important one, both sociologically and politically. Streaming according to ability (as defined by testing) has usually been associated with traditional modes of teaching. 'Progressive' teaching is more associated with mixed ability classes. The arguments in favour of mixed ability teaching are (1) it is less divisive than streaming and (2) it allows the less able to be helped by the more able, so that educational standards will be improved. Theorists of the New Right argue that the effect of mixed ability teaching is to lower standards, as 'bright' students are held back by the slowness of the less able. On the other hand streaming allows the appropriate pitching of lessons for both bright and less able pupils. However critics of streaming argue that it institutionalises failure, condemning large numbers of the less able to educational under-achievement. Thus they are suggesting that streaming is a formal way of labelling pupils as successes or failures.

Exercise 4.11

The eight paragraphs below summarise the main findings of a series of studies carried out on the effects of streaming in secondary schools. These studies include the work of Hargreaves (1967) and Lacey (1970). Bearing in mind what you have learnt from Exercise 4.10, complete the missing gaps by selecting appropriate words from the list provided.

1. Streaming is based on. . . . . . High-ability students are placed in high. . . . . . and low-ability students are placed in low streams.

2. Although streaming is supposed to be based on ability there is a strong correlation with social class. . . . . . .class students are found in the high sets and. . . . . . class students are found in the low sets.

3. There is little movement between streams.

4. Before streaming most students (working class and middle class) were committed to the school's. . . . . . For example, hard work and good behaviour.

5. Since the introduction of streaming, the high streamers have developed a. . . . . . Emphasis is given to hard work, punctuality, good behaviour and so on. However the low streamers have developed an. . . . . . . This oppositional culture rejects the norms and values of the school (and the pro-school culture) and replaces them with an alternative set of deviant norms and values. A high value is placed on. . . . . .

6. The anti-school subculture is a group response to being. . . . . . by the school as. . . . . .

7. The anti-school subculture offers a form of. . . . . . Status and respect can be earned from other group members by following the deviant norms and values of the subculture. For example. . . . . .

8. In summary, working-class students underperform in the education system because they are placed in low sets, they see themselves as failures, and form antischool subcultures that reject the value of educational success.

Missing words:

(a) Working

(b) copying, lateness, cheeking the teacher, toughness, truanting.

(c) 'failures'

(d) who can get to the lesson the latest!

(e) ability

(f) norms and values

(g) pro-school culture

(h) status recovery

(i) Middle

(j) labelled

(k) streams

(l) anti-school subculture

Teachers' expectations

Teachers' expectations of children's performance depend on a whole range of factors, such as gender, ethnicity and social class. It is argued that these expectations are important because they provide the framework within which individual pupils perform and within which they are classified as a success or failure. Thus it is suggested that powerful stereotypes operate in the classroom and in the school generally that affect the performance of those subject to the stereotypes. Thus a labelling process operates in schools, which, in changing the behaviour of those labelled, results in a self-fulfilling prophecy. A self-fulfilling prophecy occurs when individuals live up to a label that has been placed upon them. Cordingly (1993) argues that class stereotypes have 'dropped off the educational agenda', with the result that, while gender and racial stereotypes are combatted within schools, the discrimination that white working-class boys experience through teacher stereotyping is ignored. This creates, according to Cordingly, a group of frustrated, white working-class males with low self-esteem, who are easily attracted to extremist politics and/or football hooliganism.

Exercise 4.12

The diagram below offers a summary of the self-fulfilling prophecy effect that teachers' expectations have on pupils. Some of the research studies in this area include Cicourel and Kitsuse (1963), Rist (1970) and Nash (1973).

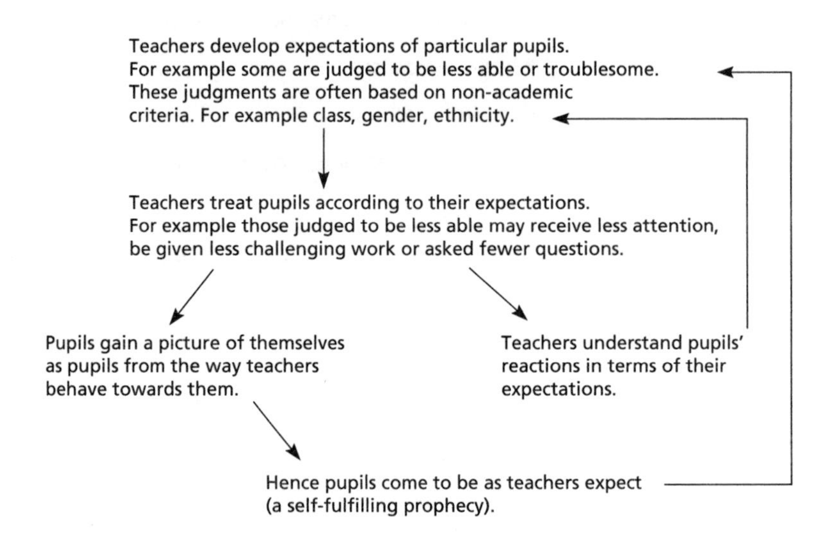

(Source: Adapted from R. Gomm, A Level Sociology, Cambridge, National Extension College, 1990.)

Using the diagram, write a brief paragraph (no more than 60 words) explaining how teachers' expectations contribute to class differences in educational attainment.

Control of the school

New Right theorists in the 1980s argued that the major reason for the underachievement of the working class was the deadening hand of the state in controlling what went on in schools (see Brown and Lauder, 1991). They began from the idea that fundamental human nature consists of rational self-interest and therefore, in a world where credentials are a clear route to success, everyone is interested in gaining the maximum qualifications possible. They therefore suggest that a free market in schools, where parents can rationally exercise their choice, will by itself get rid of educational inequality. Freeing schools from state bureaucratic control and empowering parents to make realistic choices about which school their children should attend, they suggest, will eliminate working-class parental apathy about schooling and increase their interest in education. Another aspect of this 'parentocracy' would be to shift power away from middle-class producers (the teachers) towards working-class consumers (the parents) and thus break down the middle-class monopoly on cultural capital.

One criticism of this approach is that it is difficult to see how a one-off decision about choice of school, even if it is a real choice, could, on its own, eliminate inequality. Moreover New Right theorists assume that all parents are free and equal in this educational market place (see Ranson, 1990), while knowledge, skills and access to material resources are unevenly distributed among parents.

Inside school explanations – an evaluation

Exercise 4.13

Below are a number of evaluation points of the inside school explanations. Identify which are the strengths and which are the weaknesses. Record your answers in a two-column table that clearly separates the strengths from the weaknesses. When you record your answers, rank them in order of importance. Justify your ranking to another sociology student.

1. They fail to explain the expectations of teachers. The question has to be asked, why do teachers label working-class students as less able?

2. The division between proschool cultures and antischool cultures in streaming studies is too crude. Woods (1983) identifies eight modes of adaptation to schooling, ranging from complete compliance to outright rebellion.

3. The explanations have highlighted important implications for the way teachers should be trained.

4. The interactionist-based explanations offer a fresh counterbalance to positivistic explanations. In particular they provide a useful insight into the social construction of educational failure and success.

5. The explanations are somewhat deterministic. They too readily assume that a self-fulfilling prophecy occurs after negative labelling. Some students actually cast aside their negative labels and do well educationally. It is as if the label acts as a spur to work even harder so that they can prove their teachers wrong.

6. The explanations are supported by a number of empirical studies which are high in validity.

4. A structuration explanation – Willis (1977)

Willis' work is influenced in its structural part by the theories of the French sociologist Althusser (1972), who argued that education systems are primarily 'ideological state apparatuses', concerned with the cultural reproduction of capitalism. Althusser's argument is that the main function of education is to ensure that the privileges of one generation are passed on to the next, through the ideological conditioning to be found in schooling. In Althusser's theory, individual experiences are unimportant, it is the overall effect of cultural reproduction that he found fascinating about schools. Willis draws upon the notion of cultural reproduction, but wishes to examine the processes in schools that contribute to the transfer of privilege and disadvantage across the generations.

Therefore the central question Willis attempts to answer in his book *Learning to Labour* is 'Why do working class kids fail?' To understand this phenomenon he adopted an ethnographic approach, which included observation and interviews . His approach can be considered to be innovative because he combined structurally based outside-school explanations with action-based inside-school explanations. Willis's synthesis of micro and macro perspectives is a classic example of what Giddens (1984) has subsequently termed structuration theory – structural and action perspectives combined into one set of ideas. What follows is a review of Willis' findings.

First, working-class educational underachievement can be understood in terms of antischool cultures (the action-based part of his explanation).

Second, Willis' counterschool culture has similar features to Hargreaves' and Lacey's antischool subcultures. For example its members avoid working, play truant, make use of 'sharp language' and disobey teachers. Given these characteristics the chances of succeeding in school are limited.

Third, Willis sees the counterschool culture as having very different origins from those identified by Hargreaves and Lacey. He rejects the view that counterschool culture is a product of students being labelled 'failures' at school, rather it has its origins outside school in working-class culture (the structural part of his explanation).

Fourth, working-class culture has a number of characteristics:

1. A belief that no amount of educational qualifications will produce more jobs or improve opportunities for the working class as a whole. There is an acceptance that working-class people will do manual work.
2. A belief that non-manual jobs are 'boring', 'soft', 'desk-bound', 'cissy-work'.
3. A belief that coping mechanisms should be employed to provide diversions and alternative satisfactions for menial work. For example taking unofficial 'fag' breaks at work.

Fifth, given that working-class pupils bring this cultural background into the school it is not surprising they form counterschool cultures that:

1. have little interest in academic work or gaining qualifications;
2. oppose authority and reject those who are conformist (the ear'oles);

3. emphasise having a 'laff'. For example, cheeking teachers, smoking at school.

For Willis, then, the counterschool culture (and hence educational failure) is seen as rational. Working-class kids bring into school a 'shopfloor culture' and choose not to get on in school. They make this choice because they realise that they have limited opportunities to succeed in middle-class terms and see schooling as a kind of training ground to practice ways of remaining human in the alienating factory jobs they eventually expect to fill.

Exercise 4.14

Create a flow diagram similar to the one we mapped out for teachers' expectations (see page 80) to summarise Willis' structuration explanation of working-class underachievement in schools.

An evaluation of Willis' structuration theory

Exercise 4.15

For this exercise you have to complete statements concerning the strengths and weaknesses of Willis' work. For some of these you will be able to select from the matching words provided, whilst others require logical completion by yourself.

Strengths

1. He has exposed the inadequacies of earlier explanations of class inequalities in educational achievement by recognising the need to. . . . . .

2. . . . . . . Giddens' structuration theory.

3. The use of a range of qualitative research methods such as participant observation and informal interviews means that his findings are high in. . . . . .

Weaknesses

1. . . . . . as it was based on a sample of 12.

2. He has focused too much on counterschool cultures. . . . . .

3. As with Hargreaves and Lacey, the distinction between conformist and counterschool cultures is too crude because there are. . . . . .

Some of the missing words

(a) and neglected the sociological significance of conformist subcultures (a charge that can be made of others, such as Lacey).

(b) combine structural and action perspectives.

(c) His research has had a major impact on sociological theory. For example,

One problem with Willis' work is that it was carried out at a particular time, towards the end of what the postmodernists describe as the 'modern' period and at the beginning of the 'postmodern world'. In particular, since then post-Fordist factories have transformed the prospects of Willis' 'lads' in ways they might have found disturbing. The economic restructuring of the 1980s has meant that the manual labour that underpinned the masculine culture of the Fordist factory is disappearing, and the new production heroes are computer operators, engaged in lifetime learning careers. Rather than the 'lads' of the 1990s making the transition from school to work, they are more likely to experience a world of training programmes or be reluctant post-16 students, as youth unemployment has hit hard.

Government educational policy and class inequalities in educational attainment

In Chapters 2 and 3 we gave detailed consideration to the way in which educational policies have shaped the nature of educational institutions and the teaching that takes place within them. When covering this material you may well have come to appreciate that the various policies have to a certain extent influenced or may yet influence the educational achievements of different social classes. We will now get you to apply your understanding of educational policies to the debate on class inequalities through a link exercise.

Link Exercise 4.1

For this exercise we want you to assess the extent to which educational policy has affected class inequalities in educational performance. To do this you will need to draw on material from Chapters 2 and 3. It is important that you adopt a balanced approach in your assessment. Thus you should reflect on policies that may or have widened or reduced class inequalities in educational achievement. You may find it useful to draw up a table that clearly separates the positive and negative influences of social policy. (Hint: the policies that may or have reduced class inequalities in educational attainment include the reduction of the coursework component of most examined courses to 20 per cent and the commitment to comprehensive schools; whilst student loans and the post-Dearing national curriculum may widen class inequalities in educational achievement.)

The death of class?

Social class differences in educational attainment have been one of the persistent themes of the sociology of education since the Second

World War. Yet statistics on social class performance are increasingly more difficult to obtain. The lack of official interest in class differentials is partly a consequence of the ideological notion of classlessness, in which the importance of class relationships in contemporary industrial societies is downplayed and the claim that such societies are meritocratic rather than class-based is dominant. This is reflected in sociology itself, where the primacy of class analysis has been replaced by concern about other social relationships and identities, for example gender and ethnicity.

Postmodern theories have been at the forefront of the attack on class-based analysis, arguing that it is derived from the 'metanarrative' of Marxism, in which all social relationships are reduced to class relationships. By metanarrative, postmodernists are referring to social theories that seek to explain the whole of human history and society, usually by one central theme or idea. In seeking to explain the totality of society, Marxists have focused on class analysis as a way of laying bare the 'true' and often hidden nature of capitalist societies. Postmodernists have, to varying degrees, dismissed the search for one explanation of society as a whole. They argue that such a search is not only futile, but also goes against the conditions of postmodernist societies, in which social groupings are fragmentary and fractured. For example Laclau and Mouffe (1985) argue that Marxists deny the importance of a whole range of social identities – such as gender, generation, ethnicity and nationality – when they assert the primacy of class relations. Marxists, in effect, are said to 'subsume' these social characteristics within class, thus imposing a single explanation on situations that are multilayered and complex.

According to postmodernists, developments since the 1960s have intensified the social changes that produced the conditions of postmodernity, in which all the old certainties and loyalties of class have been dissolved. The growing importance of the mass media in people's lives and the fragmentation of the working class through new forms of production and technology are important features of this process. In place of class identity, new social movements (NSMs) have emerged, and these are more likely to express the interests of postmodern individuals. These NSMs are based on issues of gender, ethnicity, ecology, sexual politics and so on and represent a fundamental shift, according to postmodernists, from the class-based certainties of modernism. In the sociology of education the demise of class is illustrated by a switch of focus away from examining differences in class attainment to greater interest in gender and ethnic differences in educational performance.

ITEMS C, D AND E

Exam questions and student answers

Read Items C, D and E and then look at the following questions on education. They are taken from the June 1993 AEB paper 1. We have focused on questions a, b, c and e, though you will come across question d in another chapter (see page 121). We have provided two answers by students for you to mark, using the marking scheme provided. Pay careful attention to the marks allocated to each part. We suggest that, when looking at any answer, you first try to locate it within a mark band (for example 3–6) and then try to give it the correct mark within that band. After the marking schemes you will find a commentary on the answers and the mark that the chief examiner awarded to the answers. Do not look at these until you have marked them yourself. Note that some line numbers are missing as these refer to part d of the answer.

ITEM C

The role of the teacher as an agent of social control is extremely important in assessing the role of the hidden curriculum in maintaining gender inequality. Obviously, teachers' attitudes towards the role of education for women and men will influence their relationship with students. Spender found that in mixed classrooms, boys received two-thirds of the teacher time, benefiting from the teacher's attention and distracting from the amount of time spent with the girls.

Just as the attitudes of teachers can play a role in reinforcing gender inequalities through the hidden curriculum so can the attitudes and behaviour of the students. Jones highlights the high level of sexual violence initiated by boys in mixed schools against females, both students and teachers. Jones argues that school is a system for legitimating male violence against women and for making this violence seem part of everyday life.

(Source: Kate Reynolds, 'Feminist Thinking on Education', Social Studies Review, vol. 6, no. 4, Philip Allan Publishers, 1991.)

ITEM D

Schools can make a difference

Although most people remain in the class they were born in, about one in three working-class children move up the social scale and about the same proportion of middle and lower-middle move down. Individual intelligence is one reason that partly explains upward movement, and going to a good school is another. But what is a good school?

Michael Rutter's study *Fifteen Thousand Hours* examined this problem. Rutter and his team looked at only twelve Inner London secondary schools so it is important not to overgeneralise their findings. Rutter's research is summarised below.

Factors measured:

- Attendance
- Academic achievement
- Behaviour in school
- Rate of delinquency outside school

Teachers' qualities linked with success in these four areas:

- Punctual
- Well organised
- Patient
- Encouraging
- Inspiring
- Willing to share extra-curricular activities with pupils
- Consistent

(Source: M. O'Donnell and J. Garrod, Sociology in Practice, Walton-on-Thomas, Nelson, 1990.)

ITEM E

The self-fulfilling prophecy

When pupils come into a school, teachers make judgements on their ability, based on many different things. These labels are, for example, 'bright', 'able', 'thick', 'less able', 'practical', 'academic', etc. However these labels are not neutral, nor do they describe the real possibilities of students, but are based on commonsense knowledge of what type of student is 'good' and which 'bad' . Thus it has been shown that teachers have stereotypes linked to class ('from broken homes'), gender ('she's just a girl'), race ('West Indians are noisy') and even physical attractiveness ('snotty-nosed kid'). Teachers then act towards students on the basis of such stereotypes – for example, those students who are labelled 'bright' are given more time to answer questions than those who are seen as unlikely to know the answer anyway.

(Source: Adapted from Tony Lawson, Sociology: A Conceptual Approach, Checkmate, 1991.)

Questions

(a) What does Jones suggest is the way in which schools 'legitimate male violence' (Item C)? (*1 mark*)

(b) Identify both factors which Item D suggests contribute to upward mobility. (*1 mark*)

(c) The concept of the self-fulfilling prophecy described in Item E has been criticised by some sociologists. Identify three ways in which the concept might be criticised. (*3 marks*)

(d) See page 121.

(e) Assess the extent to which school factors, such as those identified in the Items, explain differential educational achievement between social classes. (*10 marks*)

Student answers

CANDIDATE A

(a) Jones suggests that by not acting against male violence against female teachers and students, schools legitimate it. The school is a system that does not object to it and thus it becomes part of everyday life as high levels of sexual
5 violence continue. Schools are in fact then being negligent where this problem is concerned.

(b) Item D suggests that both individual intelligence and going to a 'good' school (characterised by Rutter as having encouraged organised teachers) contribute to upward social
10 mobility.

(c) In Item E the self-fulfilling prophecy is described as coming into force when a teacher makes judgements about a pupil based on things such as race, gender and class, and then shapes their behaviour towards that pupil accordingly. Although
15 research shows that teachers often hold an image of the ideal student (Howard Becker) it seems that such research (often interactionist) assumes that the self-fulfilling prophecy is an automatic process and thus the concept can be criticised for being too simplistic and assuming that labelling automatically
20 leads to the self-fulfilling prophecy that is said to be always a result of labelling. Labelling and the self-fulfilling prophecy do not necessarily go hand in hand either.

The concept is also somewhat unfair to teachers and
25 assumes that they have constructed attitudes about race,
class and sex merely within the interaction of classrooms.
Their ideas must have come from somewhere. Marxists say
that teachers are not, as this concept suggests, instigators
of unfairness, but rather victims of capitalism's 'ruling-class
30 ideology'. By blaming teachers we do not look at the
state's influence in maintaining a stratified, sexist, racist
society. Sharp and Green show that teachers are under
immense pressure to comply with things like the national
35 curriculum and cannot be blamed for working-class underachievement.

This concept does not do justice to pupils either. They are
viewed as passive and manipulated by the education system.
Studies of ethnicity in education for example show that
labelled black children were able to resist what teachers
thought of them.

(e) Interpretivists again focus on the school itself in trying
to explain differential achievement between social class. Ball
pinpoints streaming and banding as particularly important
115 and as in Item E, the self-fulfilling prophecy comes into
effect here. Ball's case study of a comprehensive school
shows that whilst band one pupils were 'warmed up', band
two pupils were 'cooled down'. As we can see from Items
C and D, teacher attitudes are most important and, as Ball
120 showed, middle-class pupils were more likely to be placed in
Band one. However, although Lacey, Hargreaves and Nell
Keddie all identify this same pattern, the tendency to place
middle-class students in higher bands cannot merely be
explained by teacher attitudes.

125 Functionalists in their cultural deprivation explanation of
working-class achievement see parental attitudes and
socialisation experiences as being responsible for the
underachievement of the working class.

Newsom, Newsom and Barnes see the ignorance of
130 working-class parents as hindering their child's educational
achievement. Bernstein shows that the speech patterns of
the working class prevent them from succeeding within the
system because schools, teachers etc. use the middle-class
elaborated code and not the restricted code.

135 Although such studies outline the need to look at
environmental and home factors and stress the problem
with focusing on school factors such as those in the items,
they have been heavily criticised as blaming parents and
children and seeing their culture as inferior.

140 Keddie argues that factors within the school should change, not working-class children.

Marxists argue that if the nature of the economy were to change from capitalism to communism, then schools would no longer be ideological conditioning devices, manipulated by the ruling class, and we would have a classless society. 145 Marxists effectively show us then that it is not enough to focus on such school factors as labelling, subcultures (Willis, Lacey, Hargreaves) and self-fulfilling prophecy as these are just effects of a wholly unequal society. What we need, they 150 argue, is a fundamental change in the economy. We can see from things like the 1988 Education Act that those in power do control the nature of education. Sociologists such as Clyde Chitty and Mike O'Donnell show that such Acts reinforce class divisions and effectively introduce a tiered system of education.

155 However, such Acts would effectively change the day-to-day running of schools and so would be relevant to school factors. Assessing such school factors as those in the items does explain the class differences that operate in schools. They are valuable in assessing how such Acts as that of 160 1988 directly affect schools and change teacher attitudes, and for this purpose at least they are valuable.

CANDIDATE B

(a) Jones suggests that the way in which schools 'legitimate male violence' is making this violence seem part of everyday life, that is, accept it without question.

(b) Item D suggests that individual intelligence and going to 5 a good school are reasons contributing to upward social mobility.

(c) Self-fulfilling prophecy can be criticised on the ground that because it is based on commonsense knowledge, it is changeable. Also, studies have indicated that pupils can not 10 conform to these stereotypes (Fuller) and revolt against the teacher's negative manner. Pupils have been shown (as any individual) to be non-conformist. It may be that the pupil may have outside influences that are similar to those of teachers.

(e) Explanations of the differential educational achievement between social classes include biological factors, out-of-

school factors and in-school factors.
60 Biological differences have been rejected on the ground that middle-class culture has been seen as higher than working-class culture. Also the IQ tests themselves have been problematic because they favour middle-class culture and cheating was found to have taken place. It has been shown
65 that out-of-school factors are present when it comes to educational achievement. Prosser and Weiss found that over the country, middle-class children were performing better in schools than their working-class counterparts. Coates and
70 Silburn agree, suggesting that, because working-class children come from poor home backgrounds, lacking in educational toys, and parents have little or no interest in school, these children are less intelligent.

More importantly, school factors such as those found in the hidden curriculum are becoming more and more
75 influential in educational achievement. Keddie uses education itself to show this. Those pupils who come top at school with concrete education are shunned because the sort of education that is highly regarded is abstract knowledge. These pupils are thought of as bright and
80 teachers encourage them to become more aspirational. Those with concrete education (their own personal experiences) are thought to be less intelligent. This has also fuelled labelling and self-fulfilling prophecies. Interactionists have been criticised for using too many ethnographic, detailed accounts of teachers and pupils. They rely on
85 subjective experience and lack reliability. Other factors to be considered are cultural experience, and restricted and elaborated codes (Boudon, Bourdieu, Labov).

Marking scheme for the AEB June 1993 education questions

(a) What does Jones suggest is the way in which schools 'legitimate male violence' – (Item C?) 1 mark. The mark will be given for 'making it seem part of everyday life' or any acceptable equivalent.

(b) Identify both factors which Item D suggests contribute to upward social mobility. 1 mark: Any form of words which identifies individual intelligence and a good school can score.

(c) The concept of the self-fulfilling prophecy described in Item E has been criticised by some sociologists. Identify three ways in which the concept might be criticised. 3 marks: Any reasonable criticisms can score up to a maximum of three. The most likely could be lack of consistency in applying labels, no notion of pupil resistance, the 'automatic' nature of the process etc.

(e) Assess the extent to which school factors, such as those identified in the Items, explain differential educational achievement between social classes. 10 marks.

0: no relevant points.

1–3: answers in this band may well concentrate on reproducing the factors identified in the items in more detail, or seek to apply these factors, in a minimal way to social classes. Any assessment is likely to be commonsensical.

4–7: in this band, candidates may seek to assess through juxtaposition of alternative factors. The more candidates apply these factors to an explicit critique, the higher they are likely to appear in the band. Studies cited must be interpreted well and applied to the question in some measure.

8–10: assessment should be explicit to reach this band, with alternative factors being used effectively to provide a critique of school factors. The very best will arrive at a balanced conclusion which emerges from the debate.

Commentary on the answers to parts a, b, c and e.

CANDIDATE A

(a) The candidate has interpreted the Item C well, included the appropriate phrasing (line 4) and shows a clear understanding of legitimation. (*1 mark*)

(b) The candidate has interpreted both the necessary factors (lines 7–8) and thus gains the one mark. (*1 mark*)

(c) The candidate applies her understanding well here by offering three acceptable critiques of the SFP: simplistic explanation (lines 19–23), unfair to teachers (lines 24–34) and student resistance (lines 35–39). If there is any criticism of her answer, it is that the candidate could have expressed these more succinctly, but we do not penalise her for this. (*3 marks*)

(e) There is good, explicit evaluation here (lines 157–59), and it is also presented as an integral part of the answer (for example lines 138 and 146). There is also good interpretation and application of the information in the items (lines 115–16), as well as outside information, especially the 1988 Education Reform Act (lines 151). It is a well-argued and focused response, quite amazing for the 20 minutes or so that the candidate had to devote to it. (*10 marks*)

CANDIDATE B

(a) There is good interpretation of Item C, using words from the item. (*1 mark*)
(b) Both factors are present here. (*1 mark*)
(c) The most obvious mark goes to the statement about non-conformity (lines 9–10), but the other two points made were less explicit. In the end we decided there was enough sense in the 'it is changeable' point (lines 8–9), but not enough in the last point (lines 12–14). So only limited application skills were demonstrated here. (*2 marks*)
(e) Again, the limited evaluation focused on methodological issues (lines 85–7), though there was some attempt to weigh up the importance of school factors (line 74 and 'more and more influential', line 75). However this is a classic juxtapositional approach, allowing implicit evaluation without necessarily spelling it out. That is, the candidate puts forward one type of explanation, for example biological factors (lines 61–5), and then an alternative, such as home background (lines 69–74), as an implicit contrast. Application skills are in evidence, for example Keddie's work (lines 76–84). (*5 marks*)

ITEMS F, G AND H

Structured exam questions

The following questions are ones for you to do yourself. They relate to Items F, G and H and are taken from the AEB's June 1991 A level sociology paper, parts a, b and c. We have provided some hints and ideas after each question. Make sure that the length of your responses are appropriate to the number of marks allocated to each part question.

Questions

(a) According to Item F, which type of pupil has benefited least from the introduction of GCSE? (*1 mark*)

(Hint: the question is directing your attention to Item F, so you should be able to interpret the answer from it. Be careful not to spend too much time on this part, as there is only one mark available for a correct answer.)

(b) Using only the material in the Items, summarise in your own words the patterns of differential educational attainment in Britain. (*5 marks*)

(Hint: the crucial thing to notice in this question is that you are only allowed to use the material in the items. Bringing in other knowledge cannot be rewarded, because of the wording of the question. Therefore you should focus strictly on the information in the items. However, you also have to use your own words, so be sure to read the material first and then write down your understanding of it, avoiding the wording in the items.)

(c) Item F suggests that poorer households have a 'relative lack of home provision' and Item G indicates a class bias in university entrance. Assess the extent to which home background can affect educational achievement. (9 *marks*)

(Hint: the focus of this question is on the effects of home background on educational achievement. While the bulk of you answer could concentrate on home factors, note that you are required to evaluate the extent to which home background is influential. You could do this through a consideration of the effects of home background compared with other factors. However you should be critical of the effects of home background factors in their own right and not just juxtapose home and school factors. This is only an implicit assessment – you should be explicit in your evaluations.)

ITEM F

There has been much argument about the alleged shortfall in training and resources for teachers preparing for GCSE courses. An HM Inspector's report (1988) on the first two years of GCSE, however, describes the new system as a qualified success.

On the positive side, the report noted improvements in teaching and pupil learning, and fewer pupils achieving no examination successes. More pupils also succeeded in obtaining higher grades than under the old GCE/CSE system, and 'average' students seemed to perform especially well. The report also notes, however, that more able students have not always been set work which is 'sufficiently demanding', while, on the whole, pupils at the lower end of the ability range seem to benefit least from the new arrangements. This latter point has lead to suggestions that the relative lack of home provision – of books and help with school work – in poorer households is accentuated by the new course requirements. The report also makes reference to 'mixed, and, at times, alarmist' messages in the media about the introduction of GCSE into classrooms.

(Source: Adapted from Social Studies Review, Research Roundup, vol. 4, no. 3, 1989.)

ITEM G

Percentage distribution of full-time university entrants, Britain, 1984 by social class

	Middle-class	Working-class
University entrants	80	19
All 18 year olds	35	65

(Source: Adapted from S. J. Ball, 'Education: the Search for Inequality', Social Studies Review, vol. 4, no. 2, Philip Allan Publishers, 1988.)

ITEM H

Much has been written in recent years about patterns of gender inequality in education. In particular, major studies have been conducted on the under-representation of girls and women in subjects in the sciences, engineering and technology groups. The evidence which has been presented demonstrates that, as the groups proceeding through O level (now GCSE), A level and first degree studies get smaller, so fewer women are found at each level. In particular, in higher education, women receive fewer first degrees in science, engineering and technology than in languages and other arts-based subjects. In a recent commentary, Alison Kelly (1987) concluded that chemistry now shows least sex differentiation in terms of scientific qualifications. As a consequence, she concluded that the problem of girls' participation in science is really confined to physics. However, as Kelly notes, it is not sufficient to take sex differences into account when examining such patterns; differences based on class and race should also be considered.

(Source: Adapted from R. Burgess, 'Researching Education' in Developments in Sociology, vol. 4, Ormskirk, Causeway, 1988.)

5 Explaining gender differences in educational achievement

By the end of this chapter you should:

- be able to describe gender differences in educational achievement;
- understand gender inequalities which exist in the higher education sector;
- be able to assess different explanations of gender differences in educational achievement and subject choice;
- appreciate the way government educational policies can affect the educational achievements of males and females;
- have reflected on a student's answer to an exam question;
- have practised a structured exam question yourself.

Introduction

Gender was investigated as a mainstream issue relatively late in the sociology of education. Prior to the 1970s, sociological discussions focused mainly on class differences in attainment. However, with the impact of feminist scholarship during the 1970s and 1980s the educational experiences of female students increasingly came to the fore. This chapter will start by mapping out gender differences in educational attainment and subject choice. Three sets of explanations will then be put forward to account for the observed variations in educational performance and subject choice: (1) genetic explanations, which focus on biological differences in intelligence; (2) outside school explanations (non-genetic) which emphasise childhood socialisation processes based on external cultural and structural factors; and (3) inside school explanations, which look at the sexism inherent in the hidden curriculum. We will also examine the extent to which educational policies and initiatives have been responsible for the significant improvements in female academic achievement in recent years.

Evidence of gender differences in educational achievement

When gender first began to be investigated by sociologists of education, the focus was largely on female underachievement at every level of the education system, and the ways in which traditional ideas about the proper role of women in society prevented them from achieving their full societal potential. However, females have markedly improved their educational performance during the 1980s and 1990s, so that the contemporary situation, while not without its problems and issues for girls in schools, is one where the educational opportunities open to females have possibly never been greater. Wilkinson (1994) argues that this is part of a 'genderquake' in which a fundamental change in attitudes towards women's role in society has been achieved. Prominent among the 'transformed circumstances' of women is a more positive attitude towards education as a means of improving chances at work.

ITEM A

Qualifications obtained in the UK by gender (percentages)

	Males				Females			
	1975/6	**1985/6**	**1990/1**	**1991/2**	**1975/6**	**1985/6**	**1990/1**	**1991/2**
Percentage gaining:								
2 or more A-levels or Scottish Highers	14	15	21	23	12	14	24	26
A-level or Scottish Higher(s)	4	4	4	5	4	4	5	5
5 or more GCSEs grade A–C (or CSEs grade 1)	7	10	12	13	9	12	16	17
1–4 GCSEs grade A–C (or CSEs grade 1)	24	24	25	23	27	29	27	25
1 or more GCSE/O grades D–G*	30	34	29	29	28	31	22	20
No GCSE or CSE grades	21	13	9	7	19	10	7	6
Total leavers (thousands)	423	444	338	324	400	427	323	312

* Includes GCSE grades D–G, O level grades D–E, CSE grades 2–5.

(Source: Adapted from Education Statistics for the United Kingdom (1993), Department for Education, London: HMSO.)

ITEM B

GCSE and A level results by selected subjects (as percentage of 16+ and 18+ school leavers, England, 1990)

	GCSE (grades A–C)		'A' level	
	boys	**girls**	**boys**	**girls**
English	40	57	4.0	8.5
Maths	36	33	7.6	4.4
Physics	19	9	5.7	2.0
Chemistry	14	12	4.5	3.3
Biology	11	17	2.8	4.6
Creative arts	16	27	2.1	3.8
French	16	25	1.5	3.9

(Source: DES Statistical Bulletin, December 1991, quoted in M. Denscombe, Sociology Update Leicester Olympus Book, 1992.)

ITEM C

Female students as a percentage of all students: by selected full-time degree courses, Britain 1981/82 and 1990/91

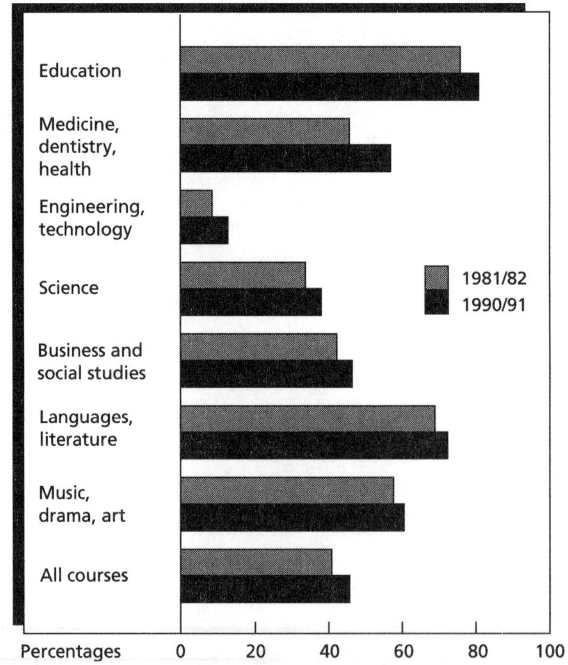

(Source: Department for Education (1993), reproduced in Social Trends, vol. 23, London: HMSO.)

ITEMS A, B AND C

Exercise 5.1

i 1. Identify the patterns of educational attainment shown in Item A.

i 2. Examine Item A. In which year did 12 per cent of females obtain five or more GCSEs grade A–C (or CSEs grade 1).

i 3. Using Item B, compare the differences in educational achievement between girls and boys.

i 4. Study Item B and identify which GCSE subject exhibits the largest gender gap in educational performance.

a 5. Item C indicates that between 1981/82 and 1990/91 an increasing number of women entered higher education to follow a first degree course. Give two reasons for this increased rate of female participation in higher education.

i 6. According to Item C, which course(s) are women least likely to study at degree level?

Having completed Exercise 5.1, you should now have an appreciation of the extent of gender differences in educational attainment and subject choice. You will have recognised that females outperform males in GCSE and A level examinations. You will also have noticed that performances at GCSE and A level vary according to the subject taken, such that females are well ahead in the arts but behind in scientific subjects (biology excepted). The relative underachievement of females in scientific-based subjects at the ages of 16 and 18 is clearly significant, for the statistics on first entry into higher education suggest that females are less likely to choose degrees of a scientific or technical nature. The gendered nature of higher-education subject choice is important, because the degree schemes females opt for are of lower status and afford fewer opportunities for entering the most powerful and well-paid occupational positions.

Higher education

The proportion of women undergraduates has risen since the Second World War, from about 25 per cent to 42.8 per cent in 1989 (Halsey, 1993), though it is in the new universities that the growth is most marked. However sociological research has shown that there continue to be important differences in the higher education experiences of men and women. For example Castleman and Poole (1990) show that there is still important gender segregation in subject choice at university level, and Mickleson (1989) shows that men receive greater rewards for the outcomes of their education than women do.

It is also the case that academics are mainly men, and women tend to occupy the least prestigious and more temporary university posts. Middleton (1993) suggests that this is because of 'academic machismo' (Morgan, 1981), whereby female academics are marginalised by academic discourses or ways of thinking that are dominated by men. For example she argues that what counts as sociology is decided by male gatekeepers – conference organisers and journal editors – who constitute the organising principals of the subject. If they are to progress in their chosen field, women academics have to 'bracket out' their femaleness and accept androcentric (male-centred) definitions.

Explanations of gender differences in educational achievement and subject choice

Let us now consider three types of explanation to account for the above patterns of attainment and choice:

1. Genetic explanations
2. Outside school explanations
3. Inside school explanations

1. Genetic explanations

Genetic-based explanations of gender differences in attainment were influential in psychology during the 1970s, though the biological determinist approach has a long history. The crucial belief of biological theories is that gender differences are natural and therefore unalterable. Educationally, then, it would be right and proper to treat boys and girls in schools differently, because their natural inclinations are towards different adult roles. Any socially constructed differences between men and women were built upon and constrained by these natural differences (see Hutt, 1972). For example theories were advanced that females excelled at language-based subjects because of their greater verbal and reasoning abilities, yet underperformed in mathematical and science-based courses because of lower levels of innate spatial ability, which restricted their understanding of shape and form.

These biological theories of innate intelligence have been strongly criticised. Kelly (1982) suggests that gender differences in spatial ability may be attributed to the types of toys children play with rather than their genetic make-up. Furthermore genetic explanations cannot adequately account for the narrowing of gender differences in mathematical and science-based subjects since the mid 1980s – if the differences were biologically determined we would expect them to remain constant over time.

A variation on this theme is represented by New Right ideologies, as put forward by Scruton (see Williams, 1989), which suggest that the biological and natural instincts of the sexes determine a particular sexual division of labour in the home and the gender segregation of the male-dominated public sphere and the female world of the private home. These gender arrangements are seen as a 'natural necessity'.

2. Outside school explanations

Feminist sociology has been influential in developing a macro approach to gender inequalities in education. Three social (as opposed to genetic) explanations can be identified within the outside school approach.

1. Childhood socialisation
2. Employment opportunities
3. Patriarchal relations

Childhood socialisation

Feminists such as Sharpe (1976) maintain that differences in child socialisation serve to generate masculine and feminine cultural identities. Secondary agencies of socialisation such as the media and peer groups are said to reinforce gender identities established during primary socialisation within the family. For example many teenage magazines targeted at female audiences present ideologies of beauty, marriage, domesticity and subordination that serve to strengthen the messages of femininity families instil into their female members. Gender socialisation of this sort is significant because it helps us to understand why females have traditionally 'latched' on to subjects such as home economics and the arts, which have a feminised image, rather than subjects such as technology and science, which are packaged in a masculine way. Therefore sex role theorists, such as Byrne (1978) have argued that the cycle of discrimination against women is created by parents and teachers reinforcing sex stereotypes, which then become the basis for discriminatory practices.

Exercise 5.2

Exercise 5.2 requires you to do some independent work. You should read some textbook accounts of outside school explanations of gender differences in educational attainment and subject choice. You should then use the material you have read to fill in the chart below. When completing the chart you need to explain how each agency of socialisation steers females away from scientific and technological subjects and towards the arts. You should also cite empirical studies wherever possible to support the points you make. We have started to fill in the chart for you to get you started.

A summary chart illustrating the way childhood socialisation affects educational attainment and subject choice by gender

Agency of socialisation	**The process by which educational attainments and subject identities are determined**	**Empirical studies**
Family role models		
Toys played with	Whereas males are given active construction toys to play with such as meccano and chemistry sets, females are encouraged to play with passive caring toys such as dolls and cookery sets. As a consequence females do not develop the kind of scientific aspirations and aptitudes that males do.	Kelly (1982)
Peer group		
Newspapers and magazines		
Adverts		

During the 1980s a series of research studies challenged the assumption that girls were socialised into one particular form of femininity, or that girls did not challenge the notions of feminine roles with which they were presented. For example Connell (1986) argued that feminism itself had helped to bring about radical changes in the ways girls perceived themselves, so that they no longer constructed their identity in mainly domestic terms. Rather women now saw themselves as much as workers as homemakers. More recently Riddell (1992) found that schoolgirls had a dual notion of their futures, linking their subject choices at schools to the local labour market (especially working-class girls) whilst also accepting that motherhood and domesticity were important parts of their identity as women. But the girls in Riddell's study were not passive in this process of socialisation. Rather they had absorbed both accepting and undermining messages about traditional female roles. In addition different gender codes were expressed by working-class and middle-class girls, with middle-class girls opting for academic education and thus gaining the approval of the middle-class female teachers whom they most closely resembled.

It is also important to note that Riddell found that parents' conceptions of femininity were also complex and varied according to class position. While middle-class parents were more supportive of the principle of equal opportunity, middle-class men were most opposed to any positive action to achieve it. Working-class men were the most supportive of traditional gender codes. In both classes, a minority of mothers strongly supported changes in women's social position. So the view that there is a uniform socialisation into one specific gender code is mistaken. Rather there are conservative and radical views concerning gender roles and different groups of parents choose elements of those agendas in different proportions, which then balance out in their children in different ways.

Employment opportunities

ITEM D

Nearly 11 million women were employed in Britain in 1991, according to the *Labour Force Survey*. Women form an increasingly large part of the nation's labour force and now account for 43 per cent of all people with jobs. At the same time the proportion of men in work is decreasing. By 1991, 71 per cent of women of working age were 'economically active', in the sense that they were either in paid employment or were actively seeking work. This figure compares with just 66 per cent in 1979. For men, the picture is quite different. Their economic activity rates are on a downward slide, falling from 91 per cent in 1979 to 88 per cent in 1991. If the trend continues, women will become a majority in the workforce before too long.

However this does not tell the whole story. The kind of work women do tends to be different from that of men. Women are much more likely to:

- **Work in the service industries**: 82 per cent of working women have jobs in the service industries compared with 54 per cent of men. This is particularly evident in the health-associated professions, personal services, and clerical and teaching occupations, where women significantly outnumber men.
- **Work part time**: 42 per cent of women with jobs are working part-time, according to the *Labour Force Survey* 1991. This involves nearly 4.5 million women workers. Married women are twice as likely as non-married women to be part-time employees; half of married women workers are part-timers compared with just over one quarter of non-married women workers.

(Source: Adapted from M. Denscombe (1993) Sociology Update, Leicester, Olympic Books, 1993.)

ITEM D

Exercise 5.3

1. By how many percentage points did economically active women of working age increase between 1979 and 1991, according to Item D?

2. In what ways do the jobs women do more than men, as described in Item D, reflect traditional views of gender roles?

3. Suggest one reason why the 'kind of work women do' (Item D) helps to explain subject-specific attainment and subject choice.

The issue of employment opportunities for girls is linked in sociology to the concept of 'cultural reproduction'. That is, sociologists are interested in the ways in which society acts to produce adults who end up with similar life-chances or opportunities to those of their parents. In the case of females, the situation is complicated by the 'domestic option'. Traditional ideology allocates homemaking and childrearing as the prime responsibility of women and 'earning' as the main activity of adult males. Clearly, in a world where adult male unemployment is high and adult female employment is prevalent, these traditional definitions of gender identity are likely to be strained. Yet while the labour market is now an acceptable goal of female education, cultural reproduction of the genders continues.

In particular, sociological focus has been on the choice of subjects by males and females and on the specific question of why girls continue to choose subjects that are likely to lead to disadvantage in the labour market, in terms of job security and levels of reward. At one level, traditional ideas about femininity and therefore 'proper' jobs for girls would seem to be the answer to this problem. However the labour market is changing rapidly and new forms of feminine identity are emerging that would seem to militate against this apparently easy relationship between the traditional notions of femininity and less prestigious jobs.

Cultural reproduction theory has shifted from a deterministic model, in which young people of either gender are slotted automatically with little choice into the appropriate job roles for a capitalist society, to one in which the active participation of individual girls and boys is recognised. Thus, while there are structural constraints in schools that form and channel subject choices, such as the options set against each other (part of the inside school explanations) or the powerful influence of parental pressure, sociologists such as Connell *et al.* (1982) stress the wide scope for individual choices within these constraints.

More recent work on cultural reproduction has challenged its usefulness in a postmodern world characterised by deindustrialisation. Weis (1990) for example, argues that postmodern societies, with their emphasis on service industries rather than heavy manufacturing, no longer require boys to follow their fathers into industrial jobs and girls to follow their mothers into domesticity. Rather, postmodern industries require flexible workers. Gender identities are therefore likely to shift under the impact of this development. The introduction of the national curriculum can therefore be seen not as a commitment to equal opportunities for girls and boys, but as a result of the need to train more young people in the scientific and technological skills needed by a postmodern economy (see Myers, 1989). The result may be to establish women as a reserve army of labour across a wider number of occupational sectors.

Patriarchal relations

Many feminists have argued that the ideology of patriarchy in society at large is a major cause of inequality in schools. The ideology of patriarchy suggests that the dominant ideas in society tend to favour men and operate to keep women in subordinate positions. For example Arnot (1991) argues that the introduction of the Technical and Vocational Educational Initiative, with its emphasis on gender equality through increasing female choices, actually did little to achieve gender equality. As she put it, 'providing equal freedoms within unequal social relations had little chance of creating equal opportunities' (ibid., p. 454). What she is suggesting is that, given a free choice, girls and boys tend to respond according to society's views of what is proper for each gender, so that girls tend to avoid choosing science and technology subjects. Therefore there should be greater compulsion in schools to ensure that there are common experiences for girls and boys, which will in turn ensure that equality of opportunity comes about.

During the 1980s the rise of New Right ideologies tended to reinforce patriarchal relationships in society as a whole and this impacted on education. However the effect of New Right ideas was not always as straightforward as might have been expected. Certainly New Right writers were hostile to the notion of equality for women, seeing it as an 'ideological extravagance', and hostile to the central importance the New Right gave to the family (see Campbell, 1987, for an account of the New Right attitude). The assumption made by New Right thinkers was that men would specialise in work in the market place and women in household work. This had implications for the type of education each gender was to receive. New Right ideas reflected traditional roles, with boys being prepared by schools to be the main wage earner and girls to be homemakers and childrearers (see David, 1983). This in turn had implications for the types of subject girls were to be encouraged to choose in schools.

However the impact of these ideologies have been blunted by several factors. Arnot (1992) argues that feminism has developed to the extent that women have been able to resist a simple 'back-to-basics' movement, in which women are supposed to be responsible for the home and men for work, so that the experiences of women after the First World War in being returned to domesticity have not been repeated. Campbell (1987) found that changes in occupational structures ensured that in the 1980s there were many middle-class career women in the ranks of the Conservative Party who could resist the simple equation of females with domesticity. As a result, women did not return to a mainly domestic role during the 1980s, despite the impact of recession and job losses.

Outside school explanations – an evaluation

Exercise 5.4

Below are a number of evaluation points of the outside school explanations. Identify which are the strengths and which are the weaknesses. Record your answers in a two-column table that clearly separates the strengths from the weaknesses. When you record your answers, rank them in order of importance. Justify your ranking to another sociology student.

1. They are an improvement on earlier genetic-based explanations as they recognise the importance of social processes.

2. The explanations have served to generate further research.

3. They neglect the effects of inside school processes and therefore act as a smokescreen for the failure of the education system.

4. Aspects of the explanations are dated. Many young females have aspirations outside the home and women are now in more powerful occupational positions.

5. They suffer from ideological bias.

6. As a set of explanations, they attempt to link the different parts of society together and show the interdependence of different aspects of society.

7. The process whereby early experience leads to later effect is never clearly stated. It is often just assumed.

8. They tend to oversimplify the effects of cultural and social forces in society.

9. These explanations stress cultural factors as well as social, for example the importance of the media in influencing views on gender.

10. They suggest that the early experiences of people are important in affecting the later course of their lives.

3. Inside school explanations

As with the outside school approaches to gender differences in attainment and subject choice, the impact of feminist theory and research has been influential in shaping the various explanations offered. Feminists claim that a powerful hidden curriculum operates inside schools that reinforces the gender-stereotyped socialisation they experience in the family and wider society. Kessler *et al.* (1985) describe the ways in which the whole of school life is permeated with messages about what is correct masculine or feminine behaviour in the school's 'gender regime'. Arnot (1982) suggests that schools use a 'gender code' to endorse or attack particular forms of masculinity or femininity, in other words, schools are involved in a legitimation process concerning appropriate gender behaviour and outcomes.

However it is important to note that feminism has become somewhat fragmented and it is difficult to discuss the impact of feminism as a whole, rather than a number of different feminisms. As the politics of identity has replaced social class as the major formative force in individual lives, feminism itself has also split along lines of identity. Thus it has become usual to refer to liberal feminism, radical feminism, socialist feminism and black feminism in analysing schools in particular and education in general. Each of these strands is likely to emphasise different explanations for the disadvantage experienced by girls in the education system. For example liberal feminism has traditionally been associated with the social democratic approach to education, in which freedom of subject choice is an important principle. Radical feminists have been more critical of schooling, focusing on the patriarchal nature of the curriculum and the 'androcentric' or male-centred nature of much of its practices. Socialist feminists have emphasised the relationship between girls' experiences in schools and their destinies in the labour market, that is, their class position also, and black feminists have focused on the distinct and double oppressions to which black girls are subject (see Chapter 6).

The solutions to gender inequality put forward by feminists therefore vary according to what type of feminist they are. Liberal feminists, according to Yates (1985), seek to change girls' feelings and attitudes towards schooling by recommending 'girl-friendly' schooling. Yates is critical of policies such as encouraging girls to take up chemistry because this is putting forward a model of girls as 'deficit boys'. The implication of this policy is that, by making girls' experiences in education as much like that of boys as possible, equality will be achieved. Radical feminists on the other hand tend to advocate more fundamental changes to the education system to ensure equality, such as girl-only schools or positive discrimination policies.

What is perhaps most significant about the hidden curriculum is the way that it ensures that science and technology have masculine images. This is of consequence because the masculine packaging of science and technology greatly deters female participation and interest.

Let us now consider the different ways the hidden curriculum affects educational attainment and subject identity. The aspects to be covered are as follows:

1. School books
2. Students
3. Teachers' expectations and attitudes
4. Patriarchal curriculum
5. Lack of positive role models

School books

A traditional feminist view of school books is that they reinforce a view of females as passive and dependent on men. Particular focus has been placed on fairy tales and the messages about gender roles they encode (or contain in their imagery and language). Some sociologists have emphasised the way that fairy tales reflect the dominant and sexist values of the society in which they have been developed (see Bottigheimer, 1987). Such views have not gone unchallenged, with sociologists such as Bettelheim (1991) arguing that children identify with the characters regardless of the gender involved. Thus neither the gender of the reader nor that of the character is important in the 'decoding' of the fairy tale. However feminist fairy tales, which seek to represent females in different ways, have not displaced the traditional stories, which continue to sell in their thousands.

In terms of textbooks, Kelly (1987) argues that there is a masculine bias in science texts, in which women are either passive or invisible. Thus the examples used in these texts tend to utilise male images and ignore famous female scientists. Similarly Culley (1986) argues that computing textbooks tend to show men in decision-making positions and females carrying out deskilled tasks such as inputting data.

In the 1980s many feminist sociologists reviewed the way that fairy tales and other teaching materials had been studied and rejected a simple 'reading' of them that cast the female reader as a passive recipient of the sexist messages in the text. Rather, research in the 1980s sought to determine readers' reactions to such literature and expose the many different functions that such texts could have for different readers (see for example Taylor, 1989). The conclusion of this reassessment is that a specific effect for fairy tales cannot be taken for granted, but rather that 'romantic' fiction has many functions for female readers, not just a gender socialisation response.

Exercise 5.5

For this exercise we would like you to carry out a content analysis of the science and technology textbooks used at your school or college. This will require you to identify, among other things, the number of times females and males are used in pictures and illustrations and the nature of their roles in them, the gender of famous scientists referred to, and the degree to which the examples used in the books are gender specific. You will find it easier to do this exercise with another sociology student so that you can share the workload. You should also consult your teacher/lecturer or a research methods book so that you are clear about how to do a content analysis.

Students

Many feminists writers, for example Kelly (1987), have focused on the ways in which boys take control of science and technology lessons, for example by monopolising equipment for experiments and creating a male-dominated space. This has affected female students' abilities to participate fully in science lessons. Culley (1986) noticed the same process in computing lessons, where male domination of the computers created an uncomfortable social space for those female students who wished to participate. Attempts to empower females in science and computing lessons have not always been received with good grace by those in the classroom.

Hostility to equal opportunity programmes has often come from the students themselves, both boys and girls. While girls may be ambivalent about such initiatives, they often see that some benefits might result from them. Boys on the other hand, have only things to lose and therefore tend to be much more against any attempt to redress the gender disadvantage. However the attitude of boys in everyday classroom life has also been a focus of feminist research. In particular, sexual harassment of female pupils and teachers has been investigated. This area is a minefield of gender relations, with opposing sides either claiming its widespread existence (Jones and Mahony, 1989) or denying its extent and importance (see Halson, 1989). It is also well documented how language use and male–female interaction in the classroom is used to deny classroom equality, and is often expressed in hostile ways, with boys using girls as a negative reference (see Spender, 1982). The strategies of denial used by boys include interruption, denigration and trivialisation of female talk.

These activities are important aspects of the identity construction of males. Conceptions of masculinity in school are forged in relationship to females (and for white children, in relation to black and Asian children). Weis (1992) shows that white working-class males in America define themselves in terms of not wanting to be like blacks or females. Their construction of their own sexuality and ideas about what is acceptable behaviour are therefore forged in opposition to other groups, at least in part. Schools are therefore not neutral in the process of identity construction, but they do operate in contradictory ways. While schools tend to encourage a male dominant ethos, they conversely allow space for females to explore their own identities, in an environment that encourages questioning as well as conformity. Schools can thus allow the possibility of an extension or alteration of gender identity as well as a reinforcement of gender construction within the family.

Teachers' expectations and attitudes

There has been a great deal of sociological interest in teachers' attitudes towards equal opportunities for women, with teachers often been seen as one of the main stumbling blocks to the achievement of equality for girls in schools. As Weiner (1985) points out, school-based attempts to combat inequality have often been met with hostility from teachers themselves. The conclusions of such studies tend to accept that there are a number of teacher ideologies and operating principles that relegate the issue of gender equality to a relatively low priority in schools. For example teachers are often in favour of individual choice of subjects as a matter of principle. They do not consider the outcomes of those choices in terms of gender equality, but accept a gender-differentiated curriculum as the natural result of individual choice. According to Riddell (1992), this ignores the social (for example peer group pressure) and ideological (for example ideas about 'proper' work for women) constraints within which individual students make their choices. Moreover there has also been a belief among teachers that sex-stereotyped attitudes are the product of family socialisation and that there is little, if anything, that teachers can do to alter or counteract such socialisation. Indeed many teachers remain opposed to the concept of even trying, seeing equal opportunities policies as ultimately political and therefore unacceptable in schools. This corresponds closely to New Right attacks on the 'political correctness' of such policies, which they see as undermining the natural order of things.

However resistance to gender equality also operates at the individual level. Hicks (1988) has found that many female teachers are in two minds about their dual role as worker and housewife, and as a consequence they often see male teachers as better educators than females, because males are able to concentrate on their careers more than women. As for male teachers, Spear (1985) has found that many science teachers are hostile to equal opportunity initiatives and express traditional attitudes supporting a subordinate role for women, both at work and at home.

Empirical research into gender relations in the classroom has shown a remarkable degree of consensus about the differential classroom experiences of boys and girls (see Wilkinson and Marrett, 1985). The conclusion seems to be that boys behave in a more assertive way, are given more teacher time and are generally more prominent in classroom interactions than girls. This is so irrespective of whether the researcher is looking at teacher–pupil interaction or pupil–pupil interaction. For example Sadker *et al.* (1991) have found that boys receive more criticism from teachers than girls, but also more praise. While other sociologists have reported that boys and girls receive equal amounts of praise (Stake and Katz, 1982), some, such as Whyte (1984) on the GIST project, have found that in some subjects girls receive more teacher attention than boys.

However Öhrn (1993) argues that these studies underestimate the resistance many girls exhibit in the classroom to their relative invisibility. This resistance, she argues, often takes the form of overaccommodation to the rules. By making very public displays of conformity to the rules of the classroom, girls achieve a situation where minor infringements are ignored or 'not seen' by the teacher. But when it comes to examining the allocation of jobs in the classroom to boys and girls, sociologists are more in agreement that these are distributed in sex-stereotyped ways. For example Platt and Whyld (1983) have found that boys are asked to move furniture by teachers, while girls are asked to make tea and wash up afterwards.

Exercise 5.6

Exercise 5.6 requires you to carry out some observational work in a science and/or technology classroom. We would like you to examine the extent to which teaching in this environment favours any particular gender and the degree to which the science and/or technology classroom is dominated by male students. It is important that you again consult your teacher/lecturer or a research methods book so that you are clear about how best to carry out the observation. It is essential that your research is ethically sound. Part of this will require you to obtain the permission of the relevant teachers in your school or college before carrying out the observation.

Patriarchal curriculum

While the ideas associated with progressive education would seem to favour gender equality, some sociologists have argued that the 'liberal' approach in schools of the 1960s and 1970s ironically had the opposite effect to that intended, and reinforced rather than undermined gender stereotyping. For example Clarricoates (1980) argues that the result of child-centred progressive styles of teaching, where children are allowed freedom of choice and speech, has been to promote gender differences, as young children reenact gender power struggles from outside school within the classroom. In this respect Walkerdine (1981) has found that not only do very young children use sexually abusive language in the classroom, but also that this is unchallenged by the teacher.

There has also been a debate amongst sociologists about the impact of the national curriculum on gender differentiation in schools. Riddell (1992) explores the issue of subject choice in terms of the way that allowing free choices tends to reinforce gender differentiation in schooling. Thus the impact of parental and teachers' expectations about the future roles of children tends to steer girls away from the high-status subjects of science and towards those subjects whose value in the labour market is lower. Therefore for some feminists, such as Byrne (1985), the introduction of a national curriculum, in which girls are constrained to study science to the same level as boys, at least until they are 16, is a step towards equality. Kelly (1988) also welcomes the introduction of compulsory science for girls as one of the ways of redressing the advantages boys have gained from an individualised curriculum.

In looking at girls and science, equal opportunity initiatives such as WISE (Women into Science and Engineering) have focused on the number of women participating in these curriculum areas and ignored the content of the curriculum. Bentley and Watts (1987) suggest that three different approaches to the science curriculum should be recognised. Firstly there is girl-friendly science, which seeks to make the science curriculum start with issues that grab the attention of girls and make the content of science lessons address girls' interests. Secondly there is feminine science, which seeks to replace 'masculine', aggressive, competitive behaviour in the science laboratory with a more supportive and collaborative approach that is more appealing to girls. Thirdly there is feminist science, which challenges the way that science is carried out and calls for a greater recognition of intuition in the scientific method, which would increase girls' chances of scientific achievement. On this last point Kelly (1988) argues that this assumes that, rather than just being 'invisible', women have not been part of scientific endeavour at all.

Feminist criticism of the national curriculum has focused on the simplistic solution to gender inequity it seems to offer. Rather these critics argue that the case for more girls doing science, which the national curriculum demands from schools, needs to be placed within the context of larger developments in society. For example Elliott and Powell (1987) suggest that the deskilling of jobs is occurring in all sectors of the economy, including occupations associated with science and technology. As it is women who tend to fill the most lowly and least-skilled jobs in all sectors, encouraging girls to take science and technology may result in yet another area of the labour market in which they could be exploited as women. Indeed Elliot and Powell argue that encouraging women to move away from the aesthetic and creative worlds in which they have often excelled and towards the world of science, reinforces both the 'deficit model' of women's achievements and the masculine view that these worlds are somehow less important than the world of science.

While the most blatant cases of gender segregation in the school curriculum have been tackled, often with some success and often involving across-the-board improvements in girls' achievements, there are still many areas in which underachievement has not been redressed. Deem (1992) points out that it is mainly white middle-class girls who have benefited from changes in schooling so far, but this leaves many working-class girls and boys, and black and Asian girls, at a disadvantage. Scraton (1987) argues that the most gender-segregated subject of all, PE, has not been seriously examined by those concerned with equality. The debate has yet to be resolved between those advocating girl-only teams as a way of increasing female self-confidence and physical skills and those who support mixed teams as a way of challenging male–female relationships founded on physical strength.

Lack of positive role models

Exercise 5.7

ITEM E Sociological evidence suggests that at all levels of the education system women are less likely to occupy the higher rungs of the professional ladder. This is supported by the two graphs in Item E. Inequalities of this sort are significant because it means that females have less positive role models than males to look up to. As a consequence female attitudes and aspirations may be less ambitious than those of males, and in turn this may depress educational performance.

1. According to Item E, what percentage of head teachers are female in secondary schools.

2. Which teaching scale does Item E indicate is the one that females are more likely to be represented in.

3. Use the chart on academic staff in universities (Item E) to support the claim that females are less likely to reach the highest occupational positions in the higher education sector.

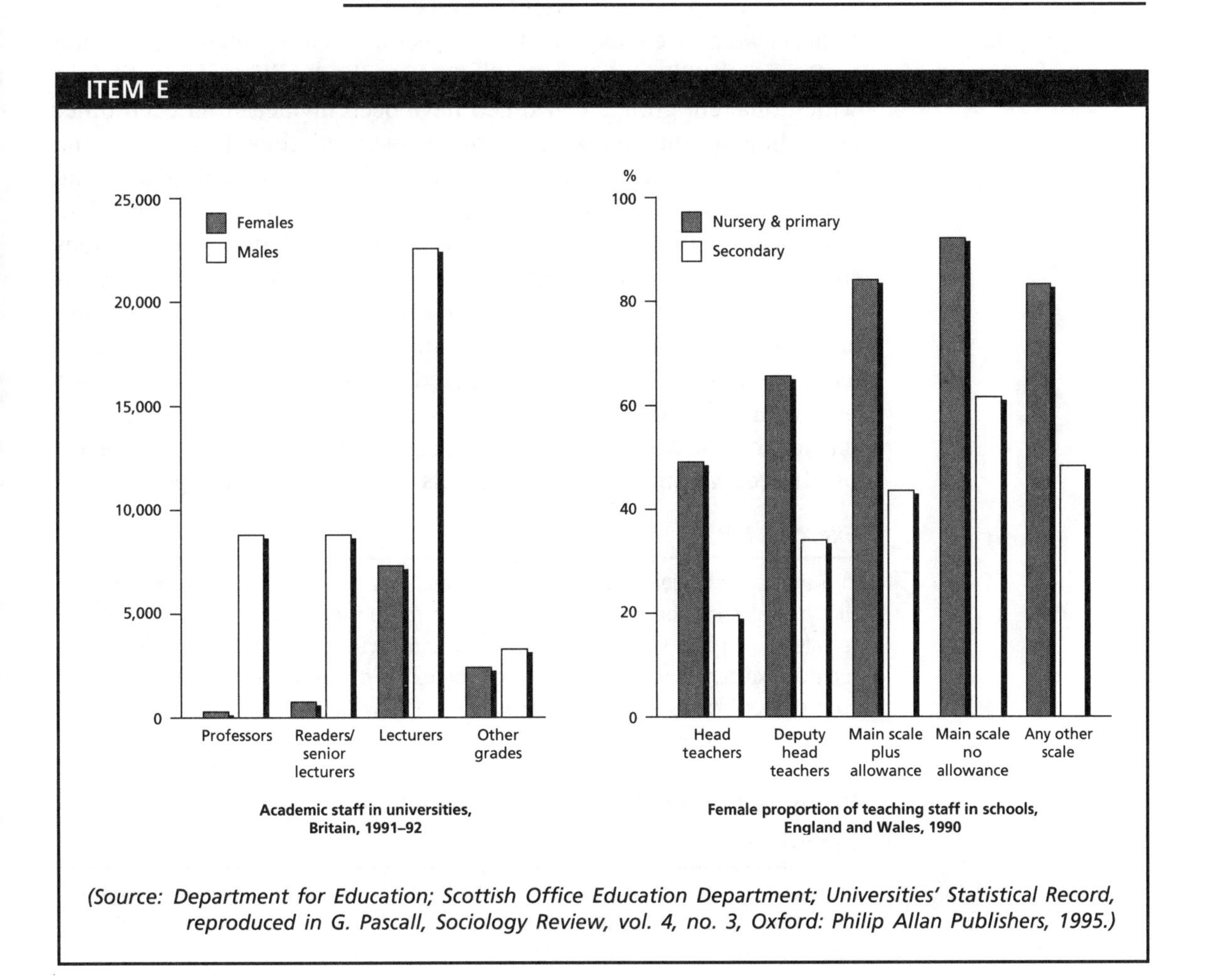

Academic staff in universities, Britain, 1991–92

Female proportion of teaching staff in schools, England and Wales, 1990

(Source: Department for Education; Scottish Office Education Department; Universities' Statistical Record, reproduced in G. Pascall, Sociology Review, vol. 4, no. 3, Oxford: Philip Allan Publishers, 1995.)

As shown in Item E, it continues to be the case that women are severely underrepresented in the senior management of schools and colleges, and particularly so in primary schools, where the overwhelming majority of teachers are female. It is also the case that black women teachers are few and far between (see East *et al.*, 1989). This lack of women in positions of power within schools is argued to be detrimental to female schoolchildren, who come to see male domination of organisations as the natural order of things.

One aspect of the feminist reaction to the lack of positive role models for girls in schools was to look to antisexist educational initiatives, not just with respect to the curriculum and female experiences in the classroom, but also to the hierarchies of schools themselves. A crucial part of the antisexist package was the development of local education authority policies that attempted to promote equal opportunities for women and men and for different ethnic groups. These included proper procedures for interviewing and quotas for the management structures of schools. While antisexist initiatives have been criticised by New Right writers in the same way as antiracist policies were (see Chapter 6), the effect of such initiatives, according to Parmar (1989), has been to introduce the 'politics of identity', in which different groups of women have been divided from each other according to the 'hierarchies of oppression' they face. Thus the experience of black women is seen as different from that of white women, and homosexual women are subject to heterosexist oppression, which their 'straight' sisters are not. Similarly Walker (1989) argues that feminism may have prised open opportunities for middle-class girls, but it has done little for working-class girls. This is partly because assertive behaviour on the part of middle-class girls is approved of as a preparation for male-dominated working life, while the same behaviour by working-class girls is seen as 'trouble-making'. The implications of Walker's work is that class is still an important influence on the educational outcomes of girls, and not just their gender.

Exercise 5.8

In a number of science and technology faculties across Britain more males than females can be found in positions of responsibility. This may account for females being less likely to identify with and excel in such subjects. Your task for this exercise is to investigate the hierarchies of responsibility that exist in your schools' or colleges' science and technology faculties and the number of males and females that occupy each position.

Inside school explanation – an evaluation

Exercise 5.9

Below are a number of partly completed statements relating to the strengths and weaknesses of the inside school explanations. Your task is to complete the statements by selecting appropriate finishing sentences from those offered to you.

Strengths

1. These offer a counterbalance to earlier structural explanations.
2. They reveal the ways in which educational . . . . . .
3. The explanations have had a major impact on social policy, ...
4. They have opened . . . . . .
5. They also emphasise some . . . . . .

Weaknesses

1. They offer an over-socialised view of people.
2. They emphasise some social forces . . . . . .
3. They are often based on small-scale qualitative research, ...
4. Despite the claim that they are interactionist in approach, ...
5. There is a tendency in some of these approaches to end up . . . . . .

Matching strengths sentences

(a) success may be socially constructed.

(b) wider social world and the way these influence what goes on in the classroom.

(c) It is reasonable to consider factors within schools as well as outside.

(d) up the 'black box' of schools.

(e) for example on the way teachers are trained, equal opportunity initiatives in school and so on.

Matching weaknesses sentences

(a) 'blaming the teacher' for all that is ill in education.

(b) many of these studies offer simplistic and deterministic views of the classroom.

(c) but do not consider other important structural causes that may influence the school.

(d) which is low in reliability.

(e) Not all females are put off science in the way suggested.

Females – the educational achievers

In the early 1990s came the first indications that the imbalance between male and female achievement was changing. The evidence for this emerged firstly from the results of the GCSE examination and then from Advanced level results. These showed that the gap between female and male attainment was widening in the favour of females in arts and humanities subjects, and in the sciences the traditional advantage of males over females was narrowing. Three interpretations have been put forward for these changes:

1. Boys falling behind
2. Social policy aiding females
3. Changing attitudes

1. Boys falling behind

This approach suggests that it is not just that females are achieving better than before, but that there is a problem with boys and education that has not yet been fully explored by sociologists. The reasons given for this falling behind are varied, but according to Barber (1994) they are connected to males developing much less positive attitudes to education than females. This negative attitude is manifested in a number of ways, including lower work rates among male students and signs of disaffection, such as increased truancy and behaviour problems among male students. It is also suggested that male peer groups tend to develop less favourable attitudes towards education and this creates peer group pressure. In 1994 *Panorama* (BBC 1, 24 October) drew on American research to show that parents spend less time reading and discussing books with their sons than with their daughters. It was suggested that this could be linked to a reluctance among males to read and their poorer standards of literacy. This view has been influential in persuading some educationalists that any agenda for equal opportunities initiatives needs to address male underachievement as much as that of females. However feminists would argue that this explanation tends to play down the real progress being made by female students and to divert attention back to boys.

2. Social policy aiding females

GIST

This view suggests that a number of policy changes have been effective in encouraging female students to achieve in those areas where they have traditionally done poorly. The first initiative was GIST (Girls into Science and Technology), which was designed to encourage female students to opt for science and technology. This included policies such as arranging visits from female scientists to act as positive role models, developing curriculum materials that reflected female interests, non-sexist careers advice and the raising of teachers' consciousness of gender role stereotyping. However critics of this explanation suggest that it is difficult to pin down a general increase in female standards to this particular initiative, as GIST was fairly narrow in scope and affected only a few selected schools. Nor were these policies necessarily always followed through because they were expensive to implement.

Single-sex classes

Another initiative that has been claimed to be successful is the introduction of single-sex classes. This builds on the arguments in favour of single-sex schools. Female-only classes provide positive role models, as, for example, the science teacher too has to be female. In science lessons, having no boys in the class removes the domination of laboratory equipment by boys, and also allows female students to answer questions and follow their interests. The positive outcomes of female-only classes are said to be an increase in female confidence and a more positive attitude towards science. Critics of this approach argue that female-only classes do not guarantee that teachers' attitudes are changed or that sexist materials are not used. As with GIST, this approach has only been adopted by a few schools as it is relatively expensive to implement.

GCSE

The introduction of GCSE, as opposed to O level and CSE, is argued to have favoured females. The principles behind GCSE are that students should be able to show what they 'know, understand and can do'. In order to achieve this, coursework has been introduced as a prominent feature of GCSE courses. This component is said to favour the consistent and conscientious work that is characteristic of female students. Similarly the increased emphasis on oral assessment is supposed to favour female skills. Also, the widespread introduction of joint science GCSEs has led to increased performance among females as their strong biology orientation has pulled up their general grade in science. However the effect of these innovations is likely to be limited. For example coursework marks are limited in GCSE, so there are clear constraints on the amount of benefit female students can be said to gain. Nor is it clear that female students possess the attributes given to them, such as working consistently harder than males. There is for example a clear link between class and females' attitude towards school work (see Chapter 4).

Link exercise 5.1

Using material from this chapter and Chapter 3 assess the extent to which the introduction of the national curriculum in 1988 may have helped to improve females' academic performances in mathematics, science and technology.

3. Changing attitudes

This view suggests that female attitudes towards education and work have changed significantly. This is partly because more young women have rallied to the feminist call for gender equality and partly because of an increase in the employment opportunities available to them. Thus it is claimed that women are now more independent minded and ambitious, and with their higher expectations they are less likely to want to marry and start a family at a young age – education, work and career have become a new focus of gender identity (Sharpe, 1994). Wilkinson (1994) also shows that employment has taken over from starting a family as the main aim of young women, and that this shift in social attitudes is having a strong bearing on educational aspirations and performance.

However it is important not to overestimate the degree of change in attitudes. Sharpe (1994) indicates that many of the females in her 1990s study, like those in the 1970s research, anticipated life as a 'dual worker', combining paid employment with family and domestic responsibilities. Sharpe also acknowledges that the desire to gain educational qualifications may partly reflect females' recognition of the fragility of the labour market in a period of recession.

We should also point out that the increased employment opportunities are less impressive than at first sight. It may be that the 'glass ceiling' has been lifted slightly, so that women are found in significant numbers in middle-management positions, but females are still underrepresented in the top echelons of management and overrepresented in the dead-end, part-time work they have traditionally dominated. This lack of gender equality is recognised by Sharpe (1994), and she sees it as potentially denting the expectations and aspirations of females in the 1990s.

Exercise 5.10

The explanations we have put forward for the recent advances in female academic attainment are some of the first to have been offered. There is no doubt that the explanations presented here will be supported and/or rejected to varying degrees, and new ones will come along. It is important that you keep yourself up to date with the issues as they appear in the press and books. Make sure you keep your eyes open and make notes on any relevant material that comes your way.

Exam question and student's answer

This exercise is aimed at helping you to order your arguments logically, so that the evaluation aspect of your response shows through. To do this exercise properly, you will need to refer to Items reproduced elsewhere in this book. Turn to pages 86–7 for the relevant Items. The question we want you to consider is taken from the AEB's A level June 1993 paper 1 (part d).

Question

Using information from the Items (pages 86–7), evaluate sociological contributions to an understanding of the hidden curriculum, as it affects female pupils. (*10 marks*)

What follows is a real examination answer by an eighteen-year-old student. However the paragraphs have been jumbled up and your task is to arrange them in a logical order. Once you have done that, highlight the sentences or passages that you think are evaluative.

Do not try to get a 'right' answer, but seek to find a logical progression. It could be useful to begin by deciding which is the introduction and which is the conclusion. By the way, this answer would have attracted full marks.

Student's answer

CANDIDATE A

Paragraph 1: Clarricoates however adds this important dimension, as she found that teachers maintained that males were intellectually more elite, despite girls getting consistently higher marks.

Paragraph 2: Stansworth takes a more holistic view of schools and sees that they are male dominated, and so until they change, female achievement will not improve. Her study is particularly useful as it shows how the whole structure and ethos of a school affects the hidden curriculum, which in turn affects females.

Paragraph 3: Shaw proposes single-sex education and Arnot single-sex classes in mixed schools. Their suggestions could be seen as a response to a worsening situation, though it must be remembered that their contributions (as far as explored here) are not empirically based and on their own provide insufficient evidence.

Paragraph 4: Since the early biological arguments of Tiger and Fox and Murdoch, sociologists have looked for social reasons why females tend to underachieve. The hidden curriculum is something that interactionists have been particularly interested in, as they see it as a central part of schooling that directly affects female pupils.

Paragraph 5: Gender inequalities and experiences shaped by a pupil's sex are issues that are not isolated to schools. Douglas and Sharp show that parental expectations affect how females regard their education. Marxists argue that teachers are unwitting agents of capitalists and that the ruling class shapes schools so that females will either be wholly domesticated or become part of the reserve pool of labour for the feminised industries. It is safe to say, though, that the hidden curriculum, practised in schools includes values that are not necessarily exclusive to schools, so Marxist and functionalist theory is relevant here.

Paragraph 6: As we see in Item C, Spender identifies boys receiving two-thirds of teacher time. This implies that teachers see it as 'natural' for boys to do well and therefore pay special attention to ensuring they achieve. Spender's research is important as it identifies one important way that attitudes of teachers affect females. However, it could be argued from this observation alone that in fact girls are more self-sufficient and require less attention, whereas boys are 'needy' and require more.

Paragraph 7: We can see then that studies that focus on the school contribute quite well to our understanding of the hidden curriculum, though they could be accused of teacher bashing and are not placed within the context of the whole society. Nevertheless they seek to uncover the experience of pupils themselves from their point of view.

Paragraph 8: However, studies that deal directly with the hidden curriculum could be successfully applied to schools and hence are valuable contributions.

Paragraph 9: Kelly shows how the formal curriculum, hand in hand with the hidden curriculum, can affect female pupils. She is concerned about the low percentage of girls in science and sees this as a result of attitudes that treat it as a boys' subject. Kelly is most in favour of GIST.

Paragraph 10: In studying the hidden curriculum (which is defined as the informal value systems, attitudes and norms within schools), interactionists and interpretivists have used qualitative methods, actually going into schools and doing empirical research to explain female underachievement. Thus their research is particularly valid as they give us insight into the day-to-day running of schools and, through the practise of verstehen and ethnographic techniques, tell us what the experiences of females actually are in relation to the hidden curriculum.

Paragraph 11: In Item E, we see that gender can be an important criterion for teachers' labelling of students which may lead to a self-fulfilling prophecy. Howard Becker also shows that the 'ideal pupil' notion that teachers have is that of a white middle-class male, not female. If it is true (as in Item D) that teachers' qualities are influential, then as females become aware that teachers have these sorts of attitudes they may feel discouraged.

Structured exam question

Here is part of a question from the June 1991 AEB's A level sociology paper (Part d). The rest of the question is in Chapter 4. You will find it useful to refer to Item H on page 95 when attempting this exercise.

Question

What explanations might sociologists offer for the different levels of achievement between the sexes in science subjects. Which explanation do you find the most convincing and why? (*10 marks*)

The question gives you a specific focus for any material you may have on gender and educational achievement. You must take care to apply any material you use to the issue of science subjects. Also, the question requires more than one explanation, so you should provide a range of explanations – as many as you can. The evaluation part of the question asks you to set out your reasons for thinking that one is more convincing than another. However you do not have to come out in favour of one explanation as you may find a combination more convincing. Nevertheless you do have to say why you have come to this conclusion if you are to gain the evaluation marks.

6 Explaining ethnic differences in educational achievement

By the end of this chapter you should:

- be able to describe ethnic differences in educational achievement;
- understand some of the problems associated with official statistics on educational achievement;
- be able to assess different explanations of ethnic differences in educational achievement;
- appreciate that the educational achievements of ethnic minority students are mediated by social class and gender;
- have reflected critically on government policies concerned with ethnic minority education;
- have practised a structured exam question yourself.

Introduction

Like interest in gender, interest in ethnic differences in educational performance began to take off in the 1980s, under the impact of renewed sociological interest in issues of identity. Prior to the 1960s, although there was some sociological interest in ethnic issues, it was largely confined to those who had a special interest in the area. However, during the 1960s and 1970s increasing numbers of sociologists began to be critical of the ethnocentric views of the white-dominated sociological establishment (see West, 1993), in which the educational experiences of all children were analysed from a mainly white viewpoint. African-American sociologist Joyce Ladner (1973) argued that this neglect of ethnic issues was not accidental but the product of the wider ideology of American society, which had consistently marginalised black experiences except when they were seen to 'deviate' from mainstream society.

By the early 1990s sociologists were increasingly interested in postmodernist issues, which emphasised the ethnic dimension as an important component of the 'new' politics of identity and difference, in which the old certainties of social class had disintegrated in the face of competing loyalties of gender, ethnicity, disability and sexual identity. For example Carol Nicholson (1989) follows up Foucault's emphasis on the 'Other' in education. Foucault was concerned with power and the way that there is always an 'Other' who is pushed aside and marginalised by dominant forces in society. Nicholson argues that we should be listening to the stories of marginalised groups in schools, such as 'people of colour', and their experiences of a curriculum and education that has disempowered such groups.

In covering this area we will follow a similar format to that of the previous two chapters. We will begin by establishing the extent of ethnic differences in educational achievement. We will then consider three different approaches that have attempted to explain the observed inequalities: (1) a genetic approach, which looks at differences in intellectual capacity between ethnic groups; (2) outside school explanations (non-genetic), which reflect sociocultural, socioeconomic and societal factors outside the school environment; and (3) inside school explanations, which address individual and institutional racism operating within schools and colleges. We will also give consideration to various social policy initiatives that have emerged in the pursuit of improving the educational experience and attainment of ethnic minority pupils.

Evidence of ethnic differences in educational achievement

A range of statistical evidence exists to support the idea that educational attainment varies by ethnic group. The statistics in Items A and B provide information on inequalities in performance from secondary schools through to higher education.

ITEM A

Educational achievement and ethnic origin in six LEAs, 1981–2 (per cent)

	West Indian	Asian	All others
CSE 1 or GCE O-level grades A-C:			
English language	15	21	29
Mathematics	8	21	21
In 5 subjects	6	17	19
GCE A-level pass in at least one subject	5	13	13
University degree	1	4	4
Other degree	1	5	5

(Source: DES (1985), Education for All (Swann Report) London: HMSO.)

ITEM B

Average performance of ethnic groups, O level and CSE results, 1985

Ethnic group	Average performance scores of children[2]	Number
African	16.9	426
African Asian	22.7	162
Arab	14.0	91
Bangladeshi	8.7	333
Caribbean	13.6	2981
ESWI[1]	15.2	10685
Greek	17.6	243
Indian	24.5	398
Pakistani	21.3	231
S.E. Asian	19.1	300
Turkish	11.9	268
Other	21.3	940
All	15.6	17058

1. English, Scottish, Welsh and Irish.
2. The performance score is obtained by allocating points for each grade, from 7 for an O level to 1 for a CSE 5.

(Source: Adapted from F. Kysel, 'Ethnic Background and Examination Results', Educational Research, vol. 30, no. 1, 1988.)

ITEMS A AND B

Exercise 6.1

i 1. Study Item A. Which ethnic group seems to perform least well in the education system?

i 2. Using Item A, calculate the percentage difference between the number of West Indians and the number of Asians obtaining at least one A level.

i a 3. Give one reason why the information contained in Item B is more satisfactory than the information contained in Item A.

i 4. Describe the patterns of differential educational achievement shown in Item B.

When sociologists are interpreting statistics such as the ones you have just been working with, it is important that they look at them critically and do not just take them for granted. An important distinction to keep in mind is the difference between 'equality of opportunity' and 'equality of outcome'. Most measures of educational underachievement are concerned with 'outcomes' such as university entrance, examination performance and so on, and it is possible that ethnic minorities may have equality of opportunity, but still (for a variety of reasons that we will explore) have inequality of outcome. One of the main criticisms of statistics about ethnic minority 'underachievement' is that they are undifferentiated. That is, ethnic minorities are all lumped together in a few categories, where important differences could be hidden. A good example of this 'collapsing' of categories is in Item A of Exercise 6.1.

Even when there is a more comprehensive categorisation, some difficulties still remain. For example, the amount of evidence about the educational achievement of Jewish and Cypriot children is relatively limited and it is therefore difficult to make comparisons (see Taylor, 1988). There is also the problem of how to break down large ethnic categories into 'real' divisions. For example, is it valid to look at the achievement of Afro-Caribbean children whose families originated from different islands in the West Indies? When does any effect associated with migration cease to be important – five years, ten years, one generation, two generations, never?

An important distinction between groups of ethnic minorities has been introduced by Gibson and Ogbu (1991). They argue that there is a real difference in the educational experiences between what they call 'voluntary' minorities and 'involuntary' minorities. For the voluntary minorities who have recently migrated into a country, education offers a way forward into a situation that is usually better than the one from which they have come. They are therefore likely to adapt to the cultural habits required for successful schooling, despite the discrimination they will also experience. Involuntary minorities are those with a caste-like position in society who already have a history of exploitation and discrimination in the 'host' country. This marginalisation of the involuntary group provokes a more hostile rejection of the education process, which combined with their structural position (such as lack of employment opportunities, even if they do gain qualifications) leads to educational underachievement.

However a large number of studies during the 1980s argued that the statistics showed that, while certain categories of South Asian children were performing at the same level as their peers, Afro-Caribbean children were underperforming significantly (see for example Verma and Pumfrey, 1988). Figueroa (1991) warns against taking these findings as the whole picture and is critical, for example, of the Swann Report (DES, 1985), arguing that its data underrepresented black middle-class children, who were likely to achieve higher qualifications than their black working-class counterparts. Other sociologists have suggested that social class, rather than ethnicity on its own, is an important factor in the levels of educational achievement attained by ethnic minority children (see Maughan and Dunn, 1988). Figueroa goes on to argue that much of the research on ethnic minority children is small-scale and has been carried out in inner-city areas where average performance is lower than the national average regardless of ethnicity. He therefore challenges the representativeness of such studies. Hence, it is prudent to be careful about these statistical findings. For example Jones (1993) argues that the educational gap between whites and ethnic minorities, in particular Afro-Caribbeans, is narrowing among the younger age groups.

Differential outcomes between ethnic groups occurs not just in education, but in government training schemes as well. The Commission for Racial Equality (CRE, 1994) has shown that, while there is little difference between the success rates of white and ethnic minority trainees in terms of getting a qualification on a government training scheme, there are large differences in the success of the two groups in gaining a job at the end of the schemes. In a government survey of the Youth Training Scheme, only one in four young blacks had found jobs after leaving the scheme compared with one in three of disabled trainees and one in two of whites (see Bevins and Nelson, 1995). Moreover there has been a trend for ethnic minority trainees to be placed on schemes that are less likely to lead to full-time employment. The Government therefore introduced 'Modern Apprenticeships' in September 1995, in which equal opportunity guidelines are built into the selection procedures.

Exercise 6.2

Try to update the statistics we have presented on ethnic inequalities in educational performance. You could start this search by referring to the most recent editions of *Sociology Update* and *Social Trends*. If your search is successful, repeat questions 1 and 4 in Exercise 6.1.

Explanations of ethnic differences in educational achievement

Having familiarised ourselves with the extent of ethnic differences in educational attainment we now draw on three types of explanation to account for them.

1. Genetic explanations
2. Outside school explanations
3. Inside school explanations

1. Genetic explanations

As in the case of social class and gender, certain psychologists have explained ethnic differences in educational performance in terms of biological differences in intelligence. In the United States, Jensen (1969) claims to have shown that blacks consistently attain lower level scores in IQ tests than whites. He concludes from this that blacks have lower intelligence levels than whites and that this is the reason why they underachieve in the education system. Despite receiving widespread criticism, genetic explanations of differential educational achievement have controversially resurfaced in the United States. In their book *The Bell Curve – Intelligence and Class Structure in American*

Life, Herrnstein and Murray (1994) conclude that blacks are genetically less intelligent than whites, who in turn are less intelligent than Asians. Herrnstein and Murray not only contend that this accounts for blacks' lower levels of achievement but also their higher levels of criminality. As with the earlier work of Jensen, Herrnstein and Murray have been subject to fierce criticism. You should remind yourself of some of the most important criticisms of genetic-based explanations of differential educational attainment by referring back to Chapter 4.

The controversy aroused by Herrnstein and Murray's book echoes a continuing debate in the social sciences between those who have argued for a large measure of inherited intelligence and those who claim that environmental factors are more important in determining levels of intelligence. What is different about Herrnstein and Murray's arguments is that they do not fix the proportion of intelligence that is inherited as high as previous biological determinists, but they do argue that attempts to improve the situation of blacks in the United States through social policy are likely to fail for the simple reason that they will never overcome the genetic differences that separate rich from poor and black from white. It is this which critics of Herrnstein and Murray have attacked, arguing that they are making a political not a scientific point in reassuring the rich (and white) that their wealth is deserved because they are more intelligent than the poor (and black). So while Herrnstein and Murray are very careful not to draw any direct racist conclusions from their data, as earlier writers have done, and indeed take great pains to argue that it is individuals and not groups that matter, their opponents have accused them of performing an ideological function – that is, justifying great inequality as somehow the natural order of things.

2. Outside school explanations

Four social (as opposed to genetic) accounts of ethnic differences in educational performance have developed from the outside school approach.

1. Family life
2. Language
3. Social class
4. Racism in society and minority youth responses: theories of resistance

Family life

This home background explanation looks inwards at the material conditions, family structures and attitudes of different ethnic groups. Early explanations for ethnic minority underachievement focused on such issues as the low incomes and inadequate housing of ethnic minority families, which like social class explanations were seen as detrimental to educational achievement. A further variation of this theme, and one which has a more contemporary impact, is the idea that the one-parent family structure that characterises a minority of Afro-Caribbean households creates difficulties for them when it comes to supporting their children's educational needs. New Right commentators have focused on the one-parent family structure as a main cause of social problems and have put forward policies that seek to discourage the formation of such families. They are seen as in some way pathological. Furthermore it has been suggested by some sociologists that Afro-Caribbean family networks place a lower value on educational success and are less encouraging of their children's education than other ethnic groups, for example those of Indian origin. On the other hand the larger family size of some South Asian families is also seen in a pathological way – that large families have a negative effect on the educational progress of the children in such situations (see Dawson, 1988). However there is some evidence from the United States that the aspirations of African-Americans are very similar to those of white Americans (see Banks, 1988), so that while there may be differences in attitudes towards education between ethnic groups, it is not the case that black families universally instil negative attitudes towards education in their children.

The effect of such explanations has been to develop a 'deficit' approach to ethnic minority children, in which their culture and life-style is seen as somehow deficient. In this way difference is defined as less. Theorists of the New Right such as Flew (1986) have argued that it is a mistake to assume that inequality of outcome is a consequence of inequality of opportunity. Rather Flew draws upon the work of the American economist Sowell (1981) to argue that group differences are not the result of discrimination, but that differences in educational outcome between ethnic groups is a result of differences in culture. However this approach has been criticised for providing a 'victim-blaming' explanation (see Massey, 1991), in which there is seen to be little wrong with the education system itself, but that the fault of underachievement lies in the background of the 'victims' of underachievement. Flew's ideas are therefore based on the notion that cultures can be judged as superior or inferior according to their outcomes, in terms of social behaviour, literature, art and so on. This has led other New Right theorists such as Scruton (1986) to argue that the solution for underachievement is for ethnic minorities to embrace British culture in the education system, whilst using voluntary associations to preserve their own.

ITEM C **Exercise 6.3**

This exercise is designed to get you to appreciate the way in which the cultural background of certain Asian families is conducive to educational success. As you complete the exercise bear in mind that some sociologists contend that the positive cultural factors you will identify are lacking in Afro-Caribbean families. Your task is to study Item C, which offers a short 'newspaper type' feature about African Asian families and school performance. When you have read the item, identify four factors that could explain the educational success of African Asian students.

ITEM C

Why African Asian students do well at school

While most of his English school friends are out enjoying themselves, Ravi Vara is at home doing homework. Furthermore he approves of the kind of discipline imposed by Asian parents on their children.

In the years since they were expelled from Uganda by Idi Amin, the Vara family have built up their own television repair and video business and now live over their shop in Luton. Ravi's father works as a maintenance engineer at Vauxhall Motors, doubling as a TV repair person in the evenings and at weekends, while his mother runs the shop and workshop with her brother-in-law.

Asian parents are very ambitious for their children and are committed to educational success. 'You have to do well at school if you are an Asian boy', says Ravi, 'otherwise you are thought of as a failure by the community.'

This attitude is reflected in recently published research that shows that Asian children out-class children from other backgrounds in education. The study, by the Inner London Education Authority (the ILEA, now abolished), demonstrates that the two groups that most often fail to develop their potential are local white children and children from Afro-Caribbean backgrounds.

The ILEA says that the results show how important it is to have parents who value education and put pressure on their children to succeed.

(Source: Adapted from R. Gomm, A Level Sociology, Cambridge, National Extension College, 1990.)

Language

This is again a home background explanation but focuses on the educational problems that arise through language. It has been argued that certain Asian students, such as Bangladeshis, experience communication problems because for many English is their second language. Thus they may find it hard to understand and be understood by their teachers. Moreover they may experience difficulties reading textbooks and examination papers. In the case of Afro-Caribbean students it is suggested they encounter educational problems because the 'creole' dialect or 'patois' they speak does not fit the standard English taught in schools. Typical difficulties they experience include misunderstanding the meaning of everyday expressions and being understood by teachers. However Taylor (1981) points out that there is a crucial difference between those who are perceived as having English as a second language (for example Gujerati speakers) and those who are perceived as speaking black British English. Whereas English-as-a-second language speakers may attract funding to help them with their 'problem', those who employ patois are likely to be seen as 'linguistically deficient' and are assumed to have no other language than low-status black British English. There is therefore some evidence to suggest that teachers label Afro-Caribbean students as less able because of the 'broken' English they speak. This has been shown to demoralise Afro-Caribbean students, with the result that they begin to resist schooling. For example Mac an Ghaill (1988) found that a group of antischool male Afro-Caribbeans deliberately used patois as an expression of rebellion against teachers and school.

The Swann Report (DES, 1985) argued that the crucial factor in language teaching was that all students should have a good command of English. The report did not like the idea of separate provision of English as a second language, arguing that it would be divisive. The committee also suggested that the maintenance of community languages should be the responsibility of the minority communities themselves. They argued against community languages as the medium of instruction, but in favour of the teaching of community languages as part of the languages curriculum of a school. Figueroa (1991) argues that this is to marginalise the community languages and undermine the idea that all cultures are of equal value, as well as placing some bilingual students at a disadvantage. Research evidence from a variety of countries suggests that mother-tongue teaching in the early years of schooling assists children in learning the dominant language of the country (see Beltz, 1985).

The concept of 'cultural capital' has been used by sociologists to explain the function of language in structuring the underachievement of ethnic minority pupils. The 'language on display' in a classroom is an important part of the judgements that teachers make about the educational performance of their students. As Thompson (1984) argues, teachers assume that they share the same language with their pupils, but teachers actually operate with a dominant form of language, to which not all students, and especially working-class and ethnic minority children, have equal access. This dominant form of language constitutes part of a cultural capital that operates to disadvantage certain groups within schools. However Bourdieu (see Chapter 4), who developed the notion of cultural capital, has been criticised by other sociologists such as Mehan (1992) for being overdeterministic about the outcomes of schooling. Bourdieu is accused of denying the importance of resistance to their disadvantage by those disadvantaged. The operation of cultural capital is seen by these critics not to be an automatic process, in which ethnic minority children are doomed to under-achievement by their lack of schooling-friendly language.

Social class

One line of argument concerning outside school explanations is that the differential educational performance of ethnic groups reflects the social class backgrounds of those groups as well as their ethnicity. It is claimed that minorities such as Indians and African Asians do well educationally because they have the economic advantages of being middle class, while groups such as Bangladeshis and Afro-Caribbeans underperform in the education system because they experience the material disadvantages of being working class. However the debate concerning the effects of social class versus ethnicity is not a simple one. Comparatively few studies have tried directly to compare the effects of these two variables (see Vasquez, 1992). However Jeffcoate (1984) argues that it is reasonable to suppose that, as the majority of Afro-Caribbean children come from manual backgrounds, they are subject to the same disadvantages as white working-class children. However Figueroa (1991) warns against any simplistic equation of class and ethnicity. He points out that the factors of class and ethnicity (as well as gender and culture) are interwoven in complex ways and that it is too simple to assume that Afro-Caribbeans and other ethnic minorities form an underclass whose experiences are all similar. Clearly there are middle-class Afro-Caribbeans who may experience racism without sharing the material disadvantages associated with the working class.

Link exercise 6.1

If we accept that social class cuts across ethnicity to account for ethnic differences in attainment, we must acknowledge the influence of material factors in determining educational performance. It is certainly true that Bangladeshis and Afro-Caribbeans are among the poorest ethnic groups in Britain. Drawing on the work you have done on social class in Chapter 4, identify and explain three ways in which the depressed educational achievements of Bangladeshi and Afro-Caribbean students can be explained by material deprivation.

Racism in society and minority youth responses: theories of resistance

This is a societal explanation that is advanced by O'Donnell (1992), among others. O'Donnell points out that prejudice and discrimination is faced by all ethnic minorities in Britain. However he argues that it is the response to this discrimination by different ethnic groups that helps us to understand differential educational performance. He observes that Afro-Caribbean males often react with anger and oppose white institutions, including education. In contrast Indians, although they are resentful of racism and show anger, do not always reject the powerful white institutions. It follows then that Afro-Caribbeans (particularly males) are more likely to underperform as they show strong resistance to schooling, whilst Indians perform well because they use the education system to their advantage – they keep their heads down.

More radical theorists have drawn on the work of Willis (1977) (see also Chapter 4) to develop resistance theory. Willis argues that subordinate groups in schools do not just passively accept their disadvantage but develop strategies for resisting the practices that lead to their underachievement. Giroux (1983) argues that these strategies may be adaptive as well as resisting, but that strategies of resistance, such as those adopted by ethnic minorities, have the potential to liberate the oppressed from their exploitation. It is by treating individuals as able to 'mediate' (negotiate or alter) their 'lived existence' that ethnic educational disadvantage may be overcome. However critics of Giroux, such as Senese (1991), argue that resistance, far from liberating ethnic minorities, may have the effect of making their situation worse. Rather than adapting to the linguistic and other demands of schooling, which may lead to success, Senese argues that resistance can lead to a further marginalisation of resisting groups, that they develop an anti-intellectual attitude and have little interest in the real world around them.

Outside school explanations – an evaluation

Strengths:

1. They have exposed the weaknesses of earlier genetic-based explanations because they highlight the need to look at the social rather than the biological causes of ethnic differences in educational attainment.
2. The outside school explanations have served to bring about

social policy initiatives to improve the educational experiences of ethnic minority children, for example provisions for teaching English as a second language.

3. A range of empirical evidence exists to support to a greater or lesser extent each of the outside school explanations. For example the Swann Report (DES, 1985) gives great weight to socioeconomic factors, as stressed by the social class explanation.

Weaknesses:

Exercise 6.4

For this exercise we want you to provide one weakness of each of the explanations within the outside school approach. Start by offering your own criticisms. You should then confirm or supplement your criticisms by referring to a suitable text.

3. Inside school explanations

As we have seen in previous chapters, inside school explanations focus on the concept of the hidden curriculum. Many sociologists believe that the hidden curriculum operating in schools is a racist one and therefore discriminates against ethnic minority students. Some debate exists about whether this racism is intentional or unintentional. Either way the evidence suggests that the racist hidden curriculum serves to create a resistance to schooling on the part of certain ethnic groups and leads to their eventual underachievement.

Exercise 6.5

Exercise 6.5 again requires you to do some independent work. It should prove to be relatively easy as you will come across ideas that have been well covered in earlier chapters. Start the task by reading school-based explanations of ethnic differences in educational attainment. You should then use the information you have gleaned to fill in the chart on page 134, which has been partially completed for you. When completing the chart you need to explain how each aspect of the hidden curriculum depresses educational performance and cite empirical studies to support the points you make. You may find some useful information in this chapter also.

A summary chart illustrating the inside school approach to ethnic differences in educational attainment

Aspect of the hidden curriculum	The process by which educational 'failure' occurs	Empirical studies
Racist books		
Racist students	Ethnic minority students experience racial harassment in schools, for example verbal and physical abuse. his may lower self-esteem and confidence. Some students play truant for fear of abuse and attack.	
Teachers' expectations and attitudes		Mac an Ghaill (1988) Gillborn (1990) Mirza (1992)
Streaming		
An ethnocentric curriculum	School curricula are ethnocentric. They fail to tap into the cultural routes and experiences of ethnic minorities. For example literature courses evolve around English authors such as Shakespeare, and history courses focus on European history. The ethnocentric nature of the curriculum ensures that black students feel *alienated*l from schools. For some ethnic groups a 'British' education may at best be irrelevant and at worst offensive. Motivation and commitment to schooling become difficult for some ethnic minority students.	
Lack of positive role models		

A selection of recent studies on inside school explanations

In the tradition identified by Cole (1992), it was history and geography textbooks that were mainly responsible for putting forward imperialist and racist views of non-white peoples. Wright (1986) suggests that two popular geography textbooks of the 1980s continued to put forward unacceptable views of blacks. Descriptions of black people in these textbooks are often negative, involving words such as coarse and drooping, while descriptions of whites are couched in positive language, such as fine and fair.

While there is evidence that some overt racial prejudice still exists among teachers (see Gillborn, 1990), Klein (1993) argues that many teachers hide behind a 'colour-blind' approach, in which they claim not to see the colour of the child, but which has the effect of denying an important part of the child's ethnic identity.

Jeffcoate (1984) argues that the evidence for teacher stereotyping of ethnic minorities is 'flimsy, to put it mildly'. He argues that there are so many problems with the research into teacher expectations, both ethical and practical, as to negate any findings in these studies. He also argues, that, while there is evidence of racist sentiments in staffroom discussion, there is also evidence (Hammersly, 1981) that these attitudes do not spill over into teacher behaviour in the classroom.

Attempts to reduce the ethnocentric nature of the formal curriculum in schools have been characterised by Hulmes (1989) as focusing on the life-styles of ethnic minorities rather than their life-chances. The result of this is a curriculum that only recognises ethnic minority experiences at the level of music, dancing, religious ceremony and cuisine.

Eggleston (1986) found that, in a study of 600 pupils in comprehensive schools, children from ethnic minority backgrounds were more likely to be placed on courses below those which might suit their abilities and ambitions.

In the United States, Kozol (1991) has shown that a large number of financial and political constraints are in operation, whose effect is to deny poor minority children an appropriate share of basic educational resources. He examines the legal and financial systems that operate in American cities to produce what he calls 'savage inequalities', and shows how attempts to redress these founder on a system that perpetuates racial and social exploitation.

Assessment of ethnic minority children, specifically Afro-Caribbean children, was found by Wright (1986) to be influenced more by the teacher's evaluation of their behaviour in the classroom than their actual cognitive ability. Therefore, rather than viewing the educational problem of black children in terms of underachievement, Wright argues that it should be seen in terms of disadvantage.

Link exercise 6.2

Using material from Chapter 3 and other sources, explain how the introduction of the national curriculum in 1988 may have served to hinder the opportunity of ethnic minorities to achieve well at school. (Hint: think about the ways in which the curriculum has been made more Eurocentric.)

Inside school explanations – an evaluation

Exercise 6.6

We are setting you two tasks for this exercise.

1. Read the evaluation statements which follow. Identify which are the strengths and which are the weaknesses. Record your answers in a two-column table that clearly separates the strengths from the weaknesses. Leave room in each column to complete task two.

2. On the basis of previous evaluations of inside school approaches (see Chapters 4 and 5), identify two other strengths and weaknesses that could be applied to inside school explanations that purport to explain ethnic differences in educational performance. Record your answers in the table you started off for task one.

Evaluation statements

(a) The approach attempts to see things from the social actors' point of view and therefore allows insight.

(b) Some research evidence (Foster, 1990) demonstrates that not all teachers are racist.

(c) The explanations have helped us to understand the nature of social inequality and injustice.

(d) Some sociologists argue that racism in schools cannot be a complete explanation because Indian and African Asian students experience such racism yet perform well educationally.

(e) It could be argued that the explanations overstate the case. A number of schools have adopted multicultural and/or antiracist approaches to education that reduce the level of racism that inside school approaches judge to exist in schools.

(f) Most of the findings are based on qualitative research and therefore are high in validity.

The interaction of gender and ethnicity

In this chapter we have already seen how social class cuts across ethnicity to determine educational performance. However we also need to consider the way in which gender interacts with ethnicity.

ITEM D

Exercise 6.7

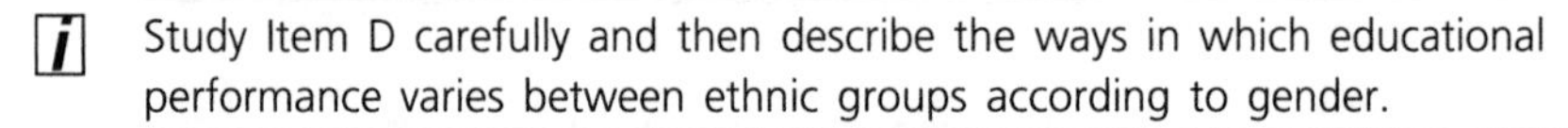
Study Item D carefully and then describe the ways in which educational performance varies between ethnic groups according to gender.

ITEM D

Highest qualification level of the population:[1] by ethnic origin and sex, Britain, 1988–90[2] (percentages)

	Ethnic origin					
	White	West Indian/ Guyanese	Indian	Pakistani/ Bangladeshi	Other[3]	All[4]
Highest qualification held[5]						
Males						
Higher	15		19	8	22	15
Other	57	58	51	40	56	57
None	29	36	30	52	21	29
Females						
Higher	13	16	13		20	13
Other	51	52	46	28	52	51
None	36	32	41	68	28	36
All persons						
Higher	14	11	16	6	21	14
Other	54	55	49	34	54	54
None	32	34	36	60	25	32

1. Aged 16 to retirement age (64 for males and 59 for females).
2. Combined data using the 1988, 1989 and 1990 (preliminary) Labour Force Surveys.
3. Includes African, Arab, Chinese, other stated and mixed origin.
4. Includes those who did not know or did not state their ethnic origin.
5. Excludes those who did not know or did not state their qualifications.

(Source: Labour Force Survey (1992), reproduced in Social Trends, vol. 22, London: HMSO.)

One of the gender differences you should have observed from the statistics in Item D is that West Indian and Guyanese women are more successful educationally than their male counterparts. Such differences have been well explained by Fuller (1980), Mac an Ghaill (1988) and Mirza (1992). All of these sociologists reach similar conclusions, which interestingly challenge the determinism inherent in the inside school approaches. They point out that Afro-Caribbean females feel and resent negative labelling and racism in schools, and like Afro-Caribbean males they develop a resistance to schooling as a consequence. However, unlike Afro-Caribbean males they do not form strong antischool subcultures, which they realise lead to educational 'failure'. Instead they adopt an approach of instrumental compliance that allows them to obtain the qualifications they desire so that they can 'prove their teachers wrong' and obtain the middle-class occupations they aspire too. To sum up, the differential educational performance between Afro-Caribbean males and females can be understood in terms of the degree of school resistance exerted. Afro-Caribbean males resist more strongly than females and are therefore less able to exploit the educational system for their own purposes.

However Mirza (1992) argues that this leaves the problem of why black girls' educational achievements do not lead to better jobs. She rejects the stereotypical views held about girls being mainly concerned about families and children. Instead, to explain their underachievement she looked at the socioeconomic location of the school, the stratified nature of local labour markets and the poor quality of careers advice. In each case, issues of gender, class and race were important in channelling black girls into career routes that failed to take their educational achievements into account.

Sociologists have therefore pointed out that ethnicity is not a separate experience from gender or class, but is nested together with those characteristics. Fuller (1980) argues that the experiences of ethnic minority girls in schools cannot be assumed to be the same as black boys or white girls, but that they will develop their own identity in response to experiences specific to them. She concludes that black girls often suffer from double or even triple disadvantage if they also come from working-class backgrounds. The way that black males construct their identity in schools differs from black girls precisely because they are male and because they have different experiences from black girls. For example Cooper *et al.* (1991) detailed evidence to show that black boys are overrepresented in special educational needs provision compared with white boys, black girls and Asian boys.

Ethnicity and educational policy

The emergence of significant ethnic minority communities in Britain after the Second World War has had a profound impact on many schools, especially those in cities, and has prompted a series of government policies on ethnic minority education. The main thrust of early educational policies vis-à-vis ethnic minorities was 'assimilation', which stressed the swiftest possible integration of ethnic minorities into the dominant culture. Lynch (1986) argues that policies such as providing special centres for those migrants whose first language was not English, were based on the idea of the superiority of the dominant culture. It would be inaccurate to regard all education in the 1950s and 1960s as an expression of this point of view, as many local authorities were concerned with equality rather than assimilation.

Ethnic minority responses to assimilationist policies were negative, and Carter (1986) documents the emergence of Saturday schools for Afro-Caribbean children as a way of motivating the children to succeed. The provision of separate schools for different ethnic minorities continues to be a controversial issue, with many Islamic groups seeking to establish state support for Islamic schools in the same way that Christian schools are supported. However opposition to such schools comes from a wide spectrum of political positions, from New Right theorists to Women Against Fundamentalism (see Klein, 1993).

The two main social policy initiatives that have emerged in Britain since the mid 1970s to meet the educational needs and problems of ethnic minority students are multiculturalism and antiracist education. As with the case of separate schooling, these are highly controversial political issues, with a great deal of disagreement amongst sociologists and politicians.

Multicultural education

Multicultural education is a policy supported by liberal sociologists and educationalists. The policy aims to encourage schools to recognise the cultural diversity of Britain's ethnic population. There is an attempt above all to move away from ethnocentric curricula. Schools that have adopted this initiative have for example integrated black authors into literature lessons, taught global history and celebrated events such as Diwali. This is seen to be a positive form of social policy that creates tolerance and understanding in society and raises the educational performance of ethnic minorities by allowing them to draw on their own cultural backgrounds. Proponents such as Banks (1988) argue that in the United States the adoption of a multicultural approach will reduce ethnic conflict in schools and aid the educational achievement of ethnic minority children.

Multicultural education has come under attack from both radical and New Right positions. New Right critics have lumped together multiculturalism, political correctness, feminism and gay rights issues as an attempt by neo-Marxists to dominate the education system and produce what they see as brainwashed students who are unable to challenge suspect ideas for fear of being damned as racist (see Siegal, 1991, as an example of the American New Right argument). In Britain, Flew (1986) also argues that multiculturalism has a revolutionary intent – maintaining ethnic minorities as members of a discontented force who are ready to act as the shock troops of some future socialist revolution. He is critical of explanations of ethnic underachievement that rely on the concept of racism, arguing that it is a vague and unhelpful concept. Beneath Flew's and other New Right theorists' attacks on multiculturalism is a concern for the preservation of a national identity, as formed by an imperialist past with no recognition of the cultural diversity existing in contemporary Britain. For example Pearce (1986) sees multicultural education as undermining the native British way of life.

Radical critics argue that multiculturalism does not go far enough and does not address directly the central concept of racism. Parekh (1986) for example sees multiculturalism as an attempt to keep ethnic minorities quiet, whilst ignoring the social and political conditions that lead to their disadvantage. Radical opponents of multiculturalism argue that it has achieved little in terms of equality of opportunity for ethnic minorities. They call for a much more proactive approach to the issue of ethnic minorities in schools, an approach that has been called antiracist education.

Antiracist education

Antiracist education is a policy that is more broadly supported by radical sociologists and educationalists. It is a more challenging form of social policy than multicultural education. It aims to examine and oppose racism in schools and society. Schools following antiracist policies have attempted to remove racism from their teaching, school organisation, curricula, reading schemes and assessment methods. This has involved them offering INSET time for raising awareness about racism and appointing a larger number of ethnic minorities to senior teaching posts. It is believed that this type of educational policy combats racism and therefore provides a more favourable society for ethnic minorities to achieve in.

As might be expected, this too has come under attack from theorists of the New Right, along similar lines to their critique of multiculturalism. In the United States Ravitch (1990) has attacked antiracist education as a threat to the common conception of nationhood – a concern that is important in such an ethnically diverse nation as the United States. In Britain, the concerns of the New Right have led O'Keefe (1986b) to argue that those involved in race relations promote disharmony, and that antiracist teachers are effectively 'race spies' in the classroom.

Exercise 6.8

Using the material above and other sources, evaluate the effectiveness of multicultural and antiracist education policies. To complete the task you will need to look into some of the criticisms that have been made of the two initiatives. We recommend that you consult O'Donnell (1991 and 1992) to help you to do this. As part of your evaluation, explain which of the two policies you feel are most likely to improve the educational chances of ethnic minorities – make sure you justify your decision.

More recent developments in the field of policy on ethnicity have drawn heavily from postmodern ideas, and in particular from the idea of 'critical pedagogy'. Critical pedagogy is critical of the Marxist assumption that there is a correspondence between the economy and schooling and the New Right's insistence on cultural uniformity as an objective of education. Instead they argue that education for children should be about their possibilities and teaching them to recognise that we live in a fragmented and uncertain world. For example McLaren (1991) argues that globalisation and increasing ethnic plurality in British society necessitates a 'decentring' (moving away from) of what is described as racist and Eurocentric discourses (or ways of thinking) in education. Instead teachers should be developing a 'postcolonial pedagogy'. This means that those who are subject to racist practices and ideology should be developing, as active agents, both challenges to racist ideas and patterns of behaviour in the classroom. Postcolonial pedagogy is therefore about the need for education to empower disadvantaged groups so that they begin to speak with their own voice. However Ellsworth (1989) describes this process as having a very high level of abstraction, with the result that postcolonial pedagogy has little to offer in the way of practical classroom management and specific techniques of empowerment.

The interrelationship between social class, gender and ethnicity

We have seen in this chapter the importance of looking at class, gender and ethnicity as aspects of an individual's being. Postmodern sociologists argue that, increasingly, it is the issue of identity that is at the centre of an analysis of the individual in society, and that characteristics such as class, gender and ethnicity are important components of individuals' construction of their identity. While individuals and groups mark themselves off from each other through the use of 'signifiers' (symbols, consumer goods, styles), it is important to note that there are structural effects on identity, such as the experiences individuals have in schools because of their significant social characteristics. The implication of the increasing fragmentation of culture in postmodern societies is that it is increasingly difficult to write about the experiences of social groups as common to all members. The interplay of ethnic, gender and class factors in the performances of different individuals is likely to lead to more complex patterns of achievement and underachievement in the education system.

ITEMS E AND F

Structured exam question

Items E and F and the question that follows are taken from the AEB summer 1994 examination, paper 1.

ITEM E

There are two obvious ways in which teachers' judgements of pupils may have an impact on the social distribution of achievement. First, as several studies have shown, teachers' expectations can colour their assessment of pupils' performance; in Goodacre's study, infant school teachers rated children whom they thought came from a middle-class background as better able to read than those whom they believed to be from working-class homes; standardised tests did not, however, reveal such a marked difference in the reading level of these two groups of children. In cases such as this, teachers' assessments of pupils reflect their views of what middle-class and other pupils should be capable of, rather than their actual performance. Second, teachers may, because of low expectations, make fewer attempts to stimulate pupils, or to overcome areas of weakness.

(Source: Bilton et al., Introductory Sociology, 1987.)

ITEM F

All the factors which produce poor school progress from working-class children also affect children from West Indian and many Asian homes. This is hardly surprising as the majority of these children are from working-class homes. But there are some problems which are faced only by children from ethnic minority backgrounds. For some of these children, the main language of the home may not be English. So their studies are carried out, to some extent, in a 'foreign' language. Although West Indian children speak English at home, it may be in a dialect that differs from standard English.

It is rare for teachers to be openly racist, but cultural differences and poor performance in some IQ tests by black children have created the belief in some teachers' minds that black children are more likely to be slow learners. This can influence the way that teachers label black pupils and so retard their progress.

(Source: Adapted from Stephen Moore, Sociology Alive, 1987.)

Question

Evaluate sociological explanations of the 'poor school progress' made by some children from West Indian and Asian homes (Item F). *(8 marks)*

The question here directs your attention directly to Item F, where specific information about the educational achievement of Black and Asian students is given. Item F therefore provides you with some of the explanations put forward which you should expand upon and evaluate with regard to their importance. You should also note that, although the author of Item E is writing about differential class achievement, there are also hints here of explanations for ethnic minority performance. The important thing is to apply the information given on teachers' expectations to ethnic minority pupils, and it would be even better if you could provide some supporting evidence, in the form of studies which specifically look at teachers' expectations and ethnic minority achievement. The lesson to be learned here is that the items often contain useful bits of information for a question, even when you are not specifically directed to go to them. It is therefore worthwhile taking a little time to make sure you have read through all the items carefully, before you begin to answer questions.

Let us look at how an answer to this question might be structured, drawing upon an answer given by a student in a real examination.

Section 1: The introduction

Consider the following introduction:

> *Overall, it is widely regarded that black and Asian children do less well in the school system compared with their white counterparts. The position of ethnic minority children is more complicated than this, as the Swann report shows that the majority of Asian children do as well as their white counterparts, but that groups such as Pakistanis and Bangladeshis do less well. West Indians are the group that tend to do the least well in the education system. Only 5 per cent have one or more A level and only 1 per cent go on to university. The explanations of these differences have concentrated on either factors from outside school or factors inside the school.*

This is a good opening paragraph because the candidate has set out some very important points that should inform the rest of the answer. The candidate has shown that she or he is aware that ethnic minorities cannot be lumped together as a whole, but that nevertheless there are important differences in educational attainment between some ethnic minorities and their white counterparts that need to be explained. They also show the marker how the answer is to proceed, by laying out the alternative types of explanation put forward.

Section 2: Genetic explanations

For the second section it would be appropriate to show why sociological approaches have rejected the biological determinist approaches of the geneticists and psychologists and looked to the experiences of ethnic minority children both within and outside the school system. The section need not be very long, but it is important to set the context. This section should have an evaluative aspect by looking briefly at the evidence for and against genetic explanations.

Section 3: Inside school explanations

The answer should then turn to explanations from experiences inside the school. It is important that you provide a range of such explanations and do not just concentrate on one. You can find a couple of explanations in the items themselves, but you must apply them specifically to the issue of ethnicity and achievement. Where possible, you should support the points you are making by refering to appropriate studies, and if there are any specific criticisms of these, you should include them to give this section an evaluative edge.

Section 4: Evaluation of inside school explanations

In this section you should consider the strengths and weaknesses of the explanations put forward, showing how they may be important in explaining certain aspects of ethnic underachievement, and also how they may be limited in fully explaining it. You may wish to consider the theoretical underpinnings of these explanations and how important these are in assessing the approach.

Section 5: Outside school explanations

Here you should consider a range of explanations that look beyond the school gates. Follow the principles contained in Section 3. However you should begin this section with a sentence that links inside and outside explanations in an evaluative way. For example: 'Because of these weaknesses in the inside school explanations, some sociologists have offered an alternative view that emphasises the experiences of ethnic minorities outside school.'

Section 6: Evaluation of outside school explanations

Continue to demonstrate your evaluation skill by considering the advantages and disadvantages of these approaches, using the guidelines in Section 4.

Section 7: Class, gender and ethnicity

In this section you should demonstrate your understanding of the complexity of the issue under discussion by looking at the complex interaction between class, gender and ethnicity. Refer back to your introductory paragraph to see where the theme should be developed from.

Section 8: Conclusion

There are many ways in which you can come to an evaluative conclusion. You do not always have to sit on the fence, but can support one or a couple of explanations, as long as you have argued for them during the course of your answer and have considered some alternatives, which you are rejecting. A straightforward 'sitting on the fence' conclusion is illustrated by the following paragraph:

> *If you join together all these explanations of 'poor school progress' it will give you a more accurate account of why some ethnic minorities do not do so well, because, as we have seen, there are many factors that help to explain 'poor school progress'.*

Now write your own response to the question, using the above structure, but come to your own conclusion as this will strengthen the evaluation of the different explanations you include. You should also try to include an introduction that sets out the route your answer will take.

7 Functionalist explanations of the role of education and training

By the end of this chapter you should:

- appreciate the ways in which the socialisation role of schools and training programmes can be seen in a positive light;
- be familiar with functionalist views on the allocation role of education and training;
- understand the views of those who maintain that education performs a positive vocational function for society;
- be able to assess functionalist approaches to the role of education and training.

Introduction

When considering the role of education and training we are concerned with examining the functions that schools and training courses perform for society. In sociology, this has traditionally been the main concern of the functionalist perspective. Functionalists see society as a system of interrelated parts, in which each part has functions to perform for the whole of society. They have therefore always been concerned with the relationship between education and the economy.

However, the relationship between the economy and the education system is not a straightforward one, in that schooling has historically not only been seen as a preparation for the world of work, but also as schooling into the wider culture of society. Industries have until recently offered their own specific training programmes, through apprenticeships, on-the-job training and so on. Though industrial training programmes have often been linked to education courses in colleges of further education, during the 1980s and 1990s the education system took on a more explicit vocational role, as the government sought to improve the preparation of young people for the world of work.

When the British economy was dominated by Fordist characteristics such as mass production and a low-skill, low-wage workforce, the amount of job training needed was limited. However Finegold and Soskice (1988) claim that the characteristics of a post-Fordist economy demand, in part, a highly skilled workforce, and that therefore the training system in Britain should change to meet the new circumstances.

While other sociologists accept that there will be a demand for highly skilled labour in the post-Fordist economy, they also warn that development will not be the same in every sector of the economy and that there are likely to be sectors in which underemployment and low skills are dominant (Brown and Lauder, 1992). Functionalists, however, offer an optimistic analysis of the role of education and training. They maintain that education and training performs a positive function for all in industrial and post industrial societies. Schools and training schemes are said to achieve this through three related economic roles.

1. Socialisation – their role in instilling norms and values.
2. Allocation – their role in slotting people into 'appropriate' occupational positions.
3. Vocational training – their role in equipping young people with practical and technical skills.

Each of these roles will now be examined in turn.

The socialisation role

Functionalist sociologists claim that schools and, more recently, training programmes act as a form of secondary socialisation that follows primary socialisation within the family. This socialisation is said to be an essential means by which modern societies perpetuate themselves. The most emphatic statements of the functionalist view on educational socialisation come from Durkheim (1956) and Parsons (1959). Both these theorists claim that educational systems perform an integrative and regulative function by transmitting socially 'agreed' norms and values. The transmission of such norms and values is said to occur through the formal curriculum (for example timetabled subjects such as English and history) and the hidden curriculum (for example the punishment and reward systems operating within schools). It is through the internalisation of society's norms and values, it is believed, that individuals learn to become good 'social citizens' and societies achieve social cohesion and stability. Acceptance of particular ways of behaving is important for the operation of the economy, because many types of work can be boring. The instillation of a 'work ethic' and the development of good work habits, such as punctuality and honesty, are important for the successful operation of an industrial economy. Moreover an industrial economy needs workers who, at the bare minimum, have the basic skills of numeracy and literacy.

However the socialisation role of schooling can be seen as more than just the instilling of basic values, skills and attitudes. Drawing on the work of Foucault, Hoskin (1990) argues that modern (as opposed to traditional) forms of government are only made possible through education. In traditional societies, compliance with government is obtained by coercion or force, while in modern societies, social discipline is obtained through the education process, which seeks to regulate the population by offering individuals 'emancipation' through education. That is, education holds out the promise of a better, freer life to those who pursue it.

Exercise 7.1

i

With the help of a Sociology textbook identify three norms and three values that functionalists believe characterise Western societies. (Hint: you may need to look under the 'theory' section of the textbook you choose.)

Exercise 7.2

i

In 1994 John Major's Conservative government launched a 'back to basics' campaign. This policy was partly an attempt to stem the alleged breakdown in social mores. Your task for this exercise is to conduct a newspaper search, possibly using CD ROMs, to find out some of the key norms and values that John Major wanted institutions such as the family and schools to instil into young people. The following example should help you to get started:

- Individuals should grow up knowing 'right from wrong'.

Link exercise 7.1

a

It can be argued that one of the reasons why Conservative governments in the 1980s and 1990s have supported the new vocationalism is because initiatives such as TVEI, CPVE, YT, ET and (G)NVQs (see Chapter 3) aim to make students and trainees 'attitudinally better employees'. This is said to be achieved by instilling key work values such as punctuality. Identify four other work values that may be socialised into students and trainees when following a new vocational course.

The allocation role

Functionalists such as Davis and Moore (1945) and Parsons (1959) maintain that education performs an important allocation or selection role by matching students on the basis of their talents or abilities to the jobs to which they are best suited. It is argued that the function of allocating people into appropriate occupational roles is essentially achieved through the certification process operating within education and training systems. Thus schools, universities and training schemes examine students at different levels and offer graded qualifications that sift and sort people into different but fitting job positions. In this way, it is believed, the most able and talented in society end up occupying the most functionally important jobs, having achieved high-status qualifications with good grades; whilst those with low status qualifications with poor grades find themselves in the least important jobs.

The role allocation function of schools is judged to be all the more important in advanced industrial societies as the occupational structure has grown and become more complex and diverse. For example James Avis (1993) argues that educational methods such as group work, records of achievement, profiling and so on are developed by what he calls 'curriculum modernisers' to meet the needs of a post-Fordist economy. Under Fordist economic conditions, manual workers were needed who would follow instructions and carry out fairly simple and repetitive tasks. Therefore the qualifications the education system needed to provide such workers with were also fairly basic and concerned limited and formal skills such as literacy.

In a post-Fordist economy there is a need for more highly skilled workers who are flexible, responsible and, most of all, committed to the aims of the organisation. Therefore the employer needs to know much more about a prospective employee than in the past and is interested in the whole person, not just her or his basic skills. For example the employer needs to know about the ability of an employee to work cooperatively, or how creative he or she is. Qualifications therefore need to reflect these attitudes and motivations, through monitoring an individual's performance in group work or problem-solving tasks. The new vocational qualifications such as GNVQ are geared towards this type of assessment, as well as sorting individuals according to core skills such as numeracy, communication and information technology skills.

Exercise 7.3

This exercise is designed to enhance your appreciation of the hierarchy of qualifications that are needed to fit into a modern, stratified society.

Copy out the table below and fill in the necessary qualifications needed to undertake the various occupations that fall under the Registrar General's social class schema. If you get stuck, try to find out the answers at your local careers library.

Social class	Example of occupation	Necessary qualifications
Class I (Professional)	University lecturer	
Class II (Intermediate)	Teacher	
Class III n (Skilled non-manual)	Police officer	
Class III m (Skilled manual)	Electrician	
Class IV (Partly skilled manual)	Telephone operator	
Class V (Unskilled manual)	Office cleaner	

Link exercise 7.2

Functionalists make three main points with regard to the allocation function of schools and training programmes: (1) the selection that takes place is conducted in an educational environment that offers equality of educational opportunity; (2) schools and society at large reward individuals on meritocratic criteria; and (3) education and training offers an important avenue for social mobility. This link exercise is designed to get you to follow through these key functionalist assumptions.

Your task is to copy out and then complete the chart provided by carrying out the following instructions.

1. Using information from Chapter 2 define (1) equality of educational opportunity and (2) meritocracy. Referring to a sociology textbook, define social mobility (note that there are different types).

2. Drawing on material from Chapters 2 and 3, explain how various educational policies have helped to create a more open society.

3. Using a sociology textbook, locate different pieces of empirical evidence to support the functionalist assumptions that equality of opportunity is offered in educational institutions; that meritocracies exist; and that schooling acts as a vehicle for social mobility.

Functionalism	**Equality of educational opportunity**	**Meritocracy**	**Social mobility**
Definition			
Underlying theoretical assumption	Schooling is neutral in that it treats all social groupings equally. It therefore allows everyone to demonstrate their talents to the full.	Structured social inequality is accepted because there is a fair contest for unequal rewards. Educational and occupational success is achieved and is based on merit.	Given equality of educational opportunity and the existence of a meritocratic society, education acts as a route for social mobility. Modern and postmodern capitalist societies are characterised by fluid social class structures.
The positive effect of educational policies: creating an 'open' society			
Empirical evidence in support of the functionalist views			

The vocational training role

The key theorist to address this function of schooling and training is Schultz (1977). The role of education and training in transmitting vocational skills was explored in Chapter 3 when we examined new vocationalism. However this key economic role of education was debated by human capital theory (a distinct branch of functionalism) long before new vocational thinkers began to discuss the need for technical and vocational education in schools and colleges.

Human capital theory rests on the assumption that education (particularly technical education) is a productive investment – a means by which societies can bring about and sustain economic growth. It is believed that schools, colleges and universities can act as catalysts for economic growth because they provide highly educated and trained workers who have the necessary knowledge and skills to make effective use of the advanced productive technologies found in modern industries. Schultz's arguments for investment in people were influential in the creation of policies to deal with Third World poverty during the 1960s. However the failure of human capital programmes to bring about development in the Third World led to the rise of alternative views of vocational training, in which the market was the mechanism behind the provision of training programmes, rather than government planning. In the 1990s, ideas about 'investment in people' and the need of the postmodern economy for highly skilled workers have revitalised human capital ideas. Indeed all the major political parties agree that there is a need for investment in training, though they differ over the means of delivering the skills the economy requires.

Link exercise 7.3

The introduction of the national curriculum in 1988 and new vocational schemes such as TVEI have been seen as an attempt to ensure that school leavers are 'skilled up' for employment in the 1990s and beyond. Drawing on earlier work you have completed, explain how the national curriculum and TVEI ensure that young workers have the necessary practical and technological competences to work in modern industries.

An evaluation of the functionalist approach to the role of education and training

Exercise 7.4

Listed below are the strengths and weaknesses of the functionalist approach to education and training. Your task is to identify whether the strength or weakness is specific to the functionalist views on socialisation, allocation or vocational training, or whether it is a general strength or weaknesses of the functionalist approach to education and training. We have completed one of the answers to help you get started.

Strengths

1. Functionalist theorists recognise that education and training systems are related to other institutions such as the family. (*A general strength*)

2. It is true that schools and training courses transmit norms and values through their formal and/or hidden curriculums.

3. The approach is sensitive to the fact that education systems are in part shaped by the economic needs of society.

4. Some empirical evidence exists to support the claim that the sorting and sifting role of schools operates under egalitarian principles, and that this helps to create a meritocratic and fluid social structure.

Weaknesses

1. The norms and values transmitted by schools and training schemes are not necessarily those of society as a whole, but those of dominant social groups. It is thus a classcentric approach.

2. The benefit of a vocational education has to be questioned. A number of sociologists point to the problem of deskilling, which is the process whereby work activities have the skill taken out of them, either through organisational arrangements or technological change. Others point out that most practical and technical skills can be learnt on the job.

3. The functionalist approach offers a rather impersonal account of the role of education and training. It does not really address the role of schools and training courses in offering a spiritual and humanising education.

4. It is questionable whether schools offer equality of educational opportunity as they slot students into a range of occupational positions. For example 'bottom set' pupils are denied certain types of knowledge and experiences, which 'top set' pupils receive.

5. Occupational selection is not always based on meritocratic principles. Social background is often a major determinant, particularly in times of recession when there is an excess of highly qualified personnel.

6. It is doubtful whether all students end up internalising the same norms and values. This is because the educational diet of students varies according to their class, gender and ethnic background.

7. The ability of the education and training system to equip young people with practical and technical skills in the 1990s has to be queried. This is because education and training in Britain is still essentially academic and many vocational initiatives have been judged to be of a poor quality.

ITEM A

Link exercise 7.4

This exercise takes you back to the new vocational initiatives – GNVQs. We would like you to use the information in Item A to elaborate on weakness number 7 above.

ITEM A

'Deep flaws in vocational courses failing students'

FRAN ABRAMS
Education Correspondent

VOCATIONAL COURSES which ministers hope will be taken up by three out of four young people are deeply flawed, according to a report to be published today.

National Vocational Qualifications (NVQs) and 'vocational A-levels', for which 70,000 pupils are already studying, are failing many students, Professor Alan Smithers, of Manchester University, says.

The courses have no syllabuses and little formal teaching, and on some modules the failure rate is 100 per cent, researchers found.

The report, compiled for a *Dispatches* programme to be shown on Channel 4 tonight, says the council that oversees the courses has shown a 'disdain' for knowledge.

The National Council for Vocational Qualifications (NCVQ) was set up in 1986 in response to complaints that Britain's training system was inadequate compared with those of its European competitors.

Three pathways were opened. The traditional academic route remains, alongside NVQs, which aim to train people in specific trades such as hairdressing or plumbing. The third route – vocational A-levels, or GNVQs – has broader-based courses that can lead into either higher education or work and focus on areas such as art and design or manufacturing. The Government wants three out of four people to take vocational courses by 1997.

Professor Smithers, director of the Centre for Education and Employment Research, found that while British students spent between 15 and 20 hours per week studying for GNVQs, their contemporaries in France and Germany spent 33 hours on similar courses.

Teachers had little or no guidance on what they should teach, but were simply handed lists of what their students should be able to do by the end of the course, he said. Conventional teaching was discouraged, and students were asked to compile dossiers of evidence that they could perform certain tasks.

There were no formal tests for NVQs. GNVQ students had to pass a test but their result did not contribute to the final mark. Literary and numeracy were neither taught nor tested as separate subjects.

Professor Smithers said that while the aim of the new system was good, it needed more work.

'Something very odd is happening and people in authority don't seem to be aware of it. All the people we contacted expressed similar concerns, but they all thought they were the odd ones out,' he said.

Tim Boswell, the minister for higher education, told *Dispatches*: 'There will be some problems, of course, at the beginning. We are always prepared to look at this and to listen to practitioners.'

John Hillier, chief executive of the NCVQ, said that the council disputed much of the information in the report. 'We are very happy to receive constructive criticism of the system and to improve it. I am surprised that the report appears to be factually inaccurate in a number of respects,' he said.

(Source: Fran Abrams, The Independent, 14 December 1993.)

8 Conflict explanations of the role of education and training

By the end of this chapter you should:

- appreciate that the socialisation role of schools and training programmes can be seen in a negative light;
- be familiar with Marxist views on the allocation role of education and training;
- understand conflict interpretations of the vocational role of education;
- be able to assess Marxist approaches to the role of education and training;
- have reflected on student answers to an exam question;
- have practised a structured exam question yourself.

Introduction

Conflict theory covers a range of different approaches to sociological issues, all of which accept that the basic characteristic of societies is the conflict between different groups within them. Conflict explanations of the role of education and training cover similar ground to the functionalist explanations we considered in Chapter 7. Thus they are concerned with examining the way in which the socialisation, allocation and vocational roles of schools and training courses perform economic functions for modern and postmodern societies. However, unlike functionalist explanations, which offer a positive analysis of education and training, conflict theorists offer a pessimistic analysis. It is maintained that schools and training programmes do not serve the interests of everyone in society, but those of a ruling minority. Feminist sociologists reflect on the way in which education and training shapes gender identities and aspirations through socialisation, and rewards, and allocates students and trainees on the basis of gender rather than merit and ability. Weberian sociologists share similar concerns. They give consideration to the way in which education and training socialises students into distinct status cultures and the way in which role allocation is based upon class and status rather than meritocratic criteria.

This chapter addresses the ideas of Marxist sociologists. Most Marxist theories on education and training start from the dual infrastructure/superstructure characteristic of Marxism. Education and training are said to be part of the superstructure of society, and that they function to reproduce (maintain across generations) and legitimate (make acceptable) the unequal social class relations that characterise the infrastructure (economic base) of capitalist societies. Exactly how schools and training courses function to serve the needs of capitalist societies in this way will be explored through a consideration of three roles:

1. The socialisation role
2. The allocation role
3. The vocational training role

Each of these roles will now be examined in turn.

The socialisation role

Marxist sociologists share with functionalist sociologists the belief that schools and training schemes transmit norms and values that create social stability in society. However, whereas functionalists believe that this stability is based upon the internalisation of socially 'agreed' norms and values that benefit everyone, Marxists believe it is based upon the internalisation of dominant ideologies that benefit a ruling minority. This Marxist position is taken by structural Marxists such as Althusser (1972) and Bowles and Gintis (1976). The important concept employed by structural Marxists is 'ideology'. Ideologies in this sense are ideas that serve the interests of a particular social group and have a 'real' existence; that is, they are not just ideas, but have a material form in the practices and processes of institutions. So a dominant ideology would be one that shaped (or, more strongly, in Marxist terms, determined) the experiences and activities of people in the major institutions of society.

Therefore Althusser sees the education system as part of the ideological apparatus of the state. He claims that education, along with other ideological state apparatuses such as the family, reproduce class-based systems of inequality by creating the belief that capitalist social arrangements are somehow 'just', 'normal', 'natural' and so on. It is the fact that new generations of workers perceive the capitalist system to be 'fair' and 'inevitable' that prevents the system from being challenged, and hence it reproduces itself. Therefore dominant ideologies are absorbed by individuals through their experiences in the important structures of society, such as the education system. The effect of the activities of the ideological state apparatus is to reproduce social relations, so that, for example, the sons and daughters of the working class tend to remain in the working class themselves, while ensuring that the members of the working class acquire a 'false consciousness' by accepting the inequality that disadvantages them.

We will now examine three ways in which Marxists believe that education systems ensure social acquiescence and cultural reproduction.

1. The ideas that are taught

Structural Marxists argue that the formal content of schooling ensures that young people come to accept the status quo. For example, in subjects such as economics, students come to internalise dominant capitalist ideology through learning about such concepts as competition and the profit motive. These concepts are taken for granted and are presented as 'natural phenomena'. Students in schools therefore rarely come into contact with ways of thinking that challenge the existing social order. For example only a minority of students leave school having learnt about Marxism, feminism, communism and so on. However, before the introduction of the national curriculum it was difficult to identify the mechanisms by which the formal content of schooling could be controlled by the capitalist class. The dominant ideology amongst educationalists following the Second World War seemed to be some kind of social democracy, in which the curriculum in a school would be settled locally, allowing minority subjects such as peace studies or world studies to gain at least a foothold in the classroom. Moreover curriculum policies with an egalitarian (making equal) emphasis, such as antisexist or antiracist initiatives, were also allowed to flourish in a school system where curriculum decisions were decentralised.

Theorists of the New Right, represented by think tanks such as the Hillgate group or the Adam Smith Institute (see Whitty, 1989), argue that control of the curriculum by teachers and educationalists, prior to the Education Reform Act of 1988 led to a lack of accountability in curriculum design, and this allowed left-wing curriculum initiatives such as peace studies to appear in schools. They therefore argued that there should be state intervention and standardisation of the curriculum throughout the country. This was a reversal of the traditional position of the New Right, which had previously argued for less, not more state intervention. The implication of central control of the curriculum, firstly through the National Curriculum Council and then the School Curriculum and Assessment Authority, is that the formal curriculum of all schools is determined by agents of the government and is therefore more open to ideological influences that support the status quo.

For example Goodson (1990) argues that the national curriculum is an attempt to reconstruct a national identity for Britain, which has been undermined by the globalisation of economic activity. It is argued that computerisation and the growth of global communications through fibre-optic and satellite communications has significantly weakened the importance of national boundaries as a source of identity. The reestablishment of traditional subjects, with traditional content, in the national curriculum is therefore an attempt by the government to isolate what is seen as 'progressive' educational subject matter and reaffirm a curriculum that asserts a British or even an English identity. This can be see in the predominance of British history in the provisions of the history elements of the national curriculum and in insistence on the centrality of Shakespeare in the core subject of English.

However New Right sociologists have pointed out that control of the curriculum by the government is not total and does allow teachers some independence in determining what goes on in their classrooms. Indeed the Conservative government argues that the national curriculum is only a framework that encompasses the two cross-curricular dimensions of equal opportunities between the genders and ethnic minorities. However, as Arnot (1991) points out, equal opportunities can only be built into schemes of work that achieve the targets, assessment objectives and content of the government-determined national curriculum. Nor is there any funding for curriculum innovations that do not meet the criteria laid down by the government. Therefore it could be concluded that the formal curriculum is now more firmly under the direction of those who support the capitalist status quo.

Link exercise 8.1

Explain how the introduction of the national curriculum in 1988 ensured that 'left-wing' ideas and thinking did not creep into the formal curriculum. (Hint: think about some of the subjects that were omitted.)

2. The values, attitudes and personality traits instilled

Structural Marxists such as Althusser, and Bowles and Gintis, maintain that schools create social compliance through the hidden or unofficial curriculum. They argue that schools socialise students into certain values, attitudes and personality traits that 'fit' the interests of dominant social classes and capitalist ways of working. This instilling of values and attitudes may be overt in certain subjects such as religious instruction, but it is more effective in the subtle and hidden ways in which values are transmitted. The values may be obvious, such as a stress on punctuality, which has a clear message for future workers. Or the values may be less directly linked to the world of work, but powerful for all that. An important area of debate concerning the transmission of values has been the teaching styles, or pedagogy, adopted by schools. Marxists would argue that schools create docile workers by giving working-class children few opportunities for independent work, while private schools offer more responsibility for their own learning to the children of the upper class.

The debate concerning teaching styles is based on two stereotypes of the way teachers work. The first is 'traditional' education, which has the image of a disciplined, didactic (teacher talking, student listening) approach, in which the expert teacher transmits his or her knowledge to the attentive student. This 'revelatory model' (a style in which knowledge is revealed to the next generation) is often presented as the way effective education was achieved in the past. The second stereotype is the 'progressive' model, in which teachers and students set out together to discover knowledge for themselves, with the student having much more control over the topics she or he wishes to pursue. Ironically the private sector is associated with the 'traditional' model and the comprehensive sector with the 'progressive' model. The problem for the Marxist is that, if the models are taught where they are said to be taught, then it is middle- and working-class children who receive the independent mode of learning and the upper-class children who are more passive in their education. However Marxists argue that these are stereotypes and do not correspond to what actually happens in the real world, in which private school students are required to develop an independent frame of mind through academic research, while children of the working class are much more controlled in their schooling than the progressive stereotype would imply.

Many postmodern sociologists, among others, have been critical of the idea that there is only one right way to teach. They point out that single pedagogical routes to educational success, whether traditional or progressive, are unlikely to be successful. This is in tune with the postmodernist distrust of 'metanarrative', that is, any 'story' that tries to explain everything in a world that is fractured, contradictory and inconsistent. For example a traditional style of pedagogy adopted in Canada and the United States – 'direct instruction' – has been criticised because it is effective only in certain situations, for example when it is used to teach basic skills (see Hallinger and Murphy, 1987). A negative effect of 'direct instruction' is that it leads to dependency and a lack of initiative amongst students, precisely the qualities that Marxists say the education system promotes in working-class children (see Smyth and Garman, 1989).

Similarly, postmodernists argue that more student-centred techniques are not just about empowering individual students in schools. On the contrary, students taking responsibility for their own learning can be viewed as an increase in the surveillance and regulatory activities of schools (see Usher and Edwards, 1994). Discipline in the student-centred model is not externally imposed by teachers. Rather it is composed of self-discipline, so that any educational failure comes to be seen as the result of the individual failing, rather than resources not being provided or disadvantage not being addressed.

Postmodernists therefore argue for multiple models of teaching, which draw upon the experience of teachers in the classroom and are not just based on the expertise of 'scientific' researchers (see Hargreaves, 1994).

Marxists such as Aronowitz and Giroux (1991) have been influenced by postmodernism in approaching this issue of teaching styles. They begin by moving away from the economic determinism associated with Marxists such as Althusser, and examine the role of teachers as active agents in the education process. They are following the traditional concerns of Marxists by primarily looking at the working class, but rather than just identifying how the working class is dominated by capitalist ideology in the education system, they are concerned with developing alternative ways of teaching that could transform working-class lives and lead to the empowerment of the working class. They arrive at the concept of 'border pedagogy', whereby teachers are recruited to transform the prospects of working-class children in schools through a different type of teaching, in which social progress and resistance to dominant ideologies are central. In later work Giroux (1994) argues for a 'post-Marxist' approach to sociological issues and identifies the pedagogies that would effect the transformation of the working class he seeks.

Giroux therefore argues that border pedagogy should seek to cross the borders of traditional education 'narratives' such as the standard English Literature texts and seek to demonstrate to students that, for example, history is never certain but socially constructed, or that the works of literature are situated in specific historical and ideological settings. He uses the concept of the postmodernists in suggesting that texts should be 'decentred', that is, understood in their historical and social context rather than just read as 'literature'. In terms of pedagogy, Giroux argues that students and teachers should be much more engaged in designing their courses, and that teachers should engage in a variety of teaching styles, including giving more responsibility to the students for their own learning. In developing 'democratic' practices in schools, Giroux is suggesting that working-class students would be empowered and more able to control their own lives within a capitalist system. He believes that the adoption of border pedagogy would change the extent of social class inequality in Britain (see Chapter 4).

However Giroux and Aronowitz have been criticised for assuming that teachers would be willing to adopt border pedagogy and that students would be open to and influenced by the new classroom strategies (see Lynch and O'Neill, 1994). Lynch (1990) argues that teachers are part of the state apparatus, and are therefore unlikely to adopt Giroux's border pedagogy. Nor is it likely that teachers would have the freedom to introduce such a radical pedagogy, especially with the increasing central control of education that took place in Britain during the 1980s. Moreover students have shown themselves to be highly resistant to classroom strategies that do not seem to be immediately relevant (see Hannan and Shorthall, 1991). They respond to pragmatic and instrumental strategies directly related to the local labour market, rather than strategies linked to concepts such as liberation or empowerment.

Exercise 8.1

Explain how the hidden curriculum operating inside schools or training schemes may instill the values of (1) obedience; (2) punctuality; (3) acceptance of authority. (Hint: think about the positive and negative sanctions that schools employ on a day-to-day basis.

3. The ways in which educational institutions are organised

Bowles and Gintis (1976) contend that the structural organisation of educational institutions, as an aspect of the hidden curriculum, has the effect of making young people accept the existing social order. Studying schooling in capitalist America, these Marxist sociologists claim that the internal organisation of schools corresponds to the internal organisation of the capitalist workplace. There is thus a 'correspondence principle' operating, in which the experiences of young people in schools is a direct preparation for their experiences in work. Hence, working-class children experience schools as systems of control, in which they are taught the aptitudes and attitudes necessary for low-skill, routinised work. Working-class children are therefore subject to a strict hierarchical control that corresponds to the type of control they will experience in their working lives. On the other hand middle-class children, it is argued, experience a less formally controlled educational environment, in which they are encouraged to take responsibility for their own learning and to acquire independence of mind rather than the habit of obedience. This hidden curriculum of school organisation has the effect of legitimating inequality. So Bowles and Gintis argue that, in the United States at least, schools do not perform the democratic function of promoting the personal development of all children. Nor do they promote equality of opportunity. On the contrary, the organisation of schools mirrors the organisation of an hierarchical and autocratic industrial system, in which workers are expected to obey without question. If working-class students are alienated by their experiences in schools, then this is also preparation for their experiences in work.

However this aspect of the work of Bowles and Gintis has come under a great deal of criticism. Brown and Lauder (1991) argue that there has never been a simple correspondence between the education system and the needs of the economy, as suggested by Bowles and Gintis. Rather the education system performs several different functions for society, not all of which are economic. For example Brown (1990) suggests that what he calls the 'first wave' of education in the nineteenth century was more to do with a way of differentiating between the elite and the masses, than with the needs of the early capitalist economy. Moreover the correspondence principle assumes that those who experience the 'hidden messages' of the organisation of the school interpret them (or, in postmodern terminology, decode the messages) in a particular way. It seems highly unlikely that participants in the education system will all 'read' the messages of hierarchy in exactly the same way.

Michael Apple (1982, 1986) developed the work of Bowles and Gintis by examining the hidden curriculum in terms of the role of teachers. He suggests that teachers are being proletarianised, as they are deskilled through the introduction of standardised curriculum packages, and that the profession is becoming feminised. This has the effect of increasing state control over teachers and more tightly defining how they carry out their functions. He is not arguing that teachers are like automatons, with no power of resistance. He believes that schools are sites of struggle and that both teachers and pupils resist the reproductive processes they are subjected to. Indeed Apple argues that the education system has 'relative autonomy', which allows this resistance to have space. However the end result is, according to Apple, the reproduction of inequalities.

He also argues that the formal curriculum is class-biased, the reproduction of high-status academic knowledge being a priority in the schooling of those who are not poor or part of a minority. Moreover, when analysing school textbooks, Apple argues that the the formal curriculum of schools neglects social conflict and distorts the causes and consequences of conflict, which contributes to the ideological reproduction of capitalism. This approach is supported in the work of Anyon (1981) who, having looked at five schools, argues that what counted as knowledge in these schools varied according to their social class basis, with working-class schools being dominated by a low-status curriculum content. However Ramsay (1983), in a larger survey of schools, found a great deal of variation among working-class schools, and as Hannan and Boyle (1987) demonstrated, the management and attitudes of teachers can make a difference in determining the ethos of a working-class school, so that not all working-class schools prepare their students for failure.

Exercise 8.2

This is the first of two exercises to help you to appreciate the way in which educational experiences correspond with work experiences. Your task for Exercise 8.2 is to identify the hierarchical systems of authority and control that exist in schools and the workplace. Make sure that you pair off equivalent occupational positions. The top and bottom rungs of the school and workplace hierarchies have been given below to get you started. You should finish with about six different levels in total.

Hierarchical systems of control

School	Work
Headteacher	Managing director
Cleaners	Cleaners

Exercise 8.3

This exercise is designed to get you to consider a number of other similarities that exist between school and work. Your job here is to identify the missing correspondences between school and work and to fill in the gaps.

School	Work
Ordinary workers have little or no control	
	Workers follow orders. They do not have a say in what goods are made or how they are made.
Acceptance of alienation	
School work rarely done for its own sake, but for ulterior motives, for example to gain praise or good qualifications.	
Fragmentation	
The curriculum is broken down and divided into separate 'subjects'. The school day is also fragmented.	
The principle that those with different talents and aptitudes require different rewards	
	The different layers of jobs (managerial, supervisory, skilled, semi-skilled, manual, unskilled) are rewarded differently by pay, conditions, etc.

The allocation role

Marxists share with functionalists the belief that education and training serves to allocate people to or select people for distinct occupational positions. However the optimistic assumptions that underlie the functionalist theory of role allocation (see Chapter 7) are hotly disputed by Marxists such as Althusser (1972) and Bowles and Gintis (1976). There are three points that Marxists make regarding role allocation by the education system.

1. The education system does not offer equality of educational opportunity

Marxists make this claim on two levels. Firstly, equality of access does not exist. It is argued that all students do not have the same opportunity to study at schools that offer an equivalent education. For example the high fees of private schools debar the vast majority of working-class students from attending them. (See Chapter 2 for further details.) During the 1980s the governments of Britain and the United States, influenced by New Right theorists, pursued policies of open enrolment and parental choice in an attempt to empower all 'parent–consumers' of education and make the education system more responsive to parental needs. Evidence suggests that these policies do lead to changes in the recruitment patterns of schools, but to the detriment of working-class children. For example Moore (1990) shows that in the United States the more popular schools have become 'colonised' by better-off parents, and that children from less well-off families have become concentrated in other schools. This is because better-off families are more knowledgeable about how to operate the system to their own advantage, as well as having the means and mobility to move to areas with popular schools. Also, as Edwards and Whitty (1992) show, popular schools begin to select their pupils on the basis of academic ability, upon which their popularity depends, thus creating a 'two-tier system' in which working-class children are concentrated in the less popular schools.

Secondly, within the state sector of schooling pupils are not treated equally. Here Marxists draw on a wide body of evidence to suggest that working-class students are 'cooled' out of the educational system. For example they make reference to the fact that many teachers hold low expectations of the working class and that this has a damaging, self-fulfilling prophecy effect on working-class pupils (see Chapter 4 for further details). Aronowitz and Giroux (1991) argue that any working-class pupils that do 'get on' in the education system have to abandon their working-class attitudes, thoughts and actions and become socially mobile. Success in higher education necessitates a change in class identity.

2. Role allocation is not conducted within a meritocratic framework

Marxists argue that educational and occupational success is based upon social class rather than merit. The process of cultural reproduction works against the meritocratic ideology that surrounds schooling in capitalist societies and ensures that working-class children get working-class jobs, if they get a job at all. The statistics of educational 'success' and 'failure' show that working-class children underachieve in the education system compared with their middle-class counterparts, and this is due, in part at least, to the non-meritocratic nature of the education system. According to the Marxists therefore, the problem facing the education system is how to offer greater equality of opportunity to meet the demand of capitalist corporations for workers with certain skills, while limiting ßthe aspirations of the majority of working-class children. Brown and Lauder (1991) argue that the concept of IQ has been used by the education system to detect 'talent' early in a child's life and to select socially on the basis of class by an apparently 'objective' criterion. The result of IQ testing, according to Evans and Waites (1981) is to further the interests of middle-class children while minimising working-class resistance to an unfair system.

3. Education offers limited opportunities for social mobility

This argument is advanced because of the belief that equality of educational opportunity is not offered in schools and because capitalist societies are not meritocratic. Thus the ideology of meritocracy is a powerful force for preserving the status quo and preventing a truly meritocratic society. Capitalist societies are not meritocratic, because the capitalist system confers huge advantages on those who own and control the means of production, and thus can ensure that the system operates to their own and their children's benefit.

Therefore Marxists maintain that schools and training programmes not only reproduce class inequalities but legitimate them as well. That is to say, they make them seem natural or somehow inevitable. It is argued that this ideological role of education and training is achieved by spreading various myths about the 'openness' of the system of role allocation. For example schools and training schemes create the belief that educational and occupational attainment is based on merit. Thus individuals and social groupings come to accept that those in powerful positions have got there by ability and effort, whilst those in subordinate positions only have themselves to blame because of lack of talent or effort.

Exercise 8.4

Below is a partly completed paragraph that summarises the Marxist view of role allocation. You should copy out the paragraph and fill in the missing words by selecting the appropriate words from the list provided.

From a Marxist point of view, schools and training courses serve to . . . . . . people for jobs. However the education and training system does not offer . . . . . . of . . . . . . opportunity, nor does it operate under . . . . . . principles, and it does not act as a route for . . . . Schooling actually depresses the . . . . . . and lowers the aspiration levels of . . . . . . students. In this way working-class pupils are . . . . . . out of the education system. It is almost as if they are supposed to . . . . . . so that they can take up . . . . . . 'blue collar' positions. The net result of the role allocation function of schools and training programmes is to . . . . . . the social class . . . . . .

Missing words

- mobility
- class
- fail
- appropriate
- meritocratic
- social
- structure
- equality
- sifted
- educational
- talents
- reproduce
- working
- allocate

Link exercise 8.2

This exercise is almost identical to one you carried out in Chapter 7. We want you to draw up a chart along the same lines as that in Link Exercise 7.2, but this time as it applies to the Marxist role allocation theory. You should begin by copying out the chart provided and then complete it according to the following instructions. There is no need to define the key terms as this has been done previously.

1. Use the material you have just read in this chapter to establish the underlying theoretical assumptions of the Marxist theory of role allocation.

2. Use information from Chapters 2 and 3 to explain how various educational policies have served to create a closed society.

3. Making use of a sociology textbook, identify several pieces of empirical evidence to support the Marxist assumptions that the education system does not offer equality of educational opportunity; that role allocation is not conducted within a meritocratic framework; and that education offers limited opportunities for social mobility.

Marxism	Equality of educational opportunity	Meritocracy	Social mobility
Underlying theoretical assumption			
The negative effect of educational policies: creating a 'closed' society			
Empirical evidence in support of the Marxist views			

The vocational training role

We have seen that the functionalists (Chapter 7) view the vocational training role of schools in a positive light, arguing that schools provide the skills and work habits that industry requires to function efficiently. Marxists have a different view of this vocational function. Structural Marxists such as Althusser (1972) do not see schools transmitting a range of practical skills to the workers of the future. Rather they see education providing working-class children with only basic numeracy and literacy to enable them to perform the routine and boring jobs they will eventually obtain. This is because Marxists such as Bowles and Gintis (1976) see schools as institutions of social control, rather than as meritocratic or empowering. Conflict theorists such as Paul Willis (1977) have developed this idea by looking at the actual experiences of working-class boys as they move into the world of work. Willis charts how the 'lads' are involved in preparing for their own future exploitation by employers, and how schools equip these boys with appropriate attitudes for boring, routine work. Therefore Marxists tend to see vocational preparation in wider 'thought control' terms than the functionalists do.

However two issues need to be addressed with regard to this vocational role and the relationship between education and society. The first concerns the concept of 'skill' and how schools actually prepare their pupils for the world of work. Marxists tend to see the development of the capitalist economy in terms of deskilling (see Braverman, 1974). By this they mean that, as technology develops under the impetus of cost-saving policies of capitalist enterprises, it tends to result in an increasing loss of skill by both manual and non-manual workers. This results in the ever-intensifying exploitation of workers who, with the loss of their skills, lose much of their power in negotiations with employers. Thus the education system, according to the Marxists, only has to provide workers with the basic skills needed for low-level work.

However there has been a great deal of debate about deskilling and whether technological development inevitably means that skills are taken away from the workforce. For example Thompson (1983) argues that Braverman has exaggerated the extent and significance of deskilling by promoting an idealised view of a skilled workforce in the past. Moreover postmodernists have argued that the development of new technologies has had a fragmentary effect on the skills of the labourforce rather than the uniform effect suggested by Marxists. For example Harvey (1989) argues that postmodern industry demands different types of worker in flexible labour markets. Firstly there are the 'core' workers, who have full-time, permanent status and the prospect of being reskilled as technology advances. 'Periphery' workers are of two types: full-time workers with skills that are readily available in the labour market, for example clerical skills; and low-skill, part-time, casual workers. Therefore it is not just deskilling that occurs under modern capitalism, but reskilling also, and education systems in the postmodern world will have to deliver workers that are differentiated by their levels of skill.

The second issue concerns the actual relationship between education and the economy. Marxists see the education system as a means of reproduction, that is, as one of the ways capitalist relations of production are maintained from one generation to the next. Vocationalism in schools is seen as an important aspect of this reproduction, because, for example new vocationalism (see Chapter 3) seeks to identify the needs of capitalist industry for certain types of labour power and to develop the educational courses that will meet those needs (see Hodgkinson, 1991). However Marxists such as Bowles and Gintis (1976) argue for a positive and direct relationship (or correspondence) between education and the economy, in which educational change is determined by the needs of the economy.

Other Marxists follow Althusser (1972) in arguing that the education system is 'relatively autonomous'. This means that the state gives it some freedom from the economic requirements of capitalism, but ultimately education does have to fulfil the needs of capitalist industry. Other sociologists such as Moore (1988) argue that there is no correspondence at all between education and industry, but rather they are autonomous (free-standing) social formations.

Brown and Lauder (1991) argue that there has never been a simple relationship between education and the economy as the Marxists suggest, and call for a new relationship to be forged between them in the light of technological and industrial change. They believe that Britain should be aiming for a high-skill rather than a low-skill economy, and therefore education should be based on the idea that all rather than just a few are capable of significant practical and academic achievements. This involves the creation of a high-trust education system, which will empower students by providing a high-ability education system for all and what they call the 'power tools' of confidence and analytical skill. This will enable all students to interpret the wealth of information available in the globalised information market of the postmodern world.

Link exercise 8.3

Many of the Marxist ideas you have just read about on the vocational training role of schools also apply to training initiatives outside the school environment. For example many left-wing writers are critical of Youth Training. It is argued that not only does YT often fail to equip trainees with 'transferable skills', but it also reproduces the capitalist status quo. Your task for this exercise is to use the material you read in Chapter 3 on YT to elaborate on the Marxist position on YT. You should try to build upon the table we have started for you.

Reasons why YT often fails to equip trainees with 'transferable skills'	Reasons why YT reproduces the capitalist status quo
1. High trainee staff ratios	1. A source of cheap labour
2. Too much working and not enough training	2.
3.	3.
4.	4.
5.	5.

An evaluation of the Marxist approach to the role of education and training

Exercise 8.5

This exercise is the same as the one you carried out for the evaluation of the functionalist approach to education and training in Chapter 7. You have to identify whether the strength or weakness is specific to the Marxist views on socialisation, allocation or vocational training, or whether it is a general strength or weakness of the Marxist approach to education and training.

We have again completed one of the answers to help you get started.

Strengths

1. The approach recognises that the education system is shaped by structural factors – the economic infrastructure of society. Recent evidence would support this view, for example the national curriculum and the new vocational initiatives have been 'shaped' by the government and industry. Furthermore, as more schools opt out of local education authorities so the control of education by the state and industry increases.

2. A lot of empirical evidence exists to support the claim that schools 'cool' out or depress the talents of working-class students. Empirical evidence also suggests that occupational position and reward is often based on social background and not ability.

3. The effect of powerful ideologies is recognised.

4. The approach offers a useful challenge to New Right thinking on vocational education. This is because the negative aspects of vocational education are addressed.

Weaknesses

1. It offers an over-socialised view of humankind. It is highly questionable whether students internalise the hidden curriculum, as described by Bowles and Gintis and Althusser. Even Marxists such as Willis are doubtful. Willis' 'lads', you will remember, resisted school and were far from obedient, docile and disciplined.

2. The explanations are too class based – they lack a gender and ethnicity focus.

3. The approach can often be 'blind' to any evidence that suggests that society is becoming more open and meritocratic.
(A weakness as it applies to allocation)

4. The positive achievements of new vocational courses in raising skill levels and individuals' control over the work process are often ignored.

Link exercise 8.4

This exercise is designed to develop your interpretation and application skills. We would like you to use material from Chapters 7 and 8 to identify the similarities and differences between the functionalist and Marxist views on education and training (make sure you cover each of the three roles they talk about). You should record your answers in a chart similar to the one we have started off for you.

The similarities between functionalist and Marxist views on education and training

Socialisation	Allocation	Vocational training
1. Schools and training programmes instil norms and values via the formal and hidden curriculum.		
2.		

The differences between functionalist and Marxist views on education and training

Socialisation	Allocation	Vocational training
1.		
2.		

ITEM A

Schools do not merely prepare children for work, they also help reproduce social norms and cultural preferences. Intentionally or unintentionally, schools play a part in the creation of adults socialised to be consumers, Britons, decent citizens, spouses and the like. That people should accept such identities and adopt corresponding patterns of behaviour is just as important to the maintenance of society as is economic production.

Schools encourage their pupils to absorb social rules, manners and values – like those which mark out gender divisions in society. Boys and girls are treated differently by their teachers who expect and encourage different behaviour from the two sexes. For instance, a group of teachers at A level, when asked what they imagined their students would be doing in five years' time, replied almost exclusively with reference to work in the case of boys, but marriage in the case of girls.

(Source: N. Abercrombie and A. Warde, Contemporary British Society, London, Polity Press, 1988.)

ITEM A

Exam question and student answers

Item A and the subsequent question are taken from the AEB's winter examination for 1994. The student answers that follow have had some of the concepts and names of sociologists taken out, mixed up and listed at the end. Your task is to place the correct concepts/names in the spaces in the answers. Both answers gained five marks for the students. You could also underline the places in which the answers are evaluative.

Question

To what extent do sociologists agree that the main function of education is to 'prepare children for work' (Item A)? (*7 marks*)

Student answers

Candidate A

For functionalists, education acts as a selection function and also economic and socialisation ones. For them, education selects the most able people and prepares them to take their place in society. They are taught the general (and occasionally, work-specific) skills required by society and its. . . . . . (mainstream dominant culture). For functionalists, the education system is designed as a system of. . . . . ., where only the successful will make it to higher education, which is academic-based. Society is therefore a meritocracy. Children are prepared for work but mainly of a higher academic kind. General work skills are more rarely taught.

For Marxists, obedience and. . . . . . to authority are the key elements of education, in a system that is designed to fail the majority of children and turn them out into low-paid employment, with no career prospects (or no employment at all). Bowles and Gintis formulated the '. . . . . .'. As Marxists they believed that what goes on in schools is closely related to what goes on in the outside world, where class differences within schools correspond to those outside. They found that children destined to become manual workers are taught that obedience is preferable to being clever or creative, that knowledge is. . . . . . and the pieces irrelevant to one another, that knowledge is consumed rather than created and that learning should be motivated by external rewards (that is,. . . . . .).

Candidate B

Although the functionalist and conflict theorists usually tend to disagree, there is a certain amount of agreement when it comes to education. Functionalists such as. . . . . . argue that school's main function is to educate and prepare children for their role in the society of the future. He believes that the whole culture of school – learning to be on time and. . . . . . and behave appropriately – is the embryo of the society of the next generation. The cleverest are prepared for high-income, high-status jobs and the least clever learn to accept their limitations and resign themselves to being underdogs.

Marxists such as. . . . . . would agree entirely with this, but he takes the view that school is part of the. . . . . ., which works for the establishment, recreating a nation of docile workers. He is indignant about this, whereas Merton nonchalantly accepts it and describes it as necessary to keeping order in society.

In the 1960s, the trendy social interactionists gained respect from the hippie movement with their view that education is only part of the function of a school. This led to many 'progressive' schools being set up. An. . . . . . was created, with children of all social classes and abilities being put together. Cooperation and tolerance were encouraged. This, however, made teaching very difficult and finally the schools closed as people could see that social education was becoming more time consuming and less time was being given to. . . . . .

Although there are other functions of a school, apart from preparation for work, most sociologists agree that it is the main function, even though they see it from different perspectives.

Missing words	
integrative environment	success and failure
Althusser	deference
fragmented	Merton
correspondence theory	academic education
qualifications and later wages	obey rules
ideological state apparatus	norms and values

Structured exam question

We would like you now to answer a question from the AEB's November 1992, paper 1, examination. Begin by reading Item's G and H on page 63. The question we would like you to do is question e on page 64. You will find the advice we gave on page 64 useful in answering this question.

References

Abrams, Fran (1993) 'Deep Flaws in Vocational Courses Failing Students', *The Independent*, 14 December.

Aggleton, Peter (1987) *Rebels without a Cause? Middle class youth and the transition from school to work* (London: Falmer Press).

Ainley, P. (1993) *Class and Skill: Changing Divisions of Knowledge and Labour* (London: Cassell).

Allan, Philip *et al.* (eds) (1994) *Focus on Britain* (Oxfordshire: Philip Allan).

Althusser, Louis (1972) 'Ideology and Ideological State Apparatuses in B. R. Cosin (ed.), *Education, Structure and Society* (Harmondsworth: Penguin).

Anyon, J. (1981) 'Social class and school knowledge', *Curriculum Inquiry*, vol. 11, no. 1.

Apple, Michael (1982) *Education and Power* (London: RKP).

Apple, Michael (1986) *Teachers and Texts: a political economy of class and gender relations in education* (London: RKP).

Arnot, M. (1982) 'Male hegemony, social class and women's education', *Journal of Education*, no. 164.

Arnot, M. (ed.) (1985) *Race and Gender; equal opportunities policies in education* (Oxford: Pergamon Press).

Arnot, Madeleine (1991) 'Equality and Democracy', *British Journal of Sociology of Education*, vol. 12, no. 4.

Arnott, Madeleine (1992) 'Feminism, Education and the New Right', in Madeleine Arnott and Len Barton (eds), *Voicing Concerns: sociological perspectives on contemporary education reforms* (Wallingford: Triangle).

Arnott, Madeleine and Len Barton (eds) (1992) *Voicing Concerns: sociological perspectives on contemporary education reforms* (Wallingford: Triangle).

Aronowitz, Stanley and Henry Giroux (1991) *Post-modern education; politics, culture and social criticism* (Minneapolis: University of Minnesota Press).

Avis, James (1993) 'Post-Fordism, Curriculum Modernisers and Radical practice: the case of vocational education and training in England', *The Vocational Aspect of Education*, vol. 45, no. 1.

Ball, S. J. (1988) 'Education: the Search for Inequality, *Social Studies Review*, vol. 4, no. 2.

Ball, S. J. (1990a) *Politics and Policy-making in Education* (London: Routledge).

Ball, S. J. (1990b) *Education, Inequality and School Reform: values in crisis* (King's College Memorial Lecture).

Ball, S. (ed.) (1990c) *Foucault and Education: Disciplines and Knowledge* (London: Routledge).

Banks, J. A. (1988) *Multi-ethnic Education: theory and practice* (Boston: Allyn and Bacon).

Barber, Michael (1994) quoted in Paul Marston, 'A-level girls pass boys for the first time', *Daily Telegraph*, 25 October.

Barnett, Corelli (1986) *The Audit of War: the illusion and reality of Britain as a great nation* (London: Macmillan).
Barton, L. and Walker, S. (eds) (1993) *Race, Class and Education* (London: Croom Helm).
Baudrillard, J. (1983) *Simulations* (New York: Semi-text).
Beltz, C. (1985) 'Review of migrant education in Australia', *Education News*, vol. 19, no. 3 (May).
Bentley, D. and M. Watts (1987) 'Courting the positive virtues: a case for feminist science', in A. Kelly (ed.), *Science for Girls?* (Milton Keynes: Open University Press).
Bernstein, Basil (1975) *Class, Codes and Control: towards a theory of educational transmission* (London: Routledge & Kegan Paul).
Best, Lesly (1993) 'Dragons, Dinner Ladies and Ferrets: sex roles in children's books', *Sociology Review*, vol. 2, no. 3.
Bettelheim, Bruno (1991) *The Uses of Enchantment: the meaning and importance of fairy tales* (London: Penguin).
Bevins, Anthony and Dean Nelson (1995) 'Blacks stranded at back of jobs queue', the *Observer*, 12 February.
Bottigheimer, R. B. (1987) *Grimm's Bad Girls and Bold Boys: the moral and social vision of the tales* (New Haven: Yale University Press)
Bourdieu, P. (1973) 'Cultural reproduction and social reproduction', in Brown, R. K. (ed.) *Knowledge, Education and Cultural Change* (London: Tavistock).
Bourdieu, Pierre and Jean-Claude Passeron (1977) *Reproduction in Education, Society and Culture* (London: Sage).
Bourdillon, H. (ed.) (1994) *Teaching History* (London: Routledge).
Bowles, S. and H. Gintis (1976) *Schooling in Capitalist America: Educational reform and the contradictions of economic life* (New York: Basic Books).
Braverman, H. (1974) *Labour and Monopoly Capitalism* (New York: Monthly Press Review).
Brown, P. (1990) 'The Third Wave: education and the ideology of parentocracy', *British Journal of Sociology of Education*, vol. 11.
Brown, P. and H. Lauder (1991) 'Education, Economy and Social Change', *International Studies in the Sociology of Education*, vol. 1.
Brown, P. and H. Lauder (eds) (1992) *Education for Economic Survival* (London: Routledge).
Brown, R. K. (1973) (ed.) *Knowledge, Education and Cultural change* (London: Tavistock).
Burgess, B. (1994) 'Education: an agenda for change', in M. Haralambos (ed.), *Developments in Sociology: an annual review*, vol. 10 (Ormskirk: Causeway).
Burke, J. (1989) *Competency-based Education and Training* (London: Falmer).
Burrows, Roger and Brian Loader (1993) *Towards a Post-Fordist Welfare State?* (London: Routledge).
Buswell, Carol (1991) 'The Gendering of School and Work', *Social Studies Review*, vol. 6, no. 3.
Byrne, E. (1978) *Women and Education* (London: Tavistock).
Byrne, E. (1985) 'Equity or equality: a European overview', in M. Arnot (ed.), *Race and Gender: equal opportunities policies in education* (Oxford: Pergamon Press).

Caldwell, B. J. and J. M. Spinks (1992) *Leading the Self-Managing School* (London: Falmer).

Campbell, B. (1987) *The Iron Ladies* (London: Virago).

Carr, H. (1989) *From My Guy to Sci-fi: genre and women's writing in the postmodern world* (London: Pandora).

Carter, T. (1986) *Shattering Illusions: West Indians in British politics* (London: Lawrence and Wishart).

Castleman, T. and M. Poole (1990) *Academic Progression, Strategies and Initiatives for Women in Higher Education in Victoria* (Victoria: Ministry of Education).

Cathcart, H. and G. Esland (1990) 'The compliant-creative worker: the ideological reconstruction of the school leaver', in G. Esland (ed.), *Education, Training and Employment, Volume 2: the educational response* (Wokingham: Adison-Wesley).

Chitty, Clyde. (1993) 'The Education System Transformed', *Sociology Review*, vol. 2, no. 3.

Chubb, J. and T. Moe (1990) *Politics, Markets and America's Schools* (Washington: Brookings Institution).

Cicourel, A. V. and J. I. Kitsuse (1963) *The Educational Decision Makers* (Indianapolis: Bobbs-Merill).

Clare, John (1994) 'Education', in Philip Allan *et al.* (eds), *Focus on Britain* (Oxfordshire: Philip Allan).

Clarricoates, K. (1980) 'The important of being Ernest . . . Emma . . . Tom . . . Jane. The perception and categorisation of gender conformity and gender deviation in primary schools', in R. Deem (ed.), *Schooling for Women's Work* (London: Routledge and Kegan Paul).

Clune, W. and J. Witte (eds) (1990) *Choice and Control in American Education*, vol. 2 (London: Falmer Press).

Cole, M. (1988) *Bowles and Gintis Re-visited* (Lewes: Falmer Press).

Cole, Mike. (1992) 'British values, liberal values or values of justice and equality', in James Lynch *et al.*, *Equity or Excellence?: Education and cultural reproduction* (London: Falmer Press).

Collins, R. (1981) *The Credential Society* (New York: Academic Press).

Connell, R. W. (1986) *Teachers' Work* (Sydney: George Allen and Unwin).

Connell, R. W., D. J. Ashenden, S. Kessler and G. W. Dowsett (1982) *Making the Difference: schools, families and social divisions* (Sydney: George Allen and Unwin).

Cooper, P. *et al.* (1991) 'Ethnic minority and gender distribution among staff and pupils in facilities for pupils with emotional and behavioural difficulties in England and Wales', *British Journal of Sociology of Education*, vol. 12, no. 1.

Cordingly, Philippa (1993) 'What about the class angle?', *The Times Educational Supplement*, 5 November 1993.

Cosin, B. R. (ed.) *Education, Structure and Society* (Harmondsworth: Penguin).

Cox, C. B. and R. Boyson (eds) (1975) *Black Papers 1975 The Fight for Education* (London: Dent & Sons).

Coyle, J. (1991) 'What will follow Key Stage 4?: Developments in Advanced Supplementary and Advanced level Sociology', *Social Science Teacher*, vol. 20, no. 2.

CRE (1994) 'Training for real jobs at last', *CRE-Connections*, no. 2 (October) (Commission for Racial Equality).
Culley, L. (1986) *Gender Differences and Computing in Secondary Schools* (Loughborough: Loughborough University Press).
Dale, Roger (1985) *Education, Training and Employment* (Oxford: Pergaman).
David, M. (1983) 'Teaching and Preaching Sexual Morality: the New Right's anti-feminism in Britain and the USA', *Journal of Education*, no. 166.
Davis, K. and W. E. Moore (1945) 'Some Principles of Stratification', *American Sociological Review*, vol. 10.
Dawson A. (1988) 'Inner city adolescents: unequal opportunities?', in A. Verma and P. Pumfrey (eds) *Educational Attainments: issues and outcomes in multicultural education* (London: Falmer Press).
Deem, Rosemary (ed.) (1980) *Schooling for Women's Work* (London: RKP).
Deem, R. (1992) 'Schooling and gender: The cycle of discrimination', in James Lynch, Celia Madgil *et al., Equity or Excellence? Education and Cultural Reproduction* (London: Falmer Press).
De Lyon, H. and F. Mignolio (1989) 'Women Teachers' (Milton Keynes: Open Univesity Press).
Demaine, Jack (1988) 'Teachers' Work, Curriculum and the New Right', *British Journal of Sociology of Education*, no. 9.
Denscombe, Martyn (1992) *Sociology Update* (Leicester: Olympus).
Denscombe, Martyn (1993) *Sociology Update* (Leicester: Olympus).
Denscombe, Martyn (1994) *Sociology Update* (Leicester: Olympus).
DES (1974) 'Work Experience', Circular 7/74 (London: HMSO).
DES (1985) *Education for All* (Swann Report) (London: HMSO).
DES *et al.* (1991) *Education and Training for the 21st Century*, vols 1 and 2 (London: HMSO).
DES Statistical Bulletin (1991), in Martyn Denscombe (1992) *Sociology Update* (Leicester: Olympus, 1992).
DFE (1993) *Educational Statistics for the United Kingdom* (London: HMSO).
DFE (1993) *Social Trends*, vol. 23 (London: HMSO).
Donald, James (1992) *Sentimental Education* (London: Verso).
Dore, Ronald (1976) *The Diploma Disease: education, qualification and development* (London: Allen and Unwin).
Douglas, J. W. B. (1964) *The Home and the School* (London: MacGibbon and Kee).
Dreyfus, H. and P. Rabinow (eds) (1982) *Michel Foucault: Beyond Structuralism and Hermeneutics* (Brighton: Harvester Press).
Durkheim, Emile (1956) *Education and Society* (Glencoe: Free Press).
East, P., R. Pitt, V. Bryan, J. Rose and L. Rupchand (1989) 'Access to Teaching for Black Women', in H. De Lyon and F. Mignolio, *Women Teachers* (Milton Keynes: Open University Press).
Edwards, R. (1991) 'Winners and losers: the education and training of adults', in P. Raggatt and L. Unwin (eds) *Change and Intervention* (London: Falmer Press).
Edwards, Richard (1993) 'Multi-skilling the flexible workforce', *Journal of Further and Higher Education*, vol. 17, no. 1.
Edwards, T. and G. Whitty (1992) 'Parental Choice and Educational Reform in Britain and the United States', *British Journal of Educational Studies*, vol. 40, no. 2.

Eggleston, J. (1986) *Education for Some: the educational and vocational experiences of 15–18 year old members of minority ethnic groups* (Stoke-on Trent: Trentham).

Elliott, B. and D. MacLennan (1994) 'Neo-Conservative School Reform', *British Journal of Sociology of Education*, vol. 15, no. 2.

Elliott, J. and C. Powell (1987) 'Young women and science: do we need more science?', *British Journal of Sociology of Education*, vol. 8, no. 3.

Ellsworth, E. (1989) 'Why doesn't this feel empowering? Working through the repressive myths of critical pedagogy', *Harvard Educational Review*, vol. 59, no. 3).

Esland, G. (ed.) (1990) *Education, Training and Employment*, vol. 2, *The educational response* (Wokingham: Adison Wesley).

Evans, B. and B. Waites (1981) *IQ and Mental Testing* (London: MacMillan).

Eysenck, H. J. (1962) *Know your own IQ* (Harmondsworth: Penguin).

FEU (1994) 'Developing GNVQ Science – FEU Evaluation', *FEU Newsletter*, November.

Figueroa, Peter (1991) *Education and the Social Construction of Race* (London: Routledge).

Finegold, D. and R. Soskice (1988) 'The Failure of Training in Britain: analysis and prescription', *Oxford Review of Economic Policy*, vol. 4.

Finn, Dan (1985) 'Manpower Services Commission and the Youth Training Scheme: a permanent bridge to work', in Roger Dale, *Education, Training and Employment* (Oxford: Pergaman).

Finn, D. (1987) *Training without Jobs* (Basingstoke: MacMillan).

Finn, Dan (1988) 'Education for Jobs: The route to YTS', *Social Studies Review*, vol. 4, no. 1.

Flew, A. (1986) 'Education against racism', in D. O'Keefe (ed.), *The Wayward Curriculum* (London: Social Affairs Unit).

Flew, A. (1987) *Power to the Parents* (London: Sherwood Press).

Flude, M. and M. Hammer (eds) (1990) *The Education Reform Act 1988: its origins and implications* (London: Falmer Press).

Foster, P. (1990) 'Case Not Proven': An Evaluation of Two Studies of Teacher Racism', *British Educational Research Journal*, vol. 16, no. 4.

Foucault, M. (1979) *The Order of Things: an archeology of the human sciences* (New York: Random House).

Foucault, Michel (1982) 'The Subject and Power', in H. Dreyfus and P. Rabinow (eds), *Michel Foucault: Beyond Structuralism and Hermeneutics* (Brighton: Harvester Press).

Fuller, Mary (1980) 'Black girls in a London comprehensive school', in Rosemary Deem (ed.), *Schooling for Women's Work* (London: RKP).

General Household Survey (1994) *Social Trends*, vol. 24 (London: HMSO).

Gibson, M. and J. Ogbu (eds) (1991) *Minority Status and Schooling: a comparative study of immigrant and involuntary minorities* (New York: Garland).

Giddens, Anthony (1984) *The Constitution of Society* (Cambridge: Polity Press).

Gillborn, David (1990) *'Race', Ethnicity and Education: teaching and learning in multi-ethnic schools* (London: Unwin-Hyman).

Giroux, Henry (1983) *Theory and Resistance in Education: a pedagogy for the opposition* (South Hadley: Bergin and Garvey).

Giroux, Henry (1994) *Border Crossings* (London: Routledge).
Gomm, Roger (1990) *A Level Sociology* (Cambridge: National Extension College).
Goodson, I. (1990) 'Nations at risk and national curriculum: ideology and identity', *Politics of Education Association Yearbook* (London: Taylor and Francis).
Green, Andy (1994) 'Postmodernism and State Education', *Journal of Educational Policy*, vol. 9, no. 1.
Greenfield, W. (ed.) (1987) *Instructional Leadership: Concepts, issues and controversies* (Boston: Allyn and Bacon).
Guy, R. (1991) 'Serving the needs of industry?', in P. Raggatt and L. Unwin (eds), *Change and Intervention* (London: Falmer Press).
Hallinger, P. and J. Murphy (1987) 'Instructional leadership in the school context', in W. Greenfield (ed.) *Instructional Leadership: concepts, issues and controversies* (Boston: Allyn and Bacon).
Halsey, A. H. (1993) 'Opening the doors of higher education', *Education Economics*, vol. 1, no. 1.
Halson, J. (1989) 'The Sexual Harasssment of Young Women', in L. Holly (ed.), *Girls and Sexuality* (Milton Keynes: Open University Press).
Hammersly, M. (1981) 'Staffroom racism', unpublished manuscript, quoted in Robert Jeffcoate, *Ethnic Minorities and Education* (London: Harper and Row, 1984).
Hannan, D. and M. Boyle (1987) 'Schooling Decisions: the origins and consequences of selection and streaming in Irish post-Primary schools' (Dublin: Economic and Social Research Institute, paper no. 136).
Hannan, D. and S. Shorthall (1991) 'The quality of their education' (Dublin: Economic and Social Research Institute, paper no. 153).
Haralambos, M. (ed.) (1994) *Developments in Sociology: an annual review*, vol. 10 (Ormskirk: Causeway).
Haralambos, Michael and Martin Holborn (1995) *Sociology Themes and Perspectives* (London: Collins Educational).
Hargreaves, A. (1994) 'Restructuring restructuring', *Journal of Educational Policy*, vol. 9, no. 1.
Hargreaves, A. and D. Reynolds (eds) (1989) *Education Policies: controversies and critiques* (London: Falmer).
Hargreaves, D. (1967) *Social Relations in a Secondary School* (London: Routledge and Kegan Paul).
Hartley, David (1994) 'Mixed Messages in Education Policy: signs of the times?, *British Journal of Educational Studies*, vol. 42, no. 3.
Harvey, David (1989) *The Condition of Modernity* (Oxford: Basil Blackwell).
Healey, Nigel (1989) 'Student loans versus grants: the debate revisited', *Journal of Further and Higher Education*, vol. 13, no. 3.
Heaton, Tim and Sarah Andrew (1993) 'Coursework: The Students' Perspective', *Sociology Review*, vol. 2, no. 4.
Hebdige, D. (1989) 'After the Masses', *Marxism Today*, January.
Herrnstein, R. and C. Murray (1994) *The Bell Curve: intelligence and class structure in American life* (New York: Free Press).
Hicks, Lesley (1988) 'Women Teachers', unpublished PhD thesis, University of York. Quoted in R. Deem 'Schooling and gender: The cycle of

discrimination', in James Lynch, Celia Madgil *et al.*, *Equity or Excellence? Education and Cultural Reproduction* (London: Falmer Press, 1992).

Hodgkinson, Peter (1991) 'Educational change: a model for analysis', *British Journal of Sociology of Education*, vol. 12, no. 2.

Holly, L. (ed.) (1989) *Girls and Sexuality* (Milton Keynes: Open University Press).

Hoskin, K. (1990) 'Foucault under Examination: the crypto-educationalist unmasked' in S. Ball (ed.), *Foucault and Education: disciplines and knowledge* (London: Routledge).

Hulmes, E. (1989) *Education and Cultural Diversity* (London: Longman).

Hutt, C. (1972) *Males and Females* (London: Penguin).

Hymas, Charles (1994) 'Student jobs market gets tougher by degree', *The Sunday Times*, 13 November.

Jarvis, F. (1990) 'The Debtor's Bill', *Education*, vol. 175, no. 11, 16, March.

Jeffcoate, Robert (1984) *Ethnic minorities and education* (London: Harper and Row).

Jensen, A. (1969) 'How Much Can We Boost IQ and Scholastic Achievement?', *Harvard Educational Review*, vol. 39, no. 1.

Jones, Anne (1993) 'General, National and Popular', *Education*, vol. 26 (November).

Jones, C. and P. Mahony (eds) (1989) *Learning Our Lines: sexuality and social control in education* (London: Women's Press).

Jones, L. and R. Moore (1993) 'Education, Competence and the control of expertise', *British Journal of the Sociology of Education*, vol. 14, no. 4.

Jones, Trevor (1993) *Britain's Ethnic Minorities* (London: Policy Studies Institute).

Judd, Judith (1994) 'National curriculum is torn up', *The Independent*, 6 January.

Judd, Judith and Fran Abrams (1995) 'Shows improvement, but could do better', *The Independent*, 1 February.

Karabel, J. and A. H. Halsey (eds) (1977) *Power and Ideology in Education* (New York: Oxford University Press).

Kelly, Alison (1982) *Why Girls Don't do Science*, course U221, unit 13 (Milton Keynes: Open University Press).

Kelly, Alison (1987) *Science for Girls* (Milton Keynes: Open University Press).

Kelly, Alison (1988) 'Towards a democratic science education', in H. Lauder and P. Brown (eds), *Education in Search of a Future* (Lewes: Falmer Press).

Kessler, S., D. J. Ashenden, R. W. Connell and G. W. Dowsett (1985) 'Gender relations in secondary schooling', *Sociology of Education*, vol. 58.

Kirby, Mark (1993) 'TECs and the New Vocationalism', *Social Science Teacher*, vol. 23, no. 1.

Klein, Gillian (1993) *Education towards Race Equality* (London: Cassell).

Koubel, Francine (1993) 'General National Vocational Qualifications: some considerations for Social Science teachers', *Social Science Teacher*, vol. 22, no. 3.

Kozol, Jonathan (1991) *Savage Inequalities: Children in American Schools* (New York: Crown Publishers).

Kysel, F. (1988) 'Ethnic Background and Examination Results', *Educational Research*, vol. 30, no. 1.

Labour Force Survey (1992) *Social Trends*, vol. 22 (London: HMSO).
Lacey, C. (1970) *Hightown Grammar* (Manchester: Manchester University Press).
Laclau, Ernesto and Chantal Mouffe (1985) *Hegemony and Socialist Strategy: towards a radical democratic politics* (London: Verso).
Ladner, J. A. '(1973) *The Death of White Sociology* (New York: Vintage Books).
Lauder, H. and P. Brown (eds) (1985) *Education in Search of a Future* (Lewes: Falmer Press).
Lynch, J. (1986) *Multicultural Education – principles and practices* (London: RKP).
Lynch, James *et al.* (1992) *Equity or Excellence? Education and cultural reproduction* (London: Falmer Press).
Lynch, K. (1990) 'Reproduction: the role of cultural factors and educational mediators', *British Journal of Sociology of Education*, vol. 11.
Lynch, K. and C. O'Neill (1994) 'Colonisation of social class', *British Journal of Sociology of Education*, Vol. 15, no. 3.
Mac an Ghaill, M. (1988) *Young, Gifted and Black: student-teacher relations in the schooling of black youth* (Milton Keynes: Open University Press).
MacLeod, Donald (1991) 'Comprehensives 'fail' at A-level', *The Independent*, 5 December.
Maguire, Susan (1993) 'Training for a Living?: the 1990s youth labour market', *Sociology Review*, vol. 3, no. 1.
Marsland, D., quoted in J. Demaine (1988) 'Teachers' work, Curriculum and the New Right', *British Journal of Sociology of Education*, vol. 9.
Marston, Paul (1994) 'A-level girls pass boys for the first time', the *Daily Telegraph*, 25 October.
Massey, Ian (1991) *More than Skin Deep* (London: Hodder & Stoughton).
Maughan, B. and G. Dunn (1988) 'Black pupils' progress in secondary school', in G. Verma, and P. Pumfrey (eds), *Educational Attainments: issues and outcomes in multicultural education* (London: Falmer Press).
McCarthy, C. and W. Chrichlow (1993) (eds) *Race, Identity and Representation in education* (London: Routledge).
McLaren, P. (1991) 'Postmodernism, Postcolonialism and Pedagogy', *Education and Society*, vol. 9, no. 1.
Mehan, H. (1992) 'Understanding inequality in schools: the contribution of interpretive studies', *Sociology of Education*, vol. 65.
Mickleson, R. A. (1989) 'Why does Jane read and write so well? The Anomaly of Women's Education', *Sociology of Education*, vol. 62.
Middleton, S. (1993) *Educating Feminist: life histories and pedagogy* (New York: Teachers College Press).
Mirza, H. (1992) *Young, Female and Black* (London: Routledge).
Modgil, S. *et al.* (eds) (1986) *Multicultural Education: the interminable debate* (Lewes: Falmer Press).
Moore, D. (1990) 'Voice and Choice in Chicago', in W. Clune and J. Witte (eds), *Choice and Control in American Education*, vol. 2 (London: Falmer Press).
Moore, R. (1988) 'The Correspondence Principle and the Marxist Sociology of Education', in M. Cole, *Bowles and Gintis Re-visited* (Lewes: Falmer Press).

Moore, Rob and Mike Hickox (1994) 'Vocationalism and educational change', *The Curriculum Journal*, vol. 5, no 3.
Morgan, D. (1981) 'Men, Masculinity and the Process of Sociological Enquiry', in H. Roberts (ed.) *Doing Feminist Research* (London: Routledge and Kegan Paul).
Müller, D. and P. Funnell (1991) *Delivering Quality in Vocational Education* (London: Kogan Page).
Murray, Robin (1988) 'Life after Henry', *Marxism Today*, 14–18 October.
Myers, K. (1989) 'High heels in the market place', *Education*, 16 June.
Nash, R. (1973) *Classrooms Observed* (London: Routledge and Kegan Paul).
Nicholson, Carol (1989) 'Postmodernism, Feminism and Education: the need for solidarity', *Educational Theory*, vol. 39, no. 3.
O'Donnell, Mike (1991) *Race and Ethnicity* (New York: Longman).
O'Donnell, Mike (1992) *A New Introduction to Sociology* (Walton-on Thames: Nelson).
O'Donnell, Mike and Joan Garrod (1990) *Sociology in Practice* (Walton-on Thames: Nelson).
OFSTED (1993) *Unfinished Business: Full-Time Educational Courses for 16–19 Year Olds* (London: HMSO).
Öhrn, Elisabet (1993) 'Gender, Influence and Resistance in School', *British Journal of Sociology of Education*, vol. 14, no. 2.
O'Keefe, D. (ed.) (1986a) *Anti-Racism: an assault on education and value* (London: Sherwood Press).
O'Keefe, D. (ed.) (1986b) *The Wayward Curriculum* (London: Social Affairs Unit).
O'Reilly, J. (1992) 'Where do you draw the line? Functional flexibiliy, training and skill in Britain and France', *Work, Employment and Society*, vol. 6, no. 3.
Palmer, F. (ed.) (1986) *Anti-Racism: an assault on education and value* (London: Sherwood Press).
Parekh, B. (1986) 'The concept of multi-cultural education', in S. Modgil *et al.* (eds). *Multicultural Education: the interminable debate* (Lewes: Falmer Press).
Parmar, P. (1989) 'Other Kinds of Dreams', *Feminist Review*, vol. 31.
Parsons, Talcott (1959) 'The School Class as a Social System', *Harvard Educational Review*, vol. 29.
Pascall, Gillian (1995) 'Women on Top?: Women's careers in the 1990's', *Sociology Review*, vol. 4, no. 3.
Pearce, S. (1986) 'Swann and the Spirit of the Age', in F. Palmer (ed.), *Anti-Racism: an assault on education and value* (London: Sherwood Press).
Platt, A. and J. Whyld (1983) 'Introduction', in J. Whyld (ed.), *Sexism in the Secondary School* (London: Harper and Row).
Plowden Report (1967) *Children and their Primary Schools* (London: HMSO).
Punter, D. (1986) *Introduction to Contemporary Cultural Studies* (London: Longman).
Raffe, D. (1993) 'Participation of 16–18 year olds in education and training', *Education Economics*, vol. 1, no. 1.
Raggatt, P. (1991) 'Quality Assurance and NVQs', in P. Raggatt and L. Unwin (eds), *Change and Intervention* (London: Falmer Press).

Raggatt, P. and L. Unwin (eds) (1991) *Change and Intervention* (London: Falmer Press).
Ramsay, P. (1983) 'Fresh perspectives on the school transformation–reproduction debate: a response to Anyon from the Antipodes', *Curriculum Inquiry*, vol. 13, no. 3.
Ranson, S. (1990) 'From 1944 to 1988: education, citizenship and democracy', in M. Flude and M. Hammer (eds), *The Education Reform Act 1988: its origins and implications* (London: Falmer Press).
Ravitch, D. (1990) 'Diversity and democracy; multicultural education in America', *American Educator*, Spring.
Riddell, Sheila I. (1992) *Gender and the Politics of the Curriculum* (London: Routledge).
Rist, R. (1970) 'Student Social Class and Teacher Expectations', *Harvard Educational Review*, vol. 40, no. 3.
Robbins Committee (1963) *Report on Higher Education* (London: HMSO).
Roberts, H. (ed.) (1981) *Doing Feminist Research* (London: Routledge and Kegan Paul).
Rorty, R. (1982) *Consequences of Pragmatism* (Brighton: Harvester Press).
Rust, Val (1991) 'Post-modernism and its comparative education implication', *Journal for Comparative Education Review*, vol. 35, no. 4, pp. 610–626.
Rustin, Michael (1994) 'Flexibility in higher education', in Roger Burrows and Brian Loader *Towards a Post-Fordist Welfare State?* (London: Routledge).
Sadker, M., D. Sadker and S. Klein (1991) 'The Issue of Gender in Elementary and Secondary Education', *Review of Research in Education*, vol. 17.
Saunders, Peter (1994) 'A social divide based on merit', *The Independent*, 25 October.
Schultz, T. W. (1977) 'Investment in Human Capital', in J. Karabel and A. H. Halsey (eds), *Power and Ideology in Education* (New York: Oxford University Press).
Scott, D. (1990) *Coursework and Coursework Assessment in the GCSE* (CEDAR: University of Warwick).
Scraton, S. (1987) 'Gender and P. E.: ideologies of the physical and the politics of sexuality', in S. Walker and L. Barton (eds), *Changing Policies, Changing Teachers* (Milton Keynes, Open University Press).
Scruton, Roger (1984) *The Meaning of Conservatism* (London: MacMillan).
Scruton, R. (1986) 'The myth of cultural relation', in D. O'Keefe (ed.), *Anti-Racism: an assault on education and value* (London: Sherwood Press).
Senese, G. (1991) 'Warnings on resistance and the language of possibility: Gramsci and a pedagogy from the surreal', *Educational Theory*, vol. 41.
Sharpe, Sue (1976) *Just Like a Girl: How Girls Learn to be Women* (Harmondsworth, Penguin).
Sharpe, Sue (1994) *Just Like a Girl: How Girls Learn to be Women: From the Seventies to the Nineties* (London: Penguin).
Siegal, F. (1991) 'The cult of multiculturalism', *The New Republic*, February 18.
Sieminski, Sandy (1993) 'The "flexible" solution to economic decline', *Journal of Further and Higher Education*, vol. 17, no. 1.
Simkins, Tim (1994) 'Efficiency, Effectiveness and LMS', *Journal of Educational Policy*, vol. 9, no. 1.

Simon, Brian (1988) *Bending the Rules: The Baker Reform of Education* (London: Lawrence and Wishart).

Smithers, A. (1993) *All our Futures – Britain's Education Revolution* (London: Channel 4 Publications).

Smyth, J. and N. Garman (1989) 'Supervision as school reform: a critical perspective', *Journal of Educational Policy*, vol. 4, no. 4.

Sowell, Thomas (1981) *Ethnic America: a History* (New York: Basic Books).

Spear, M. (1985) 'Teachers' Attitudes towards Girls and Technology', in J. Whyte, R. Deem, L. Kant and M. Cruickshank (eds), *Girl Friendly Schooling* (London: Methuen).

Spender, D. (1982) *Invisible Women: the schooling scandal* (London: Writers and Readers Coooperative).

Spours, Ken and Michael Young (1988) 'Beyond Vocationalism: a new perspective on the relationship between work and education', *British Journal of Education and Work*, vol. 2, no. 2.

SSEC (1943) *Curriculum and Examinations in Secondary Schools* (The Norwood Report) (London: HMSO).

Stake, J. E. and J. F. Katz (1982) 'Teacher–pupil relationships in the elementary school classroom: teacher–gender and pupil–gender differences', *American Education Research Journal*, vol. 19, no. 3.

Stanton, G. (1990) 'Curriculum Implications', in J. Burke, *Competency-based Education and Training* (London: Falmer Press).

Sylvester, D. (1994) 'Change and Continuity in History Teaching', in H. Bourdillon (ed.) *Teaching History* (London: Routledge).

Taylor, H. (1989) 'Romantic readers', in H. Carr, *From My Guy to Sci-fi: genre and women's writing in the postmodern world* (London: Pandora).

Taylor, M. J. (1981) *Caught Between: a review of research into the education of pupils of West Indian origin* (Windsor: NFER-Nelson).

Taylor, Monica (1988) *Worlds Apart? A review of research into the education of pupils of Cypriot, Italian, Ukrainian and Vietnamese Origin, Liverpool Blacks and Gypsies* (Windsor, NFER-Nelson).

Theodossin, E. (1986) *In Search of the Responsive College* (Bristol: Further Education Staff College).

Thompson, J. (1984) *Studies in the Theory of Ideology* (Cambridge: Polity Press).

Thompson, Paul (1983) *The Nature of Work: an introduction to debates on the labour process* (London: MacMillan).

Tizard, B., J. Mortimore and B. Burchall (1981) *Involving Parents in Nursery and Infant Schools* (London: Grant McIntyre).

Usher, Robin and Richard Edwards (1994) *Postmodernism and Education* (London: Routledge).

Vasquez, James (1992) 'Locus of control and academic achievement', in James Lynch *et al.*, *Equity or Excellence? Education and cultural reproduction* (London: Falmer Press).

Verma, G. and P. Pumfrey (eds) (1988) *Educational Attainments: issues and outcomes in multicultural education* (London: Falmer Press).

Walford, Geoffrey (1993) 'Education and Private Schools', *Sociology Review*, vol. 3, no. 2 (November).

Walker L. (1989) *Australian Maid: sex, schooling and social class*, PhD Behavioural sciences (Sydney: Macquarie University).

Walker, S. and L. Barton (eds) (1987) *Changing Policies, Changing Teachers* (Milton Keynes, Open University Press).

Walker, S. (1985) 'GCSE Social Science: the story so far', *Social Science Teacher*, vol. 15, no. 1.

Walkerdine, V. (1981) 'Sex, Power and Pedagogy', *Screen Education*, vol. 38.

Watson, I. (1993) 'Education, class and culture: the Birmingham ethnographic tradition and the problem of the new middle-class', *British Journal of Sociology of Education*, vol. 14, no. 2.

Weiner, G. (1985) *Just a Bunch of Girls* (Milton Keynes: Open University Press).

Weiner, Gaby (1990) 'What price vocationalism – the feminist dilemma', *British Journal of Education and Work*, vol. 4, no. 1.

Weis, L. (1990) *Working Class without Work: high school students in a deindustrialising economy* (New York: Routledge).

Weis, Lois (1992) 'Disproportionality, Education and Social Justice', in James Lynch, Celia Madgil *et al.*, *Equity or Excellence? Education and Cultural Reproduction* (London: Falmer Press).

West, Cornell (1993) 'The new cultural politics of difference', in C. McCarthy and W. Chrichlow (eds), *Race, Identity and Representation in Education* (London: Routledge).

Whitty, G. (1989) 'The New Right and the National Curriculum: state control or market forces?', in M. Flude and M. Hammer (eds), *The Education Reform Act 1988: its origins and implications* (London: Falmer Press).

Whitty, G., J. Fitz and T. Edwards (1989) 'Assisting Whom? Benefits and Costs of the Assisted Places Scheme', in A. Hargreaves and D. Reynolds (eds), *Education Policies: Controversies and critiques* (London: Falmer Press).

Whyld, J. (ed.) (1983) *Sexism in the Secondary School* (London: Harper and Row).

Whyte, J. (1984) 'Observing sex stereotypes and interaction in the school lab and workshop', *Educational Review*, vol. 36, no. 1.

Whyte, J., R. Deem, L. Kant and M. Cruickshank (eds) (1985) *Girl Friendly Schooling* (London: Methuen).

Wilkinson, H. (1994) *No Turning Back: generations and the genderquake* (London: Demos).

Wilkinson, L. C. and C. B. Marrett (eds) (1985) *Gender Influences in Classroom Interaction* (New York: Academic Press).

Williams, F. (1989) *Social Policy: a critical introduction* (Cambridge: Polity Press).

Willis, Paul (1977) *Learning to Labour* (Farnborough: Saxon House).

Willis, Paul (1983) 'Cultural Production and Theories of Reproduction', in L. Barton and S. Walker (eds), *Race, Class and Education* (London: Croom Helm).

Woods, P. (1983) *Sociology and the School: an interactionist viewpoint* (London: Routledge & Kegan Paul).

Wright, Cecile (1987) 'School processes – an ethnographic study', in J. Eggleston *et al.*, *Education for Some: the educational and vocational experiences of 15–18 year old members of minority ethnic groups* (Stoke-on Trent: Trentham Books).

Wright, D. (1986) 'Racism in school textbooks', in D. Punter (ed.), *Introduction to Contemporary Cultural Studies* (London: Longman).
Yates, L. (1985) 'Is Girl-friendly Schooling What Girls Need?', in J. Whyte, R. Deem, L. Kant and M. Cruickshank (eds), *Girl Friendly Schooling* (London: Methuen).
Young, M. F. D (1971) 'An approach to the study of curricula as socially organised knowledge', in M. F. D. Young (ed.), *Knowledge and Control* (London: Collier-Macmillan).
Young, M. F. D. (ed.) (1971) *Knowledge and Control* (London: Collier-Macmillan).

Author index

Subject index